America's Sexual Transformation

**Recent Titles in
Sex, Love, and Psychology**
Judy Kuriansky, Series Editor

Rock 'n' Roll Wisdom: What Psychologically Astute Lyrics Teach about Life and Love
Barry A. Farber

Sixty, Sexy, and Successful: A Guide for Aging Male Baby Boomers
Robert Schwalbe, PhD

Managing Menopause Beautifully: Physically, Emotionally, and Sexually
Dona Caine-Francis

New Frontiers in Men's Sexual Health: Understanding Erectile Dysfunction
and the Revolutionary New Treatments
Kamal A. Hanash, M.D.

Sexuality Education: Past, Present, and Future (4 volumes)
Elizabeth Schroeder, EdD, MSW, and Judy Kuriansky, PhD, editors

Sex When You're Sick: Reclaiming Sexual Health after Illness or Injury
Anne Katz

Secret Suffering: How Women's Sexual and Pelvic Pain Affects Their Relationships
Susan Bilheimer and Robert J. Echenberg, M.D.

Teenage Sex and Pregnancy: Modern Myths, Unsexy Realities
Mike Males

Monogamy: The Untold Story
Marianne Brandon

Sex, Love, and Mental Illness: A Couple's Guide to Staying Connected
Stephanie Buehler

Coming Home to Passion: Restoring Loving Sexuality in Couples with Histories
of Childhood Trauma and Neglect
Ruth Cohn

Losing the Bond with God: Sexual Addiction and Evangelical Men
Kailla Edger, PhD

In the Company of Men: Inside the Lives of Male Prostitutes
Michael D. Smith and Christian Grov

AMERICA'S SEXUAL TRANSFORMATION

How the Sexual Revolution's Legacy Is Shaping Our Society, Our Youth, and Our Future

Gary F. Kelly

Sex, Love, and Psychology
Judy Kuriansky, Series Editor

AN IMPRINT OF ABC-CLIO, LLC
Santa Barbara, California • Denver, Colorado • Oxford, England

Library of Congress Cataloging-in-Publication Data

Kelly, Gary F.
    America's sexual transformation : how the sexual revolution's legacy is shaping our society,
our youth, and our future / Gary F. Kelly.
        p. cm. — (Sex, love, and psychology)
    Includes bibliographical references and index.
    ISBN 978-0-313-39645-8 (hardcopy : alk. paper) —
    ISBN 978-0-313-39646-5 (ebook)
    1. Sex—United States.   2. Sex customs—United States.   3. United States—Social life and
customs—21st century.   I. Title.
    HQ18.U5K45   2012
    306.70973'09045—dc23   2011026313

ISBN: 978-0-313-39645-8
EISBN: 978-0-313-39646-5

16   15   14   13   12   1   2   3   4   5

This book is also available on the World Wide Web as an eBook.
Visit www.abc-clio.com for details.

Praeger
An Imprint of ABC-CLIO, LLC

ABC-CLIO, LLC
130 Cremona Drive, P.O. Box 1911
Santa Barbara, California 93116-1911

This book is printed on acid-free paper ∞

Manufactured in the United States of America

This book is dedicated with gratitude and affection to my
students and my companions in the counseling and
therapy relationship, who have always taught me
so much about life, sexuality, and myself.

CONTENTS

SERIES FOREWORD

I have been using Gary Kelly's textbook, *Sexuality Today*, in my classes about the psychology of intimacy at Columbia University Teachers College for many years. I had been impressed with how presentable and readable his text was, making the topic of sexuality particularly vital to a young generation of professionals. It is also of interest that the text has been recently published in Chinese—given that I have done trainings in China about sexuality for decades, I know how valuable it will be to be accessible to that country where sexuality is a burgeoning field.

I also knew that Kelly is a veteran in the field of sexuality who had a most unique front row seat in the development of the field, with perspectives that have not been told in the context of his more academic work.

Given all that, I was particularly thrilled when I approached Gary to write a book integrating his academic perspective with more personal views and opinions.

This resulting book delivers. *America's Sexual Transformation: How the Sexual Revolution's Legacy Is Shaping Our Society, Our Youth, and Our Future* is a fascinating tour through the lens of a sexuality expert who combines his roles as an academic, award-wining teacher (for many years), and editor (of two important journals in the field), who has a decades-long experience in the field of sexuality and also had first hand experience working with the grand names (and actually grand dames, as he tells us in one of his chapters) in sexuality—a claim not all can make. These include heroic and groundbreaking founders of organizations still thriving as crucial in the field today, like Mary

Calderone, who founded SIECUS (the Sex Education Council of the U.S.) and Pat Schiller who founded the American Association of Sex Educators and Counselors and Therapists.

Through his association with the early pioneers of sexuality, Kelly was introduced to exploring many of the topics and populations that are still challenges in the field today, including teen sexuality and gender identification. I must say I relate to these given that I too started in those early days of the field. I was one of the first psychologists to work with people with gender issues and to be on a team evaluating those requesting sex change operations. Later, as an advice show host on youth-targeted radio stations on a show that gained huge popularity, called *LovePhones*, I answered thousands of questions from young people about love and sex and gender, all documented in my book called *Generation Sex*. In his text and in this book, Kelly recounts challenges teens face, escalated in present times, that capture the angst of Generation X, and now of the Millennials.

Through all his experience, Kelly highlights for us the expansion of the definition of sex as an act to a much deeper concept of who we are. This is particularly interesting in light of his early training in biology. This background shows up too in this book, illuminating us about the interplay and importance of biological factors in sex. Given his background, it is understandable that Kelly would infuse this book with biological perspective, giving us insight into gender issues and introducing important (and new for some) terms and concepts like *autogynephilic*, a boundary-blurring mixture of erotic excitement and quasi gender bending whereby such young people usually grow up with masculine boyhood interests, eventually finding themselves fetishistically sexually interested in female clothes and female bodies. Additionally, he reminds us of the important role of neurochemical phenomena in the formation of sexuality and touches on a concept of nature/nurture that has long intrigued all professionals. He also refers to epigenetics—still a young field—which highlights the process whereby social information and other environmental factors affect changes in the individual's genome that alter gene function, that can result in changes passed on to the next generation. Hormones or other substances that enter the body through the environment can create chemical changes in the body that change brain structures and behaviors in permanent ways, which can then also be inherited. These will eventually affect our understanding of each individual's gender identity, sexual orientation, and unique sexual expression as well as the process of attraction and pairing.

Ethics is also a growing field of interest in sexuality, and Kelly, who had long had a great interest in this topic area, takes this on in his consideration of the growth of the field of sexuality. Such concerns include controversies over what makes gender and other issues like child-adult sex, sex offenders and sex abuse.

While Kelly has had a front row seat on the development of the field of sexuality, he treats readers of this book to a front row seat to his own evolution as a professional, in writing editions of his textbook, and therefore having to stay abreast of the changes and most up-to-date issues in the field

Besides all the elucidation of Kelly's book, there is another treat: that we gain insight into not only Gary Kelly the respected academic, researcher, and teacher but also how he has faced professional challenges, for example, difficulties in editing his text, which is now in its 10th edition. A most challenging topic is to identify the frequencies of various sexual behaviors practiced by various segments of the American population. Specifying how often which people do what is exactly what not only the grandfather of sex research, Alfred Kinsey, faced, but also the issue we face today. So many times, I am asked about this by media who interview me about so many various aspects of sex—whether it is the number of people who practice a particular sex act (like oral sex), how many people have affairs, or how many homosexuals there are. After years of facing this issue, Kelly offers us some guidance about the numbers of people practicing particular behaviors.

In addition, Kelly treats us to insights into his personal life that shaped his dedication to the field. Through his vignettes, Kelly demonstrates how approachable, open, and honest he is—all qualities of a good sexuality professional but also of a good human being. After all, that is his underlying thesis about sex—that it is more than "sex" and goes to the heart of what it means to "be."

Against a background of tracing the evolution of the field of sexuality from sex icons like Elvis the Pelvis and Mick Jagger to professional pioneers from Margaret Sanger in the early years of Planned Parenthood to Lonnie Barbach leading the early groups teaching women how to achieve orgasm, Kelly's book is a wonderful read about a veteran sexuality expert's view of issues that challenge our culture and youth today.

Dr. Judy Kuriansky
Series Editor

PREFACE

Although I've been thinking about this book for several years, I simply wasn't ready to write it until now. Several developments in my life converged to make this true. At the end of 2005, I retired from a career of more than 30 years as a university administrator, freeing me to spend more time with my writing, teaching, and counseling practice. My wife and I had a new home built beside a lake in the Adirondacks, providing an inspiring location for thought and contemplation. More specifically, I was working on the 10th edition of my sexuality textbook, *Sexuality Today*, able to spend more time with it than I ever had before. As I pored over hundreds of research studies and theoretical papers, it hit me that sexuality—at least in America—is undergoing a very real transformative process, quite different from and well beyond what the sexual revolution had yielded. It was the sexual revolution that opened many of the doors, but it was through the subsequent work of sexual pioneers and sex researchers that entirely new perspectives on sexuality were merging with 21st-century technology and political and economic upheavals to fuel this sexual transformation.

In the university Honors Program that I helped develop, I began to teach a course on the social and ethical implications of scientific and technological progress in which I ask students to examine moral philosophies along with some of the most vexing ethical dilemmas we face in our society today. I push these students to develop the critical thinking and reasoning skills that help them come up with analyses of these ethical conundrums. I want them to struggle not to find any single *right* answer but a thoughtful, well-reasoned response that is *better* than an impulsive, ill-considered one. And for me, one of the gratifying outcomes of teaching that course has been the honing of my own powers of reason and analysis.

When I first presented the proposal for this book to Dr. Judy Kuriansky, the editor of this series on sex, love, and psychology, she reminded me of something very important: this was a book in which I would be free to express my own opinions. As an academic and as the author of a college textbook, I spend a good deal of time holding my own perspectives in check, attempting to present fair-minded and objective coverage of many different points of view. I have my own stands on many issues, of course, but I have never seen it as my mission to persuade students to my way of thinking or any particular political position. I'm sometimes tempted, but I hold back. So the opportunity to express my opinions and predictions in these pages has been a welcome luxury and perhaps even a delicious indulgence. I hope I haven't abused the privilege.

In the background of the observations I make in this book is a wild card that could shift many outcomes if it gets played with any more force than it already has. The intensified political polarization in America, which is reflective of a wider international trend, continues to generate new barriers and bigotries and reinforce old ones. Even as we struggle to reduce hate speech and the prejudices and stereotypes it represents, there has been a marked and increasingly public display of distrust and hatred for members of the Islamic faith, for immigrants and illegal aliens, for social programs that attempt to provide care for the poor, and for anything that supports some imaginary status quo. Such sentiments are predictable during tough economic times, for when people have to tighten their money belts, they tend to loosen their tempers and their lips. Those of us who have long been observing the American sexual scene know that it has not been all that long since sexual orientations and behaviors that vary from the mainstream were subjected to terrible bigotry, social stigma, and violence. My fear is that all that negativity could easily rear its head once again and be directed toward sexual oppression. There are lots of sensitive sexual issues before us right now about which people have some reasonable differing points of view. I would hate to see the well-founded controversies and rational political debates devolve into more hatred and violence. Sexual differences have always been easy targets for intolerance and prejudice, and for those of us who have the privilege of living in a country that serves as a model of personal freedoms and human rights for the entire world, we must be vigilant not to allow such repugnant things to be perpetuated here.

All of my professional career, I have had the privilege of being with and working with young people. This is a wonderful thing, and it still fills my heart with awe nearly every day. I always look forward to talking with them about the critical issues in our society as well as the compelling stories of their own lives. While many of my age contemporaries seem to grow increasingly awkward around young people, I find myself increasingly at ease and able to be myself when I am with them. I recognize their inexperience, their naïveté, and their occasional flashes of hubris, but I also recognize the fragility of their developing egos and the burgeoning wisdom that so often amazes me about their decision making. The youth of our world truly do represent the hope for the future, and they are already in the forefront of what, in this book, I call *America's Sexual Transformation*. I trust them to do a good job with it and, in fact, a considerably better job than other generations have done before.

Gary F. Kelly
www.garyfkelly.com

ACKNOWLEDGMENTS

There are a number of people who deserve acknowledgment for helping me make this book become a reality, although it is I who take full responsibility for its accuracy and the opinions it expresses. The editor of this series of books, Dr. Judy Kuriansky, affectionately known as Dr. Judy by most of the world, was especially significant in helping me shape and focus my original proposal. She and Praeger's senior acquisitions editor, Debbie Carvalko, then, were key forces in strengthening and honing the message of each chapter. My childhood neighbor, Dr. Ronald Burkman, now an obstetrician/gynecologist with Wesson Women's Group in Springfield, Massachusetts, and Dr. Mark Regnerus the University of Texas at Austin were very gracious in checking the sections in chapters 1 and 6, respectively, where their work is mentioned. Ian SerVaas, a graduate student at the University of Indianapolis, who did research on sexuality among students at his undergraduate institution along with his internship at the Kinsey Institute, read and offered excellent suggestions on two of the chapters. Patrick Malone, public information officer at the Sexuality Information and Education Council of the United States (SIECUS) was most generous with his time in helping me sort out all the current federal legislation relating to sexuality education. Of special importance in my writing, always, is my wife Betsy. She read all the first-draft chapters before anyone else, offering her usual good insights and suggestions to improve what I have to say and my ways of saying it. With my writing, as with everything else in my life, she helps me be the best I can be.

Chapter 1

RISKY BUSINESS: SEXUAL REVOLUTION TO SEXUAL TRANSFORMATION

I was oblivious to the societal sexual developments taking root all around me in 1955 when I was 11 and my pal Alfred Bloomer showed me a matchbook advertisement featuring the shapely legs of a woman. I would never be a leg man, so I didn't get why he found the picture so appealing, but I didn't tell him that. He was a year older than I, so I thought it might be something I'd grow into. I was just beginning to discover my sexuality and its power over me, but I had already figured out which sexual matters you talked about and which you hid. Mostly, in 1955, you hid.

My parents tended to gingerly sidestep sexual issues in my presence. It was clear that my father was less comfortable with sexual content than my mother. Once, as the three of us rode in the car together, they talked about the daughter of family friends who had recently "had to get married." From the backseat I stupidly ventured, "She's pregnant?"

My father's ire was swift, and his face reddened. "You're too young to be talking about such things," he sputtered.

My mother tried to defend me by saying, "He doesn't even know what he's talking about." They were both wrong, of course, but I learned to keep my place in such matters and to listen unobtrusively when I wanted to know what was going on. Little did I know that the sexual awakenings I was coming to feel within my own pubertal body were about to meld with the sexual upheavals of the entire nation and that my own personal unfoldings and the wider sexual revolution would at times get somewhat out of control.

SEX IN BLACK AND WHITE

Sex is bedded with many human conceits, including the assumption that we are immune to the catastrophes that befall others. Another is the tendency toward finger pointing when we discover that we aren't so immune after all. These are age-old blind spots of the human psyche, fortified with big doses of egocentrism and ethnocentrism. When King Charles VIII of France invaded Italy in 1494, the French soldiers who were garrisoned in Naples during the following winter began noticing syphilitic chancres on their penises, eventually breaking out in rashes and fever. The disease took such a toll on the troops that the army collapsed and fled, blaming Italian women for their defeat by microbe. The Italians dubbed it the French sickness as the disease spread throughout Europe and then into Africa and Asia. Muslim Turks would call it the Christian disease, and the Chinese pointed their accusatory fingers at the Portuguese. Popular wisdom holds that Columbus and his crew brought sexually transmitted disease to the New World, yet recent examination of pre-Columbian bones in the Americas has demonstrated the presence of a syphilis-like disease far earlier than the time when that libidinous band of Spanish sailors began to spread their infected seed. In fact, it was probably Columbus's men who carried the disease back to Europe.[1]

Sex can be fraught with unpleasant and unwanted consequences, and those risks are also conflated in the service of moralists trying mainly to quell sexual flames. Yet it is the very power of the sexual instinct that has captured the imagination and unease of philosophers and theologians since the time of the ancients. Classical Greek philosophers made a distinction between *philia*, a friendship kind of love through which friends seek only the good for one another and try to improve each other's virtuousness, and *eros*, the more passionate and physical kind of love. Plato (427–347 BCE) divided *eros* still again into the lofty erotic longings for spiritual unity with the gods and the more vulgar human longings of lust and possession. It was the latter that could lead to crude wantonness and enslave us if we gave in to it. Better that we eschew sexual pleasure in favor of striving together for virtue. In truth, Plato believed that weakness of the will over sexual desire would lead us down the path to personal powerlessness and subservience to others, a threat to freedom and happiness. Although Aristotle (384–322 BCE) had less to say about sex, he had plenty to say about the need for moderation when it came to appetites of the flesh that can undermine our virtue.[2] The polarized nature of Western ways of thinking was taking shape.

Some 750 years later, the Christian philosopher St. Augustine (354–430 CE) again bemoaned the risks of becoming overcome by sexual hankering, to which he thought we could lose our personal peace and self-mastery. He believed that it was only through the grace of God that one could resist the power of sexual temptation. Augustine's views about sex grew out of the theological debates of the time concerning whether Adam and Eve had engaged in sexual intercourse before their fall from grace, and he took a somewhat moderate approach between the conservative and liberal factions that warred around him. The upshot of it all was that sex should be confined to marriage and then only for procreation, not pleasure. While St. Thomas Aquinas (1225–1274) would, nearly 900 years later, concede that since God created sexual pleasure, it must be good, he also held that sexual acts should only be of the kind that could result in babies. In other words, the kind of sex involving the human penis depositing semen into the human vagina would be just fine, but sexual pleasures derived through other means represented vices. He did qualify his admonitions with an interesting reference to "any *complete* sex act," referring specifically to completion through ejaculation. Engaging in sex acts without ejaculating seemed oddly exempt from judgment. He rated the various "completed" forms of unnatural sex in terms of their degree of sinfulness, with masturbation rated as the least serious of the nasty business.

So early philosophical stances about sex came along in fits and starts, confined mostly to the tortured reason of intellectuals who were not paid much heed by the common folk. There are plenty of other historical thinkers who could be cited here, but I'll mention only three. René Descartes (1596–1650) did an especially polarizing job on human nature when he split us into mind and body, helping to perpetuate centuries of disconnect between thought and feeling, will and action. He reminded us that our desires may not represent what is best for us. Moral philosophers continued to debate the issues over the centuries but almost always with the Cartesian bias that sexual longings and sexual acts, as expressions of body, were never as good or pure or virtuous as the mind's willful denial of sexual pleasure and the seeking after more lofty intellectual and spiritual pursuits. We became trapped by the framing of sexuality between its good and evil aspects, the way of the mind-spirit versus the way of the flesh.

As the methods of science became increasingly popular and people began to realize the significance of solid, observable experience in arriving at new knowledge, Immanuel Kant (1724–1804) tried to forge a compromise between the rationalists who had long believed the mind's reason alone to be sufficient in gaining knowledge and the empiricists who were arguing that experience was the only reliable path to knowledge. Kant insisted that experience *and* the rational analysis of it were *both* vital to gaining fresh insights and knowledge. Still there seemed to be little room for heart or compassion in the equation. Stalwartly feminist John Stuart Mill (1806–1873) bucked the puritanical Victorian tide of his time to maintain that the consent of women for sexual activity should be of primary concern and that sex between consenting partners that harms no one should be tolerated. The philosophies that descended from Kant and Mill, tempered with the Aristotelian view that moderation in all things is the most virtuous path, have tended to dominate Western secular philosophies about sex, while Augustine and Aquinas still hold sway today in some religious circles, at least within Roman Catholic dogma. In the Western world, the philosophical roots of our sexual nature got tangled in dualistic perceptual models that emphasized inner struggle, a push and pull between base instinctual desire and the will to rise above that desire in action. A battle of wanton lewdness against the striving for something more pure and ethereal—a conflict between body and mind, between evil and good. The essence of Western thought and philosophy—dualism—found easy examples in human sexuality.

As Eastern philosophical traditions were building on a much older lineage of viewing the universe and human nature in more holistic, unified terms, seeing the good and bad of all things as two different sides of the same coin that could ultimately be accepted and integrated, my own philosophical ancestors were pushing good and bad into two alienated camps that must ultimately do battle. Our contemporary culture wars once again clearly demonstrate the paralyzing effects of this persistent polarization of beliefs.

Several 19th-century European physicians added their own pseudomedical judgments about sexual activity when the cultural imperatives called increasingly for labeling and categorizing. Their amalgam of unscientific and moralistic pronouncements about sexual behaviors and human health would influence the public psyche until well into the 20th century. German physician Richard Krafft-Ebing (1840–1902), in his book *Psychopathia Sexualis*, claimed that hereditary "taintedness" was at the root of most sexual activity other than intercourse and branded masturbation as the cause of most physical, mental, and sexual malaise.[3]

One of the other influential thinkers of the time was Sigmund Freud (1856–1939), who invented a type of talking therapy during one of Europe's most sexually repressed times. The founders of psychology believed then that introspection was the only way to understand the experiences of the mind. Even though Freud wanted to do research, he was more skilled in rationalist knowledge making than empirical methods, which had not yet quite caught on in medicine. His concept of psychoanalysis had captured the American imagination by the 1950s; it was a concept that had become more appealing to the New World's intelligentsia than it had ever been in Freud's Europe. Psychoanalytical abstractions became fundamental to American plays and movies, perpetuating several themes in psychological drama, public opinion, and rudimentary attempts at psychotherapy. One of these core beliefs was that we were at the mercy of our upbringing by our parents and whatever quirks and kinks that got built into our unconscious minds along the way. Our personalities might well become stuck or stymied if our libidos didn't successfully mature through the purported stages of psychosexual development. The dynamics of our childhood relationships would then play themselves out in our adult sexual attitudes, orientations, and relationships.

It was also in the 1950s that the newly invented developmental periods of adolescence and youth were mythologized as times of brooding discontent and identity confusion, manifested in teen anger, rebellion, and forbidden sexual behavior. The mystique of troubled youth persists today, even though the evidence projects a far more positive reality. The trump card of psychoanalytic thought was that we could be freed from our psychic pain, angst, and self-destructiveness only by identifying the inner conflicts, roiling emotions, stuck libidos, or hidden sexual longings that lurked in our unconscious minds and that only by resolving their torturous riddles could we escape neurosis or insanity. If we succeeded, we would indeed be saved. But that could take several years of analysis. Not a very rosy outlook, yet this was the overpsychologized template on which we were supposed to build our sexual lives, salted and peppered with ample portions of guilt and shame and a collective, unspoken vow of secrecy about what was really going on in our sexual lives. To a large extent this unscientific mythos remains with us today and many still fall victim to its lore and lure, even though the theories and techniques of contemporary psychodynamic therapy have largely adopted more scientific grounding.

THE DOORS BEGIN TO OPEN

What chance of withstanding the impending sexual revolution did I have as an adolescent boy growing up in an isolated village in the northernmost part of New York State—a boy who, in spite of having learned on his own how to masturbate with some expertise and to look with secret longing at classmates, had never heard the word *sex* mentioned by parent, church, or school? I already felt condemned to a sexual life shrouded in secrecy and guilt, even though no one had ever explained to me why or if I should feel guilty about my lustful pleasures and fantasies. Augustine and Aquinas and Kant and Mill had not been on my reading list. Perhaps if they had been, I might at least have had some frame of reference. As it was, I had none. And I wasn't alone in this risky state of ignorance and bewilderment. There were two generations of people lined up much like myself, trying to grasp what their sexuality was about and trying to figure out the complexities of what was right or wrong about it all. We were ripe to be swept away by revolution and to oscillate with its reverberations.

If one observation could be made about the period during which I've lived, it is that the doors of new awareness, perception, and information have constantly been opening. My small-town isolation was first breached in the 1950s by towering rotor-powered television antennas on rooftops, soaring high enough to capture snowy television signals from a hundred miles away. It was television that brought us the early symbols of the impending sexual upheaval, even though we didn't realize it at the time. In those early days, most of television's images and ideas were laundered of eroticism, but that was about to change.

Even with the cameras focusing above his waist, Elvis Presley managed to become the sizzling representation of raw, grinding, lusting sexuality, the steamy kind that had been secreted away, the kind that had been portrayed in the books *Peyton Place* and *Lady Chatterley's Lover*, both of which I managed to ferret out of my mother's hiding place. We boys were unsure how to feel about this guy Elvis with the seductive curl in his lips and thrust in his hips that made girls dissolve in their own confusing and forbidden frenzy for his unbridled physicality. We had been trying to emulate the chaste and clean-cut khaki look of Pat Boone, someone we thought was seen as the perfect boyfriend. But the safe, superficially polite and comfortable world of the devoutly Christian and devoutly republican Pat Boone's "April Love" was about to give way to the hard, pulsing, pushing, and risky sexuality of Elvis, the Beatles, Mick Jagger, and a spate of other musicians celebrating raw sensuality and sexuality. We were lined up and ready.

The counterculture sexual movement that was engulfing me with a mixture of confusion and elation in my own hormonal youth seemed mostly to be an invitation to orgasmic fun. I was a reluctant sexual rebel myself at first, bored with sex-for-one, eager enough and arrogant enough not to want to get left behind, but terrified of the physical and emotional intimacy that would be required of me. Many of my youthful comrades—and the wannabe youth who envied the growing freedom they saw taking shape—were not so reticent, choosing to cast caution, guilt, and good judgment to the wind. Sometimes that worked and sometimes it didn't. As with any revolution, it was the abandonment of prudence that would eventually boomerang and knock many revolutionaries off their moorings. The early sexual revolutionaries were emboldened enough by their ill-defined causes that the risks tended to either be overlooked or minimized. Standard revolutionary strategy: fire the cannons and full speed ahead! But the more the cannons fired, the more energized antirevolutionary forces become.

If we had indeed been able to see beyond our own self-centered motivations as the sexual revolution took root, we might have noticed some things changing, making us ripe for new ways of looking at sex. We who were the early revolutionaries were oblivious to those factors that had set the stage; we mostly just wanted to get our rocks off.

THE SEXUAL REVOLUTION UNFOLDS

I was finishing high school and absorbed in college as the revolution was taking hold. We were among the last few in swanky liberal arts colleges to live in single sex dorms where women had to obey curfews and be "called on" in the lobbies of their residence halls by men, then to be signed out and in like a library book. The other sex was never allowed in rooms, even with the doors open. They didn't make sex easy for us, which was one way of keeping us under control. It didn't work perfectly, of course, but it did work to an extent. We thought it stupid and constraining, which primed us even more acutely for the sexual revolution heading our way.

This was less than a couple of decades after veterans had flooded campuses on their return from World War II. I took all of my psychology classes in the long, temporary buildings with creaky wooden floors that had originally been constructed to house married veterans. After years of crippling economic depression and a savage but exalted—almost mythic—war, these guys were ready to settle down and slice out their piece of the American pie. They had seen the world and its wilder erotic ways but hid their secrets in order to return to a tamer way of life.

While the soldiers were away, Alfred Kinsey at Indiana University was managing to get some 16,000 Americans interviewed about their sexual behaviors. Just after the soldiers returned home, anxious for the good life to begin, Kinsey's books revealed some startling truths about the sex lives of American men and women.[4] The revelations helped everyone to understand that they weren't so different—or perhaps so bad—as they had imagined themselves to be. Everybody was indeed quite sexual. But the country was uneasy about all of this truth in the early 1950s, especially at a time when Senator Joseph McCarthy's fearmongering hearings in Washington were making us suspicious about communists and homosexuals around every corner. My sister told me wide-eyed that even our minister might be a commie behind the closed doors of the manse, and we would never have known it. So by 1953, when his second study (on the sexual behavior of women!) appeared, Alfred Kinsey found that even very sturdy, respectable empirical data and the strong reputation they could temporarily build could crumble under the weight of public discomfort with frank talk about sex. The Rockefeller Foundation pulled its funding from Kinsey's work. Maybe we couldn't handle the truth!

Before William Masters began his research in the early 1960s, which involved observing hundreds of people engaged in various sexual behaviors so that he and his staff could measure their physiological responses, he made certain that he first established a solid, unblemished career as a respected gynecologist and researcher. He had learned from Kinsey's fall. In 1966 and again in 1970, Masters and his assistant/wife Virginia Johnson published their groundbreaking works on the body's sexual responses and the treatment of sexual dysfunctions.[5] Their successes may also have been buoyed by a couple of decades of increasing openness about things sexual that the revolution had already wrought.

There were many others who haltingly entered the world of sexual science and technology, but one development stands out among the many. I was in high school when I read of the new birth control pill that would offer a new level of personal sexual freedom to all of us as it rendered sex less—and more—risky. I'd have given most anything just to have had the option of taking the risk. I wonder now if, had I been availed of that opportunity, I would have given any thought or action toward reducing the inherent risks. I suspect I would not have done so. Other than my talks with a few peers, guilt-ridden masturbatory reading of *Peyton Place* and *Lady Chatterley*, and furtive and mostly futile searches among the library stacks for something more instructive, I never received any formal sex education, not even the warnings about venereal disease, not even when I majored in biology in college. The only graphic representations of sexual matters I had stumbled across in high school and college were a couple of early issues of *Playboy* and 8-millimeter films that my older brother kept in a dresser drawer, some nudist magazines my college roommate shared with me, and a copy of photographer Edward Steichen's *The Family of Man*. It included a few sensual, seminude images mindful of a boy's trusted bathroom companion at the time, *National Geographic*.

It has often been asserted that the Pill spawned the sexual revolution, and there was indeed concern that it would lead to sexual anarchy. The Pill actually came on the market in 1957, but since 30 states still had laws on the books banning the promotion of birth control, it could be prescribed only for "female disorders" because it could ease menstrual discomforts. Suddenly physicians were writing prescriptions for the ovulation-blocking medication under the guise of treating these discomforts. The government and the American Medical Association seemed to be colluding at a more formal level to keep a lid on American sexual desire, for once the Pill was approved as a method of birth control in 1960, it could still only be prescribed as such for *married* women. So, while it may well have heralded a new age of sexual freedoms, the Pill was more a product of many social forces that were creating epochal social change: rejection of the polarization of the nation into black skin and white that had fueled stereotypes and injustices, generational conflict as boys grew their hair long and girls began to look at careers beyond housewifery, restlessness about gender stereotypes, and clashes of church and state. As these stirrings dovetailed with the growing availability of psychoactive street drugs that brought the younger generation unexplored terrains of perception and cognition and the unpopularity of a war mushrooming out of control in Vietnam that was killing our children, friends, and lovers, the stage was set for a fierce rally against the status quo. By the 1980s, 10.5 million American women were taking the Pill, including single women who could finally exercise control over their educations, careers, *and* their sexual lives. This was truly revolutionary.[6]

No wonder so many people were feeling stifled. No wonder the nose-to-the-grindstone, grin-and-bear-it-for-the-good-of-the-nation ethics that the greatest generation fostered as its primary legacy began to sour and falter for new generations that were being weaned on individualism and self-centeredness.

All the while, science was giving us better means to avoid unwanted pregnancy and antibiotics that were able to cure the unfortunate infections that might result from ill-considered couplings. Pornography and erotica were breaking loose from their legal loopholes, and renewed support for First Amendment rights was underscoring our freedom to read about or view just about any kind of sexual activity imaginable. The sexual revolution was gaining steam, and the chaste, squeaky-clean Pat Boone mirage was being pushed into the background by the lusty sex appeal of rock and roll. Woodstock and all that it symbolized sexually was just a roll in the mud away.

SOBERING EVIDENCE

In the 1960s, a neighborhood mother of three young children who lived a couple of houses away from my family suffered a massive and terribly debilitating stroke. The cerebrovascular catastrophe left her barely able to walk and unable to utter coherent words. The family was devastated, and the story became fodder for the wide-eyed gossip of tragedy, at once frightening us with the specter of sudden and unpredictable health calamities and reassuring us that since it had happened so close to home, it would not likely happen again so near.

We were falsely reassured. A few months later, another mother just four houses away on another street was struck down by a stroke as well, a four-inch-long blood clot still lodged in one of the blood vessels leading into her brain. She had been taken unconscious to a larger hospital a couple of hours away, and we heard the stories of how the doctors kept having to sedate her each time she emerged from her brain-swollen haze into consciousness because she became hysterical at the stark gravity of her condition. Weeks later, she would return home, rehabilitated enough to be able to throw her paralyzed leg in front of the other in order to navigate. Her speech and other cognitive faculties had not been damaged.

Following my graduation from St. Lawrence University, I was doing genetics research under the tutelage of a pathologist, and I got my first clue about what had happened to these women. My mentor had just finished an autopsy on a woman in her late 20s who had the night before died suddenly of what he discovered to be a major pulmonary embolism. He sat at his desk and shook his head. "Another blood clot in a woman taking the Pill," he said to me. "I think there's something going on here."

All over the country, pathologists and gynecologists had been noticing the same correlation with alarm, and the Food and Drug Administration convened an advisory committee to look into the problem. This panel not only called for further surveillance of the Pill's side effects but also commented that never before in human history had so many people taken such potent drugs for so lengthy a period for reasons other than to treat a disease—the risks that people will take to minimize the reproductive potentials of sex, risks that have been borne largely by women! Pharmaceutical companies that explored various hormonal and chemical combinations to halt sperm production in the testicles found in their marketing studies that men were not as anxious to manipulate their reproductive processes, so there was less financial incentive for developing them.

By 1969, research in the United States and Great Britain had demonstrated that the amount of estrogen in the Pill did indeed increase the risk of clot-related disorders in the women who took them and that the Pill's contraceptive effectiveness could be maintained with considerably safer, reduced dosages of the hormone. Lower-dose pills became available quite quickly, minimizing the risks of strokes and heart attacks, although a small percentage of women curiously remained on the riskier, high-dose estrogen pills until those pills were voluntarily removed from the market in 1988. I can't help but wonder who didn't notice or didn't care. With today's low-dose oral contraceptives, the risk of blood clots is substantially lower than the risk of blood clots with pregnancy.

MORE BIRTH CONTROL RISKS

Just a couple of houses away from the home where the first neighborhood woman had suffered her second stroke and next door to Alfred Bloomer's duplex lived Ron Burkman, born five months to the day before me. After graduating from St. Lawrence a year before me, Ron went on to medical school to become a gynecologist, and I lost track of him. While he was aiming at a distinguished career in medicine, I had finally found my keys to the kingdom of shared sex, and I luxuriated in it. I thought I was being pretty careful and responsible, but that didn't keep me from a pregnancy scare that turned out to be a false alarm and a nasty infection that didn't. And there were some emotional upheavals for a couple of women whose pain was worse for me than my own. All in all, I found the world of sex to be very satisfying.

I had become a teacher, and after completing my graduate work in counseling and human development, I was hired to establish a counseling center at a college. For my most serious eventual relationship, the riskiest part was dating a former student, 10 years my junior. Although we had entered less constricted times, it was probably best that I had changed jobs at about the same time our relationship was becoming more public. My early practice with hiding sexual secrets had come in handy, but I was also learning that when it comes to sex, little remains hidden for long. Betsy, who would become my wife, was as eager and adventurous as I. We faced the perennial human struggle to prevent pregnancy before we married or were ready. Although the risks of birth control pills had been reduced by this time, we were both still reluctant. Betsy finally decided to try them, but their hormones tended to create nausea and discomfort for her in the mid-afternoon every day.

In an effort to relieve this suffering for sex, her gynecologist inserted an intrauterine device (IUD). The new IUDs were being touted for the freedom they brought to sex and the lack of worry or need to do anything on a regular basis except to have sex when you wanted to. Betsy's uterus had other plans. It writhed and cramped painfully for a few days until it managed to spit out the device as if it were a piece of gristle. Fortunately, she neither got pregnant nor suffered any ill effects beyond the nasty cramps. Back to the Pill we went, nausea or not.

Dr. Ronald T. Burkman was by then moving up the academic ranks at the Johns Hopkins University School of Medicine. He was one of the first physicians to note on the record that women with certain IUDs seemed to be at greater risk for serious, sometimes fatal pelvic inflammatory disease. Between 1980 and 1983, Ron authored eight papers in medical journals that fueled a mountain of lawsuits against the IUD makers, who finally withdrew all the devices from the market. Some birth control experts would claim that the baby had been thrown out with the bathwater, and as pharmaceutical companies invented contorted legal strategies for incorporating separate IUD manufacturing divisions in order to protect the parent companies from being bankrupted by further litigation, two intrauterine devices eventually became available once again. They are still today, though they have been rebranded as intrauterine *systems*.

It has always been difficult to ignore the fact that sex has some risks, but so do the various approaches we've come up with to reduce those risks. It can get discouraging.

THE COUNTERREVOLUTION GAINS A NEW WEAPON

During high school, I had my most open and searching conversations about sex with my friend and classmate Chad. There was little personal experience for either of us to talk about beyond fantasy and masturbation, but it was at least a relief to have someone to commiserate with about such things in venues other than locker rooms. Chad, I would discover, had learned out of necessity to hide more of his sexual secrets than most of us. Both of us were virgins at the end of high school, and he—by far the more adventurous—moved to Los Angeles after graduation to follow his dreams of eventual fame. Those dreams seemed silly and impractical to me, more the pragmatic scientist, but I respected his courage and bravado. While I would never see him again, we kept in touch for a time. He would eventually admit to me that he was gay, the first time anyone ever came out to me, and he continued to enlighten me about the gay lifestyle he had discovered quite by surprise in California. Same-gender sexual orientation and lifestyles carried a strong stigma then and remained largely hidden, so his reports made me feel like an ethnologist, fascinated by a faraway culture that was entirely foreign to me. His life consisted of an exciting sequence of sexual exploits that I envied for their utter bounty and abandon. Eventually, we lost touch.

About the same time Ron Burkman was writing about the risks of IUDs, there was a development on the West Coast that sparked curiosity in the medical community. A few papers appeared in medical journals recounting cases of gay men whose immune systems seemed to collapse over time, making them vulnerable to the rare Kaposi's sarcoma and a variety of other opportunistic infections. Their health would eventually deteriorate until they withered away both physically and mentally and died. The condition would eventually be labeled acquired immunodeficiency syndrome or AIDS.

Since AIDS spurred more finger-pointing as the "gay disease," it was not paid much heed by those who had no connections with the gay community. As soon as the human immunodeficiency virus had been identified and it was determined that it could be transmitted by any unprotected shared sex, the broader implications became more obvious and a level of sexual hysteria began to develop. The counterrevolutionaries who had for so long used fears of disease in attempts to scare young people away from sex grabbed onto HIV as the most powerful new weapon in their arsenal. The ethic of sexual abstinence that had largely been stymied by the sexual revolution's pursuit of individual sexual pleasure, found a fresh raison d'être. Ironically, as HIV/AIDS education became the newest call to arms in the war against sex, the incidence of other sexually transmitted diseases was reaching epidemic proportions.

I would learn eventually that Chad had been one of the early AIDS casualties, dying after the risks of searching for fulfilling sex had turned against him and his bravado.

Just as other sexually transmissible diseases had earlier become ammunition for sexual scare tactics, HIV/AIDS was exactly what the sexual temperance people needed to puff up their antisex arguments. It could now be said glibly that having sex could kill you. No fooling around this time. One misstep, one bow to temptation, and you could be dead because of sex. Truly risky business, and I had even known one of its first victims. It would be another decade before University of Chicago researchers who conducted the National Health and Social Life Survey proposed that person-to-person sexual transmission of HIV was not nearly as efficient as originally feared and that the U.S. epidemic was confined largely to inner cities, with only a weak sociological bridge to the outside.[7] The misinformation and exaggerations persist today, fostered in part by tactics used by well-intentioned but poorly informed sexuality educators.

Once the facts about HIV transmission had become clearer and thousands of gay men and intravenous drug abusers had fallen as the first AIDS victims, the gay community became mobilized for the fight. They established hostels to care for the dying, created effective ad campaigns to promote safer sex, and became activists in the fight for research funding. The percentage of new HIV infections among gay males dropped and continued to do so for nearly two decades. Since 2001, however, "men who have sex with men," as the Centers for Disease Control (CDC) classifies them, constitute the only group in the United States in which the number of new infections has risen annually. Among the 13- to 24-year-old group of gay males, the yearly increase in new HIV cases has risen by double digits, averaging 12 percent per year. Coupled with the realization that the number of HIV infections in the United States had been underreported by as much as 40 percent, the situation in the young gay male community is clearly not improving. Despite alarms that continue to blare, some younger gay males are not listening and are becoming more prone to risky sexual behaviors such as "barebacking," anal intercourse without a condom. Sexual desire often seems to trump prudent decision making. There is hubris in this risk taking that researchers are struggling to understand.[8]

Each time American society comes face-to-face with the fact that sexual behavior carries risks of harm in various guises, tides of activism rise up to discourage people from having sex, especially young people. We seem to retreat into a cocoon of sexual negativism that assumes that the only solution to avoiding the risky consequences of sex is abstaining from sex altogether, a strategy that runs counter to the realities of human nature and the power of sexual desire. Unfortunately, these periods calling for sexual abstinence are often followed by a realization that the warnings have been exaggerated, which then may be followed by a rebellion of sorts in the form of backlash risk taking.

We seem to retreat into a cocoon of sexual negativism that assumes that the only solution to avoiding the risky consequences of sex is abstaining from sex altogether, a strategy that runs counter to the realities of human nature and the power of sexual desire.

WHITHER THE SEXUAL REVOLUTION?

Just as the Pill has been simplistically cited as the trigger for the sexual revolution, HIV/AIDS has been declared its death knell. In fact, the Pill evolved out of several dynamic trends that had been unfolding for at least two decades, and this early hormonal method of birth control became possible only because the sexual revolution was already under way. It took another decade for revolutionary pressures to make it legal in all states and to be able to prescribe it to any sexually active woman who wanted it, whether or not she was married. The early waves of the sexual revolution paved the way to contraceptive access, not the other way around. The next revolutionary development in reproductive choice would be the Supreme Court's historic and still controversial *Roe v. Wade* decision in 1973, rendering it legal for women to seek abortion up to 24 weeks into pregnancy from qualified physicians. This surely was also spawned by the ongoing revolution.

Those first 20 to 25 years of the sexual revolution were characterized by a certain amount of "take what you can get while you can get it" sentiment. After all, the lines of people ready to be freed from sexual captivity had only grown longer. But it was far more than a time of heightened freedom for sexual activity. It was also a period during which the bedcovers were thrown off an entire spectrum of alternative (to heterosexual intercourse, that is) sexual behaviors, orientations, and lifestyles. The American Psychiatric Association (APA) depathologized homosexuality by removing it from its former categorization as a mental disorder. It was simply another variety on the wide spectrum of sexual proclivities. The television talk shows relished exposing sexual differences that shocked audiences and shook convictions about gender, sexual attraction, and the very concept of "normalcy." Everything we had believed, practiced, and hidden sexually was exposed to the light of examination. It was as unsettling a time as it was freeing.

There can be no doubt that HIV/AIDS sobered us up about the riskiness of the sexual revolution, although the newly recognized viral sexually transmitted diseases, such as genital herpes, human papillomavirus, and hepatitis B, had already begun the reality slap in our faces. When the hope of being entirely free of unwanted pregnancy or nasty infection was unmasked as the risky myth it was, most sensible people naturally pulled back a bit. But revolutionary inertia can be difficult to stem, so the doors to new dimensions of sexuality did not entirely close. We simply tried to keep them open more safely and sensibly. Unfortunately, there are still those who continue to replicate the more risky and reckless behaviors in fundamentally narcissistic and self-centered ways, some of whom then escape into the spurious "sex addiction" underbrush.

The sexual revolution gradually morphed into a more integrated and informed phase that was with us for another 20 or so years. It was a time of consolidation during which we began to make sense of all that had come our way in the first wave before we had been quite prepared to make good use of it in our lives. With the hope of overcoming nagging sexual dysfunction and phobic bigotry against a spectrum of sexual interests, people began to focus on the refining of their sexual lives into more satisfying, individualized patterns. Striving for good sex and seeking whatever help was needed to do so became acceptable. This pursuit would soon be aided by the marketing of medications, devices, and herbal potions that could help us get erections, feel more interested in sex, and last longer during sex.

As the Internet increased in popularity and use and the acceptance of human cultural diversity became an almost cardinal social requirement, we began to see heightened levels of awareness and honesty about the vast diversity of human sexual attractions and gender identities, greater freedom to exercise this diversity, and far greater access to others with similar interests and proclivities. The gay, lesbian, and bisexual groups around the country began to add letters to their former GLB acronyms: T for transgender, Q for queer or questioning, I for intersexed, A for allies, and so on. Everyone who didn't fit America's heterosexist parameters began to have a home and others of similar interests to communicate with.

Behind the scenes, sexuality research was ramping up the new understandings of the sexual nature of human life in ways never before imagined. How Alfred Kinsey would have loved to have had these more solid empirical data about human sexual behaviors and attitudes. How he would have marveled at the advances in our understandings of the genetic and neurohormonal templates on which human sexuality and gender are built, along with solid theory with which, for the first time ever, we could conceptualize sexual phenomena within some integrated, comprehensible frameworks. For the first time, solid theory about human sexuality took shape, theory to help us pursue whole new sets of hypotheses and flesh out critical details. In short, our sexuality was no longer the mystery it had been 50 years before. It no longer needed to be mostly a source of shame, confusion, conflict, or hidden behaviors. Its secrets would no longer be contained by laws, regulations, or even by human will. The stage was set for the real sexual transformation of America to begin.

THE 21ST-CENTURY SEXUAL TRANSFORMATION

During the first couple of years of the 2000s, I began to see renewed emphasis on global concepts of sexual health and sexual rights. Perhaps most surprising of all was the appearance of articles in professional publications that began to highlight the importance of sexual *pleasure*! It wasn't that the idea of sex being pleasurable was new, but writing about it as a legitimate and even sacred part of the human experience was refreshingly new. Perhaps the marketing of the erection drugs had played a role in creating acceptance of the idea of doing something intentionally to increase sexual pleasure. Whatever the reason, the manufacturers of condoms and personal lubricants have now rather unobtrusively begun to market products for increasing sexual pleasure. There are lubricants for women and men, marketed with the promise of intense sexual sensations and orgasms to knock your socks off. The Church and Dwight Company, manufacturers of Trojan brand condoms, have come out with a whole new line of vibrating products to enhance sexual pleasure. These include rings that fit over the penis that can be programmed to four different vibrating intensities and can be used with or without a condom. They also sell several different models of vibrators for clitoral and vaginal stimulation. Several other condom manufacturers have produced similar lines of vibrators. They are advertised on MTV and other channels and sold in mainstream drugstores from racks right beside the toothpaste and Dr. Scholl's. Sexual pleasure has become acceptable and legitimate, and you no longer have to go online or to a dingy sex store to purchase the aids that can help intensify that pleasure.[9] If you compare this with a couple of decades back, the transformation is really pretty remarkable.

Additionally, sexuality theory is enabling us to transform our understandings of human sexuality into the legitimate branch of science it deserves to be, with consequent expectations that its findings be used to help shape social policy. Sexuality is simply too big and overarching a phenomenon to be subsumed as a peripheral specialty, an amusement for a few giggles or a source of amazing facts with which to shock your friends at parties. It is a scientific field in its own right. Its findings are relevant to other models of human nature and human social conduct. Like physics, mathematics, psychology, or anthropology, it must also be somewhat of an art, tinted with the subtleties of human emotion and the lovely and horrible complexities of relational dynamics.

The foundation on which this sexual transformation is now building is an impressive one, characterized by far more startling discoveries than we have ever before known about this intriguing aspect of being human. The enormous progress in neuroscience is one example. In a relatively short time, we have pieced together an amazing array of information about how our neurons work, how neurotransmitters in the brain shape our moods and intensify or mute emotions, how various portions of the brain become active during the mysterious experiences of love and sexual pleasure, and how our genes and hormones weave their way through the workings of our minds and personalities. The fields of neurophysiology and psychology have likewise been revolutionized. They are whole new sciences now. So is the science of human sexuality.

While our comprehension of the mechanisms of inner human experience takes on entirely new dimensions, social and cultural reformations reflect both the fresh realizations that emanate from us and the changing ways of thinking that we absorb from them in a wonderful, interactive dance. As our political parties shrank into polarized camps of conflicting ideologies, so paralyzed by the fear of compromise that they were unable to act at all, the public cried out in frustration and desperation for something better, a way to let down artificial boundaries of rigid dualistic thinking so that we could move again as a nation. When it comes to sexual matters, most everyone now understands that things just aren't as simple as white and black. It is time to put that understanding into practice.

One of the more interesting social perspectives that has taken hold is the way people now define what is meant by "having sex." Years ago, when I used terms such as "sexually active," I was referring to any form of shared sexual activity. In more recent times and as a wider range of shared sexual activities has become acceptable, we've had to become more careful about the meanings of our terms. While I doubt that Bill Clinton was solely responsible for this shift when he claimed that he "did not have sexual relations" with Monica Lewinsky, meaning specifically that he had not had sexual intercourse with her, his very precise legalistic strategy made us more acutely aware that young people were becoming craftily more exacting about their meanings of "having sex" too. A study of nearly 500 university students has found that 98 percent of them considered penile–vaginal intercourse to be "sex," and 78 percent defined penile–anal intercourse as such. However, less than 20 percent considered oral–genital contact to constitute sex, and the figures were even lower for every other sexual activity.[10]

We also now have an unprecedented ability to retrieve digitally stored and sorted information about any sexual topic. If there was ever any hope of controlling how much kids could find out about sex, that hope has surely been dashed. In my opinion, we're all the better for it. Why should anyone be kept from any information about human sexuality? Why don't we all have a right to learn everything we can about some sexual topic that has come to our attention? Are there things that we really shouldn't know until we've reached a certain age, and how could such a prohibition be implemented now anyway? Perhaps we'll also have to modify our ideas about the "readiness to learn" something to include the motivation and ability to access it. But we develop those motivations and abilities sooner rather than later. Any hope of preserving the presumed "innocence" of childhood for long, if indeed that innocence involves relative ignorance about sexuality, is mostly a vain hope. We must accept the fact—whether we like it or not—that sex information, like all information, is now largely uncensorable. It cannot any longer be contained or controlled; it is there for all to see.

Our constant interplay with cyberspace renders this true for most everything we used to call private. We can still close and lock the bedroom or bathroom door, for sure, but almost everything else we think about and enjoy and dream about having will be known by others. When our thoughts and dreams become expressed on search engines and website purchases, the gnomes of cyberspace sneak into our communication devices to root this stuff out and pass it on to others who want to know. In many ways, personal privacy is a thing of the past. This doesn't upset me as much as it does most people. I see the waning of privacy as one of the changing aspects of our world that simply must be accepted and adapted to—for the better, it is hoped. What else can we do? When it comes to matters of sex, privacy has often been synonymous with secrecy and hiding, and much of the time these habits are reflections of alienation from ourselves, of not being at home in our own skins, and I would like to see less need for such personal covertness. I also recall the fears that raged for a time about the Internet destroying our sense of community when in fact it has created all sorts of new communities and new abilities to stay in close touch with those we care about or have something in common with. If anything, it has created a greater sense of community—locally and globally—than the world has ever before known.

But there is a paradoxical side of privacy too. When I was a teenager, our home had but one telephone. It represented the only viable way, other than face-to-face communication and the U.S. Postal Service, to stay in touch with my friends. We would try to get the telephone cord to reach into another room or the nearby coat closet in order to have a modicum of privacy, but there was usually a giggling little brother spying on us or a parent yelling at us to stop tying up the line. Today, nearly everyone has a personal telephone/texting/photo-sharing device that can be used in complete privacy, almost anywhere, anytime. So, while many of the details of our hopes and dreams stream around the Internet, an entirely new level of private communication has quickly and irrevocably been commandeered for communicating with those we love and also for erotic purposes such as "sexting" and pornography viewing. This should hardly come as a surprise; every information or entertainment technology ever invented has found its erotic uses.

In professional circles, one of the most fascinating signs of transformation is represented in the changing judgments about what is "normal" sexually. After 1973, when the APA depathologized homosexuality, many other sexual attractions and practices and transgender identities continued to be considered mental disorders worthy of psychological treatment. The new edition of the APA's *Diagnostic and Statistical Manual of Mental Disorders* (*DSM-5*) will delist many of them. Transgender disorder will now be referred to as gender incongruence or dysphoria, and, in fact, as more and more children are declaring themselves to be transgendered earlier in their lives, the Endocrine Society, the nation's oldest and largest professional organization of clinical endocrinologists, has promulgated guidelines for hormonal treatment that will delay puberty for transgendered adolescents until they are ready to choose a final biological direction for their bodies.[11] This is a remarkable change in medical practice as well as a stunning affirmation that as society has become more aware of and open about the spectrum of sexual and gender differences, even children and adolescents have clearer identity signposts with which to understand and define themselves sexually. This is a luxury of development that has never before existed.

Many of the kinky sexual attractions, save the potentially harmful ones such as pedophilia, have been removed from the *DSM-5*, with mental health professionals finally declaring that if society wants to judge such behaviors as wrong, then society should make and enforce laws about them, but that if psychological data do not suggest that they are pathological or dangerous and there is no known way to alter them, they should not be considered treatable disorders. Again, this is a major shift within the mental health community as we decide no longer to assume that sexual kinkiness is, by definition, sick.

Another long overdue shift in perceptions is taking shape from recent studies of child and adolescent sexuality that have begun to bear fruit. The National Longitudinal Study of Adolescent Health started following 20,000 adolescents in grades 7 to 12 beginning in the mid-1990s, and its findings have been emerging over several years. The long-standing National Survey of Family Growth finally started asking questions about sexual behavior in 2002, as has the CDC study called the National Youth Risk Behavior Survey, so we can now spot trends in youthful sexual behaviors. The CDC closely coordinates this study with the Health Behaviors in School-Aged Children study that surveys sexual health issues in 35 areas around the world. For the first time, we are getting reliable data about the sexuality of kids, and entirely new concepts and perceptions are emerging.[12]

We are finally getting a clear and honest look at the sexual development parameters of adolescence and youth, and an entirely new conceptual model is taking shape. We now recognize—or perhaps *admit*—that normative adolescent development involves the exploration of sexual feelings and behaviors and that there is a continuous flow of this individual evolutionary process into adult sexuality. We are beginning to shed the outmoded and unsupportable assumption that all adolescent sexual behaviors are risky and harmful instead of being normal developments on the path to adulthood that may have positive as well as negative consequences. As Carolyn Tucker Halpern, associate professor of maternal and child health in the Gillings School of Global Public Health at the University of North Carolina, has said,

> If we accept that healthy sexuality is central to general well-being and that healthy adolescence entails active exploration of identity, values, goals, and behavior, then our research must include meaningful efforts to identify and understand life-course pathways to sexual well-being. For some adolescents, a fine line may divide exploratory sexual activity that ultimately contributes to positive sexual identity and competence, and sexual activity that significantly increases risk of harm. We do

not know how to help youth navigate this line, or even exactly where or what that line is for individuals of diverse physical, psychological and cultural characteristics (e.g., biological sex, physical disability, sexual orientation and gender ideology) who are exposed to varying experiences at different points in the life course.[13]

So let's stop wasting our time and money on desperate and largely unsuccessful efforts to persuade the adolescents and youth of America to avoid sex and instead put our resources toward figuring out what is and isn't sexually harmful for them. Then we could legitimately offer them helpful guidelines for navigating their sexual lives.

THE RISKY BUSINESS THAT KNOWS NO END

When we're lucky, the sudden and drastic changes of revolution beget the more gradual and substantive shifts of social transformation, and that is indeed what is happening with American sexuality. Our sexuality is no longer the mystery or the secret it was 60 years ago. Researchers are finally feeling free enough to look into questions of sexuality that were previously taboo. Yet most disheartening for me in the face of this remarkable level of social change, including easy access to the most explicit views of human beings engaged in any sexual behavior ever imagined, is the fact that we in America have not yet settled on suitable means for preparing our children and adolescents for healthy, happy, comfortable, and satisfying sexual lives. We have not yet implemented the ways to permit our youth to integrate, without guilt or self-deprecation, their perfectly normal sexual needs and behaviors into their personalities and relationships in healthy and responsible ways.

We have for the most part left the youth of this country to their own devices, and they pay the price. To me, this is a travesty of neglect and irresponsibility of epic proportions and one of the riskiest sexual choices our society has ever made. We seem to forget that the desire and capacity for sexual pleasure are hardwired into the human brain and that they represent the inner forces behind the constant defiance of the risks. Evolutionary psychologists maintain that survival of the species is a prime directive of human nature, intertwined

We have for the most part left the youth of this country to their own devices, and they pay the price.

along the helices of the oldest DNA strands in our genes and expressed constantly in our strategies to connect sexually, risks be damned. Why not give kids all the information they'll need to see all sides of their sexuality?

Sex has always had its risks no matter how hard we try to minimize them. It always will. Regardless of how much we try to frighten the young with lurid stories about the dangers of raw physical connection, divert them with alternatives in an effort to sap their time and energy, or warn them about the emotional toll that sexual relationships can reap, they are still going to believe that the risks seem worth it in the face of crazy love and passionate desire. Along the way, they'll experience some of the bad things that sex can bring their way, but they'll also learn about the wonderful side of it. Realistic sexuality education and preparation for life that opens them to *all* the complexities of human sexuality, sexual choices, and human relationships are the strongest options we have for protecting them as best we can ever hope to do. The best evidence we have at present is that thoroughgoing, honest sexuality education that delivers repeated, consistent, and scientifically supportable messages about careful decision making, along with the various methods of protecting oneself from pregnancy and disease, is most likely to persuade young people to postpone shared sex until they are more emotionally ready *and* to get them to use condoms and other forms of protection when they ultimately decide to proceed with a sexual encounter.[14] I don't think there is more we can hope for in our culture.

MANAGING THE AMERICAN SEXUAL TRANSFORMATION

A student of mine recently commented to me that the study of human sexuality is odd among the sciences in that it lacks clear definition and identity, and he was absolutely right. Even though German researcher Iwan Bloch coined the term "sexual science" in 1906 and professionals in the field today call themselves sexologists, that term was always underlined in red by my spell-checker until just recently. That's progress. But sexology is still quite underdeveloped, unassertive, and naive. Even our theories are mostly rudimentary. We still lack documented agreement on what facts, principles, and life skills should be taught to the young in order for them to have the best chance of developing as sexually healthy individuals. We have no canon that holds sexuality educators responsible for providing a basic, solid foundation of sexual knowledge.

My student wondered what would happen if the scientific world were too afraid or embarrassed to teach the fundamentals of physics: gravity, the relationship of energy and mass, or quantum mechanics. There would be no physics departments and only an abbreviated course or two in most colleges, leaving us to hope that the young would discover the realities of gravity and inertia before they were maimed or killed as a result of their ignorance. Self-appointed physicists might offer clandestine classes in church basements at night, but Einstein and string theory would be broached only in whispers. We do indeed still have a long way to go in sexology.[15]

In the pages of this book ahead, I will be developing these and other points that I have had the extraordinary opportunity to explore in my various life roles. In every one of those roles, sexuality has been, at various times, central. That is because it is a central part, a central truth, of being human. As such, it is a force of human nature that makes us nervous. For centuries, religions have felt the need to contain and control that sexual nature, to separate the good from the bad, the black from the white. Societies have felt the need to codify what sexual orientations and behaviors will be considered acceptable and who will be marginalized or ostracized. Lawmakers and social policymakers have attempted to corral our sexual natures into boxes that create unjustified smugness about who is right and who is wrong.

One of the most obvious outcomes of the sexual revolution was to make external control of sexuality almost impossible. The usual powers of repression, oppression, and even good judgment were largely rendered impotent and ineffectual. This has had many positive outcomes, but it also created a dizzying array of options and opportunities that can appeal to our more selfish instincts and fleshy fickleness. That is the risky part.

All the more reason that as a society we must live up to our responsibilities for preparing our young people for life as sexual beings. And we must face facts as we do so. Those persons whom we might like the young to look to as models of propriety, good sense, responsibility, and ethical behavior—government officials, priests and other leaders of our faith communities, teachers, coaches, and athletes—all too often make headlines with their sexual feet of clay. Nothing seems to destroy a reputation or role model faster than sexual scandal, and scandals happen to some of the most respected people we know. Secret sexual liaisons rarely remain secret for long, and we find some glee in unearthing those secrets.

So do we search for other role models, more upstanding adults who manage to keep their zippers zipped and their pants and blouses on? Or do we help young people understand how powerful and capricious sexual energies can be? How much strength and will it can take to be true to one's own sexual ethics? How even essentially good grown-up people can make risky and stupid sexual misjudgments?

How do we help kids understand the power of sex in their lives while still feeling good about themselves? How do we begin to accept the legitimate pleasures of sex and leave old, unfair guilts and uncertainties behind? How do we as adults manage the confusion, risks, and sexual constrictions that our own lack of good sex education has wrought? This is what America's sexual transformation now needs to be all about.

Chapter 2

THE GRANDES DAMES OF SEX: THE WOMEN WHO MADE IT HAPPEN

Revolutions are usually marshaled by men, their masculine energies thrusting swords or pointed words into the guts of other men to overcome oppression or lay claim to some real or philosophical landscape. Revolutions can be bloody, loud, and deadly as men who perceive themselves to be noble and clearheaded strive for new freedom and fresh thinking while stomping out the echoes of what they see as narrow-mindedness and outmoded ideals. As I made my way through the battlefields of the sexual revolution, my captains—the leaders who set the pace with the beat of their sensible words—were nearly all women. I eventually concluded that this particular period of social change, in its revolutionary roots as well as in its evolutionary longevity, has been sustained in many significant ways by feminine energies.

Geert Hofstede, who is a man and a Dutch organizational sociologist, has been comparing personal values and behaviors, along with the way institutions and organizations tend to operate, in 74 countries or regions of the world based on their Masculinity Indices (MAS).[1] The MAS measures the degree to which people of both sexes tend to endorse goals that are generally more

---

This chapter is adapted from a lecture I delivered at Wellesley College, sponsored by the Phi Sigma Lecture Society. The lecture was titled "Positively Sexual," and because Wellesley is a women's college, I featured a series of quotations and biographical details from significant women in the field of sexuality.

popular among males. In other words, it is a measure of how much the society values traditional, stereotypical masculine qualities. The United States ends up somewhere in the middle of the pack, but there are some very telling characteristics regarding sexual behavior in those countries that have a high MAS, meaning that they lean toward valuing traditional male qualities. Attitudes about sex are more moralistic, sexual double standards and sexual harassment are rife, homosexuality is not well accepted, young people are influenced more by their peers than by their parents, and sex is quite ego oriented (it's all about the success of the performance). The United States is far less like this now than it was at the beginning of the sexual revolution, but some of these high-MAS qualities remain in play to some extent.

By contrast, Hofstede has found that in countries where there is a low MAS, where feminine traits and goals are held in higher esteem and are less upstaged by traditional masculine approaches to things, the sexual atmosphere is much less constrained and rigid. Attitudes about sex are more matter-of-fact, homosexuality is simply viewed as a fact of life, there is no double standard and women enjoy sex more, kids are more influenced by their parents, and the focus of sex is on relating to others in intimate ways rather than as a way to show off. The nurturing emphasis of the feminine is allowed to have a higher priority. Within sexology, I have noticed that male-directed work often—not always but often—has the focused, analytic quality of male scientists. While female sex researchers and leaders of the field can be just as empirically adept and analytical as the males, their work is also often tempered with more nuanced global insights. I am convinced that while men were surely good soldiers for the sexual revolution, especially in bravely tackling some controversial areas of sex research, women have been the more important agents of change and are now crucial to propelling the sexual transformation.

I surely do not mean to diminish the contributions in sexology of men who have been essential and trendsetting in their own right. Their work has at times represented major leaps forward. Alfred Kinsey gave us the earliest survey data that provided windows into the sexual lives of American men and women, and the shades on those windows have never again been closed. William Masters, who designed his sexual studies before he hired Virginia Johnson as an assistant, courageously studied the physiology of human sexual response and cleared up centuries of unanswered questions. But Kinsey and Masters approached their subjects with the same scientific objectivity and precision they had brought to their previous nonsexual research, Kinsey to his study of gall wasps, Masters to the treatment of postmenopausal women with hormone replacement (which we know now wasn't such a grand idea). They gathered data with dispassionate interviews and sterile instruments, aligning the numbers in neat tables and preparing tasteful drawings and charts while cautioning their research teams not to allow their emotions to get the better of them. Plain, raw science in service of the truth. That's just fine to a point, but as a powerful and somewhat mysterious part of the human psyche and personality and as an aspect of human nature that has raised the hackles of political, religious, and cultural movements for centuries, sexuality is a topic to be nurtured with delicacy and sensitivity as well.

My wife likens the awareness of men, in their loving and family relationships, to a spotlight that searches around them, bringing into focus those things on which the circular glare of the spotlight falls. They can see those things with the greatest of clarity, and they can examine them, think about them, and talk about them with precision and depth. They can strategize and philosophize about them with ease. On the other hand, she says that women survey their surroundings as if they had short- and long-range radar, seeing all the many quandaries and predicaments that need attention and help. They are sensitive to the complications that lie in the penumbra of the spotlight. They grasp the nuances of negotiated persuasion that may be necessary to foster new perspectives. So while men may understand quite clearly that reservations must be made for a getaway weekend, women will see all the preparations yet to be made, from arranging a sitter for the kids to getting the clothes washed before they can be packed. This is not to say that either approach to awareness is necessarily better than the other, although that may be so for some tasks in life. A precise and objective focus on a problem can be as enlightening as it can be incomplete, and the expansive view can be as intimidating and overwhelming as it can be illuminating. But in the transformation of society's attitudes and mores relating to sexuality, it has often been women's perspectives and patient persistence that have woken us up and brought us along.

As a powerful and somewhat mysterious part of the human psyche and personality and as an aspect of human nature that has raised the hackles of political, religious, and cultural movements for centuries, sexuality is a topic to be nurtured with delicacy and sensitivity.

FREEING WOMEN FROM SEXUAL BONDAGE

Margaret Sanger (1879–1966) was one of those early change agents. Born in Corning, New York, of Catholic parents, her mother had 18 pregnancies and died at age 50 because of the toll that these pregnancies had taken on her body. Sanger trained to become a nurse and began working in Brooklyn, where she saw desperate women unable to cope with their large families and dying from botched illegal abortions. Yet she and all medical professionals were prohibited by federal laws from disseminating even information about birth control in the United States, the only Western nation in the world at that time to have criminalized contraception. In her autobiography, Sanger wrote of an incident in July 1912 when she cared for a woman who had nearly died from a self-induced abortion. After a three-week convalescence, the woman's doctor had come for a final visit, and Sanger drew him aside to tell him of Mrs. Sach's fears:

> "Mrs. Sachs is worried about having another baby."
>
> "She may well be," replied the doctor, and then he stood before her and said, "Any more such capers, young woman, and there'll be no need to send for me."
>
> "I know doctor," she replied timidly, "but," and she hesitated as though it took all her courage to say it, "what can I do to prevent it?"
>
> The doctor was a kindly man, and he had worked hard to save her, but such incidents had become so familiar to him that he had long since lost whatever delicacy he might have once had, "You want to have your cake and eat it too, do you? Well, it can't be done."
>
> Then picking up his hat to depart, he said, "Tell Jake to sleep on the roof."
>
> I glanced quickly at Mrs. Sachs. Even through my sudden tears I could see stamped on her face an expression of absolute despair. We simply looked at each other, saying no word until the door had closed behind the doctor. Then she lifted her thin, blue-veined hands and clasped them beseechingly, "He can't understand. He's only a man. But you do, don't you? Please tell me the secret, and I'll never breathe it to a soul. *Please!*"[2]

Secrets. Sexual secrets have heaped mountains of guilt on people, interfered with their abilities to protect themselves effectively from unwanted sexual consequences, and kept them ignorant of some of the most fundamental aspects of being human—secrets held by people who are convinced that they know best and believe that their guardianship of sexual knowledge and practice is divinely or morally ordained. Women know that they must be wary of secrets.

Margaret Sanger was summoned three months later to the Sachs' dingy apartment for the same reason, but this time Mrs. Sachs quickly bled to death, leaving her agonized husband and three small children behind. It was this tragedy that caused Sanger to vow that she would work to change the destiny of such women. Even in 1912, she was dreaming about the possibility of an eventual "magic pill" that could prevent pregnancy, and in 1914 she coined the term "birth control." She would be arrested more than once and would exile herself for a time in Europe before returning to Brooklyn to open a birth control clinic among the tenements. She founded the American Birth Control League in 1921. As her struggle to liberate the secrets of contraception continued and the Great Depression created new economic necessities for limiting family size, the number of birth control clinics in the United States grew to 800 by 1942. This was the year that Sanger's Birth Control League changed its name to Planned Parenthood Federation of America.[3] It is an organization that encounters misunderstanding and opposition to this day. There are still many who want the sexual secrets to be kept.

FINDING A FEMININE VOICE IN A MAN'S WORLD

Anais Nin (1903–1977) was a diarist and author whose writings influenced feminist thought and perceptions of the erotic in literature. Born in France, her mother brought her to New York City as a girl. She was one of the first women to write about sexuality from a woman's perspective. Although she was well acquainted with the fine erotic literature of Europe, she was concerned that no good writer in the United States had ever tried to explore sexuality, only the second-rate writers and never women. In the 1940s, Henry Miller—author of famously sexually explicit books himself—told Anais Nin about a male customer who would pay a dollar a page for sexy stories, his own private store of erotic literature. She needed the money and soon had earned $100 for her efforts. But Miller warned her that the guy wanted her to leave out the poetry, analysis, and philosophy and just stick to the sexy stories. That, I think, reminds us again of the masculine approach to the erotic, and I make that statement only as an observation, without negative judgment. Nin's recollections of her erotic writing, published as *Delta of Venus* just a year before her death in the midst of the sexual revolution, remind us of the need to listen for one's own language of sexuality, to hear one's own erotic voice:

> I had a feeling that Pandora's box contained the mysteries of woman's sensuality, so different from man's and for which man's language was inadequate. The language of sex had yet to be invented. The language of the senses was yet to be explored. D. H. Lawrence began to give instinct a language, he tried to escape the clinical, the scientific, which only captures what the body feels. . . .

> Women, I thought, were more apt to fuse sex with emotion, with love. . . . But although women's attitude toward sex was quite distinct from that of men, we had not yet learned how to write about it.

> Here in the erotica I was writing to entertain, under pressure from a client who wanted me to "leave out the poetry," I believed that my style was derived from the

reading of men's works. For this reason I long felt that I had compromised my feminine self. I put the erotica aside. Rereading it these many years later, I see my own voice was not completely suppressed. In numerous passages I was intuitively using a woman's language, seeing experiences from a woman's point of view. I finally decided to release the erotic for publication because it shows the beginning efforts of a woman in a world that has been the domain of men.[4]

Women's sexuality couldn't be fully explored or addressed until it had found its voice, and it would take many other women to refine its language. The resurgence of feminist thinking that accompanied the sexual revolution went beyond the usual demands for equal rights and treatment. It also raised questions about the very origins of gender and the sex dichotomous stereotypes undergirding the rigid roles that often did not suit either women or men particularly well. A few European women wrote influential books about the emancipation of women from overly confining gender roles, including Simone de Beauvoir's *The Second Sex*, but American critics and commentators remained reluctant to admit that these issues affected those of us on the other side of the Atlantic. In fact, de Beauvoir was accused of not understanding what life was all about and of talking only about French women. It took an alert, well-educated American housewife named Betty Friedan (1921–2006), in her book *The Feminine Mystique*, to capture the essence of what was constraining American women and to encourage them to break out of roles they no longer found fulfilling.

Reflecting how hidden or perhaps unrecognized the issue was, Friedan's opening chapter was titled "The Problem That Has No Name."[5] In it, she described the inner dissatisfactions and yearnings that mid-century American women were experiencing, soul stirring but unspoken doubts about whether their roles as wives, mothers, cooks, cleaners, and caretakers were really enough. These women had "heard in voices of tradition and of Freudian sophistication that they could desire no greater destiny" than to revel in such roles. "They were taught to pity the neurotic, unfeminine, unhappy women who wanted to be poets or physicists or presidents. They learned that truly feminine women do not want careers, higher education, political rights." Women were marrying at younger and younger ages by the end of the 1950s, anxious to embark on their appointed path to household femininity. It was Betty Friedan who gave American women the permission not to ignore their inner voices that said, "I want something more than my husband and my children and my home." Talk about revolutionary!

Three years after *The Feminine Mystique* was published, Betty Friedan helped found the National Organization for Women (NOW) and became its first president. It remains one of the most influential organizations in support of women's rights even in times when American youth have grown increasingly skeptical about a feminism they tend to perceive in the most radical of terms.

In 1993, Friedan turned her attention to the needs of older people. She wrote in the *New York Times*, "Once you break through the mystique [air of mystery] of age and that view of the aged as objects of care and as problems for society, you can look at the reality of the new years of human life open to us."[6] This attitude has been integral to the sexual revolution's recognition of the sexual nature of human beings even into old age.

Several women sexologists have played key roles in helping us to understand feminist perspectives on sexuality. When I was editor of the *Journal of Sex Education and Therapy*, I received a number of fine papers from Naomi McCormick, who was getting her start in the field as an assistant professor of psychology at the State University in Plattsburgh, New York. She was a clearheaded and articulate author as well who became president of the Society for the Scientific Study of Sexuality in 1995. In her presidential address, she reminded us that feminism is not antimale or antisexual and emphasized the need for women to affirm sexuality research in their own right. She said that "feminist sexology is not limited to the study of men's sexual aggression or exploitation of women. Yes, feminist sexologists study rape, child sexual abuse, and domestic violence. Yes, some of us examine the possible harmful effects of pornography. . . . Feminist sexologists also study sexual pleasure, promote sex-positive attitudes, and affirm positive benefits to women from sex work and erotica."[7] By the turn of the 21st century, women of every ilk, including the women of sexology, had come into their own.

SEXUALITY EDUCATION AS A SOCIAL RESPONSIBILITY

One of the key women in the sexual revolution was Mary Steichen Calderone (1904–1998), daughter of photographer Edward Steichen and niece of poet Carl Sandburg. Born in Paris of artistic parents and raised among the great European artists and thinkers of the time, Calderone received her secondary education at the Brearley School in New York City. After earning her degree in chemistry at Vassar, she studied acting for three years and married an actor. She had two daughters with him, and when one of them died at age eight, she abandoned acting, divorced her husband, and sank into a deep depression. As she put her life back together, she decided to attend medical school at the University of Rochester and received her MD in 1939 at age 35. She remarried in 1941 and became medical director of Planned Parenthood Federation in 1953. Her tenure there was prolific and successful, but she was becoming increasingly alarmed about the prevailing lack of accurate sexual information in our culture and concluded that "handing out contraceptives was not enough." She was a devoted Quaker, mindful of the need for social awareness and social action even for the advancement of unpopular causes, and determined to do something about the problem. In 1964, at age 60, with the help and support of several male colleagues who were outspoken advocates for openness about sexuality, Mary Calderone founded the Sex (now Sexuality) Information and Education Council of the U.S. (SIECUS) and became its first leader. She would be a leading voice in the movement to improve access to thoroughgoing sexuality education for the next 20 years, and the organization's publications became a primary site for highlighting cutting-edge sex research. SIECUS remains an influential organization today.

In 1974, Mary Calderone wrote the following in the introduction to a book she edited titled *Sexuality and Human Values*, demonstrating again the integrative power of the feminine perspective:[8]

> The mythologies about sex simply have to go. . . . There are too many other shibboleths in modern society that need to be cleared away, to permit continued existence of the ridiculous ones that hem in or distort this one human faculty—especially one so important in the evolution of people toward full capacity to relate to each other in warmth, tenderness, care, and joy . . . the fear of the erotic in human behavior has to go.

> Right here is where I find it easiest to shift my focus from the understandings of eroticism as a scientist to the celebration of it as a religious person. . . . I find that I simply cannot convince myself that the erotic aspect of human life is not as truly integral to "that of God in every person," as is, for instance, the intellectual, the cognitive. Descartes' *I think, therefore I am* cannot be considered without the complimentary *I feel, therefore I am*. [And this] inescapably requires consideration, and celebration, of the erotic.

My friendship with Mary began in 1970 when I coordinated her visit to a conference on sex education in northern New York State as our keynote speaker. In one of the conference sessions, she held sway with hundreds of students who had been bused to the event from many schools. They submitted questions about sex that Mary deftly answered with honesty, humor, and sensitivity. She was an inspiration for them and for the educators who looked on. I would come to admire her dedication to the cause of sexuality education. On Easter morning of 1980, my wife and I met her for brunch in New York City at the St. Regis Hotel's Old King Cole Room. The night before, Mary had seen *Grease* on Broadway. She huffed and rolled her eyes, asserting, "It's about fucking, plain and simple!" And one thing about which she was adamant was that sex had to be about a lot more than fucking.

In addition to recommending to a publisher that I write a book for teenagers about sexuality and writing a foreword for that book, Mary served as a key mentor for me until she was into her 80s and Alzheimer's began to rob her of her sharp gaze and radiant mind. She was the one who had rightfully berated me for not having been more sensitive to the needs of gay teens in the first edition of the book that she was responsible for my writing and who had sent my wife and me a beautifully illustrated book on baby massage when our first child was born. Her judgment was impeccable, her courage in the face of constant attacks by the religious right inspirational, and her intelligence and personal warmth always evident.

In 1967, another organization was forged that had somewhat broader objectives than SIECUS. It was originally called the American Association of Sex Educators and Counselors but eventually grew into the expanded title of American Association of Sexuality Educators, Counselors, and Therapists (AASECT). Its founder was Patricia Schiller, JD. Pat Schiller would become my friend and mentor too, although she and Mary Calderone had very different styles, both leading increasingly powerful sex organizations.

Just as deliberate and strategic as Mary Calderone was in setting up and running her organization in a New York City office suite, Pat Schiller was energetic and motivated for getting things going from the kitchen table of her home in Washington, D.C. Mary was an elegant presence who was articulate and precise in her language, always with a dramatic flair and measured tone; Pat was a tall and gangly woman who wandered around in her garden of words, warmly delivering her message in a loud monotone. I would occasionally catch indications that they didn't care much for each other. I gathered that Pat thought that Mary was snooty and spent too much of her funding on fancy trappings (SIECUS had a grant from the Rockefeller Foundation for a time), and my impression was that Mary felt that Pat had bitten off more than she was qualified to chew. Perhaps both of them were a bit right and a bit perturbed by the other's successes, but both ultimately had significant roles to play in bringing more structure and professionalism to the sexual revolution. In one abiding goal, the two of them were of like mind. They were convinced that the children and adolescents of America needed and deserved thorough and ongoing exposure to high-quality sexuality education. Their commitment to this end was unwavering.

For all her bluster and dither, Pat knew what the profession needed, and AASECT eventually began to offer certification for sexuality educators, counselors, and therapists who could meet the qualifying criteria. It was a major undertaking as well as a tremendous responsibility for any organization to manage over time, but it assured AASECT a central and enduring role in the sexuality professions. I directed several AASECT summer workshops on my campus for educators and therapists who were anxious to earn the necessary credits for certification, while the central organization was being strained by its diverse directions and pressures. Pat asked me once if I would consider coming to AASECT as its executive director because she thought I had good organizational skills. She knew, I think, that she was getting in over her head and wanted to be freed up as an idea person who would not have to be occupied daily with mushrooming administrative details. I wasn't interested in doing that either, so I declined, although I eventually agreed to take over the editorship of AASECT's *Journal of Sex Education and Therapy*, a volunteer job that lasted for eight years.

Mary Calderone and Pat Schiller would both eventually lose control of the organizations they founded and retreat from them, but their contributions forged a new level of awareness about sexuality, new criteria for those who wanted to teach or offer therapy in the field, and a new sense of legitimacy for those who believed that the fight for sexual truth was worth fighting. Pat Schiller was quoted as saying in 2009, at age 96, that "a substantial part of sex education is nonverbal and much of what people learn about sex is not from what is said, but by what is not said."[9] And what is not said is often what young people pick up on and learn *not* to talk about, at least with adults. I've heard many a parent brag about how they've told their kids, "You can ask me anything about sex." They sometimes wonder why their kids have seemed reluctant to take them up on the offer. I fear that only too often, the offer has come too late and the young person is uncertain how the parent will judge their already established sexual behaviors. The additional unspoken parental message may be, "But I'll be upset if you're sexually active."

Debra Haffner was one of Mary Calderone's successors as president and chief executive officer of SIECUS, and one of her most important legacies was organizing a coalition of organizations concerned with human sexuality in youth and convening the National Commission on Adolescent Sexual Health. When the United States was getting caught up in the big-government give-away to support abstinence-only sexuality education, Haffner was one of the most powerful voices to remind us that in fact we were missing an opportunity to tell young people about the very positive and healthful aspects of sexuality. In the commission's report, after reaffirming the obvious value of encouraging "adolescents to delay sexual behaviors until they are ready physically, cognitively, and emotionally," she wrote,[10]

> Society must also recognize that a majority of adolescents will become involved in sexual relationships during their teenage years. Adolescents should receive support and education for developing the skills to evaluate their readiness for mature sexual relationships. Responsible adolescent intimate relationships, like those of adults, should be based on shared personal values, and should be consensual, non-exploitative, honest, pleasurable, and protected against [unwanted consequences]. . . .
>
> Parents are the primary sexuality educators of their children. . . . In homes where there is open communication about contraception and sexuality, young people often behave more responsibly. At a minimum, such communication may help young people accept their own sexual feelings and actions. With open communication, young people are more likely to turn to their parents in times of trouble; without it, they will not.

Debra Haffner spent 12 years at SIECUS, increasing its budget and staff, but eventually felt a broader calling. She received a master of divinity degree from

Union Theological Seminary and was ordained as a Unitarian Universalist minister. Like Mary Calderone, her religious convictions are a significant part of her beliefs about human sexuality. She eventually cofounded the Religious Institute on Sexual Morality, Justice, and Healing and has continued to offer workshops around the world. She has been a leading force in bringing new religious and moral perspectives to complex sexual issues, another of the remarkable directions that the sexual transformation has been taking.

EVELYN HOOKER TAKES ON THE 1950s PSYCHIATRIC ESTABLISHMENT

Evelyn Hooker (1907–1996) may well have been one of the most unsung heroes of sex research since she did not gain wide name recognition outside the professional community. She was a faculty member of the Department of Psychology at the University of California, Los Angeles (UCLA), when a gay male friend implored her to study homosexuality. In 1953, at the height of McCarthyism's hysteria about communists and homosexuals, she applied for a grant from the National Institute of Mental Health (NIMH) to begin that research. This was one of the darkest periods in terms of human rights and unbridled public bigotry in the United States. The NIMH sent its chief of extramural grants to check her out since the topic was considered so sensitive. She was told that while the agency wanted to award her the grant, she should be prepared to be investigated by the FBI and that if they were not satisfied with her personal character and respectability, the grant might never actually come through. She and her English professor husband had fought against having to sign UCLA's "loyalty oath," an activist stand that Hooker feared might ultimately be used against her in such tenuous times. Ultimately, though, the grant was awarded, and she received several subsequent grants until 1961 when she was given a Research Career Award.

In locating and working with her gay male subjects, Hooker had to contend with the stigma of mental illness and deviance with which they had been branded. She had to promise privacy and anonymity to the men she studied and ultimately met with many of them in the garden room study of her own home. The committee that oversaw her research insisted that since she was working with a psychopathology, she would need a psychiatric consultant. She was asked by the chair of UCLA's Department of Psychiatry about her research, and when she said she was studying "normal male homosexuals," he stood up behind his desk and declared, "What do you think you are doing? There is no such person."[11] She eventually found a more sympathetic adviser in Dr. Frederic Worden, a newcomer to the department. Nevertheless, during the course of her research, she received personal threats and was even falsely charged with a criminal act by the Los Angeles Police Department, which spent much of its time arresting homosexuals. The case against her was thrown out by a judge.

Ultimately, Evelyn Hooker's findings were among the most important scientific facts fueling the transformation of the existing professional beliefs and stereotypes about homosexuality. What she found, in essence, was that gay men were relatively free of psychopathology, no more prone to emotional or mental disturbances than heterosexual people. In 1969, the director of the NIMH at the time, Dr. Stanley Yolles, summoned her to Washington to "tell him what we ought to be doing about homosexuality." After a panel of experts supported her views with only a few exceptions, the American Psychiatric Association deleted homosexuality from its diagnoses of mental disorders in 1973, and the American Psychological Association followed suit in 1975.[12] Again, it would be simplistic to ignore the other political and social forces that were swirling about the sexual revolution during these high-spirited times of liberating the sexually oppressed, but Evelyn Hooker supplied the scientific ammunition that convinced some of the most influential minds to begin perceiving same-gender sexual orientation as a normal variant on a continuum of sexual interests. This was, I believe, one of the most important turning points in the practical application of sexual science. Suddenly, millions of American citizens were liberated from illness invented by moral bigotry and were made well!

TRANSFORMING DATA INTO SUBTLETIES OF SEXUAL PLEASURE

Women have repeatedly softened and made practical the scientific data of sex, which in themselves have not always been entirely supportive of the more subtle aspects of female sexuality. Following the Masters and Johnson research that first modeled human sexual response in carefully quantified terms (1966) and then proposed a highly structured set of therapeutic protocols to treat sexual dysfunctions (1970), a number of women researchers stepped in to fill the gap between the science and how its findings could be of use to the neighbors down the street.

Helen Singer Kaplan (1929–1995) was one of the first. As founder and head of the Sex Therapy and Education Program at New York Hospital, she realized that there was a component of sexual responsiveness that Masters and Johnson had overlooked. It was the psychological preparatory stage so crucial for the physical reactions to unfold naturally. She called it the *desire phase* of sexual response.[13] How could we have missed that? Of course, people need to *want* to be sexually involved before their bodies will fully respond. Desire was indeed essential and sometimes slower to manifest itself in women. Kaplan freed sex therapists to move beyond the routines and sequences of exercises that Masters and Johnson had prescribed as standard for any dysfunction and opened the doors to continue trying to understand how sexual desire—or the lack of it—impacts our sexual lives.

Four other women have been influential in pushing the model of female sexual response even further. Julia Heiman, who is presently director of the Kinsey Institute, was one of the first American researchers to compare the physiological sexual responses of men and women to their more subjective verbal reports of their experiences. She used penile strain gauges to measure penile erection and vaginal probes to measure the increase of blood volume in vaginal walls while men and women listened to explicit sexual excerpts and to less sexual, romantic stories. She found that both sexes were more physically aroused by the erotic material but that women were much less likely than men to verbally report that they were sexually aroused.[14] This groundbreaking study led to further study of women's unique patterns of sexual arousal, their reactions to arousal, and their motivations for sexual involvement, all of which seem to show subtleties of degree and substance that are markedly different from men. This exploration continues today, as we elucidate new theories of sexual arousal for both women and men.

Lonnie Garfield Barbach was a sex therapist at the University of California Medical Center when she published *For Yourself: The Fulfillment of Female Sexuality* in 1975.[15] She was a pioneer in helping women who could not reach orgasm. In her work, she pretty much ignored the approaches of Masters and Johnson and their declaration that women achieved orgasm solely through clitoral stimulation, opting instead to encourage women to explore their sensuality on their own, emphasizing that they were as deserving of sexual pleasure as their partners. She combined group therapy approaches that helped women become empowered by sharing their concerns and frustrations with other women with "homework exercises" that involved bodily exploration and masturbation. She wisely coined the term "preorgasmic" for the women, in contrast to the widely accepted male-centric term "frigid," establishing a positive expectation that women who entered her treatment program would indeed become orgasmic. And most of them did. Lonnie Barbach's work stood above most of the sex manuals that began to flood the market in the 1970s. She approached her work methodically and scientifically but with a clear sensitivity to the physical, emotional, and relational complexities of female sexual response.

How well did the new models of sexual response actually fit women's experience? That was exactly the issue that troubled Leonore Tiefer, who is currently associate clinical professor of psychiatry at both New York University School of Medicine and Albert Einstein College of Medicine. She was one of the first sexologists to suggest that the Masters and Johnson model of sexual response, with its expectation of orgasm, might be more applicable to men than to women. She was a leading voice in questioning whether the model's orgasmic focus was really all that applicable to female sexuality or whether, in fact, it had been too much influenced by male-centered physiology and fantasy. She raised the attention of the sexology community to the nuances of female sexual responsiveness and expressed concern about the increasing medicalization of sex therapy, perhaps at the expense of recognizing and resolving individual psychological stresses.[16]

Canadian physician Rosemary Basson has been a leader of a call for a more nuanced model of female sexual arousal and response. Basson is clinical professor in the Departments of Psychiatry and Obstetrics and Gynecology at the University of British Columbia and director of the University's Sexual Medicine Program. The insights she has gained in treating women concerned about their low levels of sexual desire have caused her to move beyond both the Masters and Johnson and the Kaplan models of sexual responsiveness in women. She has recognized that sexual desire in women tends not to be rooted in the genital stirrings more typical for men but instead is far more *contextual*. She believes that female sexual desire is contingent on motivations that have far less to do with releasing sexual tension and far more to do with the relationship, feelings of self-esteem and energy, and emotional intimacy of the current sexual context. This includes such factors as the techniques of sex that are employed, the degree of privacy, how safe the woman feels in the relationship, and a variety of psychological motives that often have little to do with sex per se. Basson also believes that biological and medical influences must be carefully assessed and treated. Her work has led to entirely new concepts of female sexual response and reconsideration of the standard classifications of female sexual dysfunctions. In short, Basson is reshaping the science of women's sexuality.[17]

THEORISTS OF SEXUAL TRANSFORMATION

Rosemary Basson is a good example of a theorist whose work is part of the sexual transformation we are experiencing. The focus is no longer simply about how and with whom to have sex; it is about understanding how the sexuality of each one of us becomes an expression of who we are and how each one of us can live comfortably and peacefully with the sexual choices we make throughout our lives. The theorists of sexual transformation have not been content to rely on the long-accepted standards of the early researchers. They have expanded on early data that emerged from the sexual revolution to refine, individualize, and humanize our perspectives of sex. They have led us closer to truths that have always been in front of us but that have been obscured by the blinders of old allegiances and yellowed classroom notes. These theories represent the starting point where our appreciation of America's sexual transformation truly may begin.

Revolution and transformation need philosophy as well as science to flesh out their meanings. Trouble is, the philosophy too often gets lost in esoteric texts or

The focus is no longer simply about how and with whom to have sex; it is about understanding how the sexuality of each one of us becomes an expression of who we are and how each one of us can live comfortably and peacefully with the sexual choices we make throughout our lives.

buried in the less mainstream academic departments. Such has been the case with *queer theory*, a set of ideas worthy of everyday application even though it tends more often to get thrashed about on intellectual pommel horses. Nevertheless, queer theory has legitimately called into question our enduring tendency to translate sexuality into binary systems—female or male, feminine or masculine, or straight or gay—when there are so many variations on the XX–XY biological themes and the spectrum of gender roles and sexual orientations. Teresa de Lauretis, now Professor Emerita at the University of California, Santa Cruz, coined the term "queer theory" at a conference there on gay and lesbian sexualities in 1990. For obvious reasons, queer theory has tended to be associated with sexual orientation issues since that time, even though its concepts have a far broader reach. Judith Butler, professor of rhetoric and comparative literature at the University of California, Berkeley, is a poststructuralist philosopher who has been influential in applying queer theory to gender and sexual performance.[18]

While it is tough to do much justice to a whole school of philosophical thought in a paragraph or two, here is my take on queer theory as it relates to sexuality. Teresa de Lauretis argued early on that by accepting categories such as "straight," "gay," or "lesbian," we were essentially boxing people into categories and labels that had been culturally created and that such constructions had little real meaning for authentic human experience. Queer theorists posit that it is the discourses, or thinking and writing of particular fields such as medicine or psychology, that invent these categories in the first place, and then they gradually become established as "truths." It didn't take de Lauretis long to become discouraged that mainstream institutions were doing exactly the same thing to queer theory, so she soon abandoned the term—thwarted by the very forces that she was trying to resist, as it were. Judith Butler has argued that all the trappings of sex, gender, and sexual performance—such as the assumption that men are attracted to women and that their bodies are meant to perform sexually with women—constitute examples of culturally constructed identities that coerce us into living up to certain gender and sexual rules and expectations. As such, these identities wield great power: the power to constrain and the power to find pleasure.

Some queer theorists reject the "essential" or built-in nature of biological sex, insisting that male and female, along with masculine and feminine, are also social constructions that constrain human identity. They insist that if we can "queer" these coercive traps, including the limiting labels of male and female—in other words, seeing more clearly that masculine and feminine are but cultural inventions that have no particular innate meaning—we can see beyond their limits and boundaries to a truly individualized and free existence. It should be noted that some contemporary cultural theorists have softened their social-constructionist views enough to suggest that we cannot view biology and culture as completely separate entities and that they do indeed interact in making us who we are.[19]

I have never seen science so much as a friend or an enemy as I see it as *one* way to understand *some* aspects of the universe around me and to organize that universe into somewhat understandable and manageable bits. Yet I agree with the queer theorists that we sometimes overdo the politics of classification and labels. The more we become invested in them, the more they can restrict our insights and understandings. The discourses of science can indeed create human traps that are difficult to escape; this has been repeatedly demonstrated in medicine and psychiatry. For me, the trick is to remember that our lists and cubbyholes are simply a way of organizing things and that they could as well be reorganized into entirely new lists and cubbies. That is why I believe that queer theory can be one of our important pathways to sexual transformation. Where I disagree, however, is in my conviction that science has given us important insights into the essential (biological) character of gender, sexual orientation, and sexual performance that should not and cannot be ignored or discarded. True, we should not allow them to coerce us into ill-fitting identities or into trying to be something we are not. Neither should we reject what emanates from deep within us as the very nature of our sexual being.

Coming down to earth again, one of the most compelling of contemporary sexual theories involves the sexual orientations of women. Again, the anecdotal evidence has been right in front of those of us who have worked in the field of human sexuality. I've even commented on it but only infirmly because I had no theoretical ground to stand on. After working with people as a counselor for more than 35 years, it has been obvious to me that sexual orientation seemed more solidly established in men than in women. Whether straight, gay, or bisexual, men almost always got in touch with the objects of their attraction quite early in their lives. There are plenty of cases of men who leave their girlfriends or wives for another man, but I've never run across one of those men who didn't know even before he was in the straight relationship that he was sexually attracted to males. Women are an entirely different story. I've observed many situations where a presumably straight woman (even she thought so) has suddenly fallen in love with another woman and pursued a lesbian lifestyle or subsequently returned to heterosexual relationships. Alternatively, I've known women who declare themselves to be lesbian and then have eventually ended up in relationships with men. Current theories of sexual orientation don't accommodate such cases gracefully, opting instead for a more rigid view of our attractions to other people and tending to cast aside these anecdotes as anomalies.

More than a decade ago, Roy Baumeister, a social psychologist at Florida State University, wrote a couple of articles about what he called *erotic plasticity*. He claimed that women seemed to be much more variable over time in their sex drives, gender attractions, and preferred erotic activities than men were. He conceptualized women as having a greater level of erotic plasticity or flexibility but didn't pursue the topic further.[20] Lisa Diamond, a researcher in psychology and gender studies at the University of Utah, has brought greater focus to the sexual orientation part of this phenomenon by studying nearly 100 women and their sexual attractions over a 10-year period. She concluded that women have a good deal of what she calls *sexual fluidity*, manifested as unanticipated and apparently involuntary shifts between same-gender and other-gender sexual attraction and involvement. This knocks holes in all our present theories about the origins of sexual orientation, at least as they relate to women.

Especially exciting in Diamond's work is her application of *dynamical systems theory* to her findings. This approach has been applied to a variety of human characteristics that seem to be able to emerge in the individual during development and then stabilize, change, and restabilize all over again, sometimes quite suddenly. These fluid processes are mediated by *both* innate biological templates and environmental-social influences, rendering meaningless any differentiation between the two. The bottom line is that events and experiences seem to have the potential to entirely "reorganize a woman's sexual thoughts and feelings, sometimes producing altogether new desires."[21] I will be particularly intrigued to see whether any similar kind of sexual reorganizational processes might eventually be identified in men or whether their erotic developmental processes build in a stability and rigidity that is simply not subject to fluid change. Maybe men's perceptual spotlight has sexual limits as well. Perhaps it is cultural rigidity that channels males into inflexible sexual roles. Or perhaps it is neither and the plasticity of men will eventually be realized as well.

BUILDING BLOCKS FOR SEXUAL TRANSFORMATION

This chapter has outlined some of the research findings and theories that have been critical in retooling our views of human sexuality. They have been honed by visionary women who have been willing to see beyond facts and figures, beyond pronouncements that the final answers have been found, and beyond social strictures that maintain the confining status quo. I know that men have been important in making these things happen as well, but I felt that it was time to celebrate the subtle but strong female energies that have played such a key role. The contributions of other women and of men will unfold in subsequent chapters.

What I want to highlight here at the conclusion of this chapter is a summary of some of the most significant tenets on which the new template of sexual transformation is based:

- The sex research that grew out of the sexual revolution's legitimization of the study of human sexuality is being mined and elaborated in entirely new and exciting ways.

- Fresh and relevant theories about sexuality are emerging and being refined in ways that are enriching our understandings of the human experience.

- While the seesawing of emphasis between nature and nurture will surely continue as we refine our views of sexuality, it will be the interactive mechanisms between our biological predispositions and environmental influences that now attract the most focused attention.

- Sexual concepts and labels can ensnare us in outmoded ways of viewing human nature and behavior unless we maintain the ability to look at things with fresh eyes and new maps.

- The sexual nature of individual human beings is a dynamic quality, open to some degree of change and exploration as human development unfolds.

- In times of rapidly growing knowledge about sexuality in human life, the sexuality education of new generations should not be simply an option but also a solemn responsibility that is taken as seriously as any other aspect of education.

- It will always take some measure of courage to advocate for change or action when it comes to sex-related issues and to embrace the many intricacies of one's own sexuality.

Chapter 3

THE WOMAN WHO CAME TOO SOON AND THE MAN WHO COULDN'T COME AT ALL

Neurologist and author Oliver Sacks reminds us that when we look more deeply into the lives of patients who become our cases and our case studies, we find "richly human clinical tales."[1] Sacks is fascinated by the people who experience unusual states of mind, as well as the neurobiology behind them, so he has often been able to see beyond the "pathology" to the person and the pain. This is not an effortless leap for most of us who have been schooled in the professions that label, diagnose, and treat people, for once we have been inculcated in the vocabularies, classifications, and protocols of illness, disorder, and therapy, those influences tend to overshadow all else. We begin acting out the role of therapist or healer as professionally as possible. On the one hand, this is an advantage because we can conveniently draw on the remarkable and growing body of knowledge and skill sets that can be so effective in helping people overcome physiological and psychological problems. On the other hand, if we are so attuned to protocol that we become blind to the human being and the human story present in the "case" or if we fail to listen artfully to the empathic voices and intuitive hunches inside ourselves that could move us beyond the inflexible barriers of our treatment models, we may miss unparalleled opportunities for human connection and personal growth.

The sex research spawned by the sexual revolution charted the basic road maps of sexual responsiveness, sexual orientation, and sexual behavior. Therapies that emerged from those roadmaps emphasized how to get people back

*If we fail to listen artfully to the empathic voices
and intuitive hunches inside ourselves that could
move us beyond the inflexible barriers of our
treatment models, we may miss unparalleled
opportunities for human connection and
personal growth.*

to the on-ramps for the erotic roads from which they had strayed. However, those of us who were early sex counselors and therapists found ourselves confronted with another intriguing phenomenon. As it became known that we were treating sexual "problems," we began to be sought out for all manner of fascinating sexual detours that people had taken in their sexual lives, many of which simply weren't covered in any of our how-to manuals. This, I think, is where the mundane parts of sexual therapies began to become transformative. For me, my work over the past 40 years with people who have sought me out for help with the unusual things that troubled them sexually has been the most significant way that I've been able to learn about human sexuality. And while not all those people could fit into a neatly defined category or be labeled with an apt term and diagnostic number, what they have taught me about the blind spots of therapeutic models has been startling.

In the first chapter of the highly regarded text she edited through four editions, *Principles and Practices of Sex Therapy*, the late Sandra Leiblum wrote, "Sexual problems are no longer regarded as symptoms of hidden psychological defects in maturity or development. Rather they are understood as perennial themes in the human drama."[2] This, in itself, is a dramatic statement of a paradigm shift away from the assumptions of classical psychotherapy. It is, instead, a resounding acknowledgment of how the twists and turns of our own behavior patterns and social relationships can mold our erotic lives. The fruits of contemporary sexual science are just beginning to offer hope for people who are dissatisfied with their sexual lives because they fall on the outlying tails of the behavioral bell curves of sex or must struggle to find a sexual lifestyle that will fit them comfortably while being socially acceptable.

My clients in sex counseling and therapy have, by the way, been predominantly male at a ratio of about two to one. This is mostly because of the academic context in which I work, where men outnumber women nearly four to one.

The fruits of contemporary sexual science are just beginning to offer hope for people who are dissatisfied with their sexual lives because they fall on the outlying tails of the behavioral bell curves of sex.

The fact that my case studies represent more males probably also reflects the fact that unusual sexual kinks are more common in males than in females, by a ratio of about three to one. As I reviewed the human clinical tales that I will later share in this chapter, I began to realize how many of the most challenging and unusual ones grew out of my therapy contacts with people a decade or more ago. Reflecting on the possible reasons for this, including the reality that I had reduced my availability as a sex therapist in the 1990s because of other time-constraining responsibilities, I came to an obvious conclusion. Many of the interesting sexual proclivities and concerns I dealt with more than 15 years ago were brought to me by people who felt terribly alone and isolated with their sexuality. They knew of no others who had experienced similar desires or had pursued the same unusual activities. They were frightened of their self-perceived perversity, desperate to find reassurance of their essential humanity, and hopeful for some sort of explanation or direction that might be of help. And the main reason that at least some of those people would not need to seek out professional help today is that with a couple of clicks of the mouse, the Internet can provide them with much of what they sought from me or other therapists. Cyberspace is now the refuge for all who might feel out of step with mainstream sexuality, and that fact has truly been transformative.

But before we get to the erotic clinical tales I have in store for you, I need to offer a brief overview of some of the important things that have happened within the therapeutic professions with regard to perceptions of human sexuality.

Cyberspace is now the refuge for all who might feel out of step with mainstream sexuality, and that fact has truly been transformative.

SOME SEX COUNSELING HISTORY: DARK SEXUAL MYTHS AND MEMORIES

There are plenty of examples of how the therapeutic professions have gone awry when it comes to human sexuality and of how the energies that could have been used to help others became misdirected toward warped and harmful ends. The fulminating antimasturbation theories of Victorian times that spilled over into the first half of the 20th century resulted in generations of children and adolescents being either physically bound by torturous devices to prevent them from touching their own genitalia or emotionally fettered by guilt and fear of their own desires and activities. The pathologizing of same-gender romantic and sexual attraction caused decades of unspeakable anguish, self-concealment, and clandestine couplings for a substantial proportion of the population, leaving in their wake saddened, guilt-ridden, broken, and self-medicating victims. Behavioral psychologists prodded them to change with punishing electrical shocks only to find that sexual orientation is amazingly persistent and resistant to torture, so the professional torturers finally admitted their grievous error. Likewise, the long-standing reluctance of our professions to deal openly with the issues of transgendered or intersexed persons and our tendencies to coerce them into roles and identities that would help them adapt to our binary gender biases have stymied countless individuals who wanted only the right to be themselves.

Fortunately, these barbarities have been left behind for the most part, although there was a dark and embarrassing period in the 1980s and 1990s—recent enough to still be fresh in some memories—whose victims of unresolved bitterness and accusation continue to haunt us. The counseling and psychotherapy professions of that time became infiltrated with well-meaning but terribly misguided practitioners who initiated what could only be equated with a witch hunt. Coming on the heels of a movement to educate children about the dangers of adults who might want to molest them sexually, some therapists became convinced that all manner of adult symptoms, especially those typical of depression and anxiety, might well be—these therapists believed with great vigor—the result of sexual abuse during childhood, the memories of which had been repressed in the unconscious mind. The practitioners who became trained in this model began using hypnosis and related techniques to help clients resurrect their "memories," so convinced of their authenticity that they helped create the very memories through suggestion that they thought their clients were unearthing. Research eventually began to show that many of the "repressed memories" that tore families apart and alienated adult children from their parents were actually "false memories," pieced together from a rogue mythology of childhood sexual abuse, vagaries of human suggestibility, and a desperate need to understand unpleasant psychological symptoms. Today, we might say that the phenomenon went viral, but the electronic means for that were still nonexistent at the time.

I recall that one of the counselors who worked under my supervision re-ceived an angry letter from a former client, criticizing him for not having realized that her symptoms had clearly been the result of sexual abuse by her father, memories of which had recently been unearthed with the help of her new therapist through hypnosis. I worked with several fathers during that pe-riod who were crushed by an adult daughter who had announced they would no longer maintain any contact because of newly remembered sexual abuse during their childhoods. And then there were the fathers in the throes of divorce whose wives claimed that young kids had told them, sometimes with rather leading prompts, of sexually abusive behaviors on the part of their fa-thers. Whether real or invented, such charges were difficult for judges to ig-nore. The horrible and frustrating part of these times was that we really had no way to distinguish between the very real instances of sexual abuse at the hands of a parent or other adult and the false memories that could so easily and subtly be planted in an adult's (or child's) mind, especially when the social hysteria about child sexual abuse had been whipped into such a fervor. We had little to go on except our intuitions and gut reactions and a certain responsibil-ity to help our accused clients through their pain regardless of their guilt or innocence.

I was editor of the *Journal of Sex Education and Therapy* during the height of this modern-day witch hunt, and a paper was submitted by Dr. Joan Nelson of the Center for Sexual Concerns in San Anselmo, California, titled "In-tergenerational Sexual Contact: A Continuum Model of Participants and Experiences." In the paper, Dr. Nelson suggested that society's automatic condemnation of intergenerational sex could be contributing to the confu-sion and harmful consequences that children experience and called for clearer guidelines for differing levels of outcomes from sexual encounters between children or adolescent and adults. This perfectly reasonable position did not sit well with the advocates of the condemnation models. Soon after the paper was sent out for peer review, I began to get phone calls and letters from people who were aware that the article had been submitted. They strongly urged that it be rejected, and some of the members of the board of directors of the jour-nal's sponsoring organization let me know, plain and simple, that the paper should not appear in the journal. I finally reached a compromise in which the article was accepted for publication but only with a disclaimer statement that its ideas did not reflect the position of the American Association of Sex Edu-cators, Counselors, and Therapists and with an accompanying response article that refuted its assertions, claiming instead that all sex involving children was, by definition, abusive and harmful.[3]

Once the flak had died down a bit, I received a nicely reasoned phone call and follow-up letter from well-known sexologist and sex therapist at the Uni-versity of Hawaii, Dr. Milton Diamond, stating that he was disappointed that the journal had attached so many disclaimers to Dr. Nelson's basically sound article. He reminded me that we always assume researchers' assertions to be their own and not the organization's and that even unpopular views should be allowed to stand or fall on their own merits. I realized that he was entirely right and came to regret my cautious and somewhat spineless political response to the situation I had faced. Were I to be in such a position again, I would fight harder for publishing unpopular ideas that might just soon prove to be the voice of reason. Yet it is easy to fall into the trap of not wanting oneself or one's reputation to seem too closely associated with some unpopular or unsavory point of view, even when it's legitimate!

This was a sad and difficult social time that left much unresolved pain behind. It also set back the study of child sexual abuse in ways that have yet to be entirely overcome. Literally hundreds of studies appeared in the journals that correlated histories of sexual abuse with a litany of psychological and physical ills. The lack of cause-and-effect conclusiveness that is the hallmark of correlational studies was mostly ignored for a long time, and child–adult sexual contact was demonized to the point that some called for capital punishment of offending adults. There have been other voices of caution and reason concerning the interpretation of data about child and adolescent sexual abuse, but they too have been met with suspicion and condemnation. A careful meta-analysis of data was published in 1997 by Dr. Bruce Rind, who taught statistics to graduate students in Temple University's Department of Psychology, and Philip Tromovitch, a researcher and doctoral student in the University of Pennsylvania's Graduate School of Education, in the *Journal of Sex Research*, demonstrating that child and adolescent sexual abuse did not necessarily cause intense or pervasive psychological harm in all cases, but in such a specialized journal, it did not get wide attention. However, when Rind and Tromovitch teamed up with University of Michigan researcher and statistician Robert Bauserman to publish a similar 1998 article in the *Psychological Bulletin* of the American Psychological Association (APA), all hell broke loose.

The authors had made it clear in both publications that even if this sexual conduct might not result in serious harm, it did not mean that it was not wrong or morally repugnant, and it did not mean that any laws or prohibitions against it should be changed.[4] This was not sufficient to appease the strong forces of opposition that led to some hasty, sidestepping clarifications by the APA, debates about the study's methodology, self-serving condemnatory statements from a few congressmen, and a unanimous resolution from the U.S. House of Representatives that sexual relations between adults and adolescents or children were indeed abusive and harmful! If only we could get them to reach such bipartisan consensus on things like the economy. Of course, the representatives were partly responding to some groups on the other side of the debate that were trying to subvert the findings of the study for their own purposes into evidence that it was okay to have sex with kids and that consent laws should be repealed. Rind, Tromovitch, and Bauserman got a taste of how professional reputations can suffer when controversial sexual issues get put on the line.

Somewhere in all of this lie some important truths. Truths about adults who really were sexually abused as children by trusted adults and what the consequences of that abuse have been. Truths about the intractability of sex offenders and how difficult some of them may be to treat and prevent from future offending. Truths about the value—or lack of it—in painting all sex offenders with the same brush and posting their locations and histories for all in the neighborhood to see. Truths about whether there is any possibility of nonharmful sexual interactions between children and people who are older than they are. Unfortunately, our impassioned but legitimate efforts to protect children from sexual abuse became misguided by their own fevered intentions and methods, and the science of the matter is still trying to rebound. It has righted itself in many ways, but raging biases fade reluctantly, and we still have some distance to go. It is now difficult to separate fact from myth and to distinguish between the actual consequences of sexual abuse and those that have grown out of assumptions and bitterness spawned by flawed therapies, overzealous helpers, and scientifically clueless politicians.

THE EROTIC CLINICAL TALES

As I discuss the erotic clinical tales from which I learned so much, I will also share with you a tiny fraction of what I was able to scout out online for people who might today be experiencing similar woes. For better or for worse, I suspect that many more people now find solace in these safe and anonymous electronic contacts than they do in therapy. I have mixed feelings about that since I believe strongly in the value of face-to-face human sharing and exploration, but that is beside the point. Ultimately, our ways of finding what can work for each of us in getting through life are always changing. All we can do is try our best to keep up.

As you would expect, I have altered the names and other identifying information in these stories to protect the anonymity and confidentiality of my clients.

HOW DO YOU KNOW YOU'RE A WO/MAN?

One of the earliest sex-related cases I had as a beginning counselor was a young woman who came to my office claiming that she felt like a male inside. This was even before there were television talk shows featuring transsexuals and well before I knew much of anything about the transgender phenomenon. I had recently read a little about Dr. John Money and the Gender Identity

Clinic that he headed up at Johns Hopkins University Hospital, so I wrote him a letter, describing Darlene and asking for advice. Much later, Money would be one of the clinicians who was tainted by the scandal that emerged in 2000 about the boy who had been reassigned to be a girl but never felt that female gender suited him. My own long-distance impressions were that John Money was the consummate scientist who did his best to resolve complex human gender incongruencies with the best knowledge he had available at the time. He wrote me a kind return letter, suggesting that Darlene did indeed fit the criteria for transsexualism and offering a suggested reading list for me. I soon became quite well informed about the topic and felt comfortable enough to continue working with Darlene. Before I achieved much of that knowledge, I went through all the naive trials and errors that might be expected of a novice, but most of all I tried my best to understand what it would be like to feel like a male while living in a female body or vice versa.

Darlene looked and dressed in traditionally masculine ways. She was stocky and gruff and walked with a manly gait in her jeans and flannel shirt. She had inwardly felt masculine as long as she could remember. She once asked me, "How would you feel if you had to undress in the woman's locker room? That's how I feel all the time." How would I feel indeed. Not very happy. And neither did she. Given her personal and financial situation, there was little hope that Darlene would be able to pursue sex reassignment treatment and surgery in the near future, but she was determined to save her funds for that eventuality. She eventually moved out of her parents' home and to a city a few hundred miles away where she became a short-order cook—and a man named Bart. Not that Bart ever did get the surgery, but, as it turned out, that didn't matter. He simply kept his hair in a manly style and continued to dress the part, and before long he had a girlfriend who accepted him for who he was: a man in a woman's body. Bart was at heart a simple guy, and he never would set the world on fire financially. After working so hard to find the life that fit him best, I also knew him as one of the bravest and most courageous persons I've ever known, and one of the happiest.

A couple of years after Bart had established himself elsewhere, his (Darlene's) parents called me and invited me to their humble home. I went somewhat reluctantly but thought I should honor their request since they obviously knew what had transpired in their child's life. (Today, this would not be considered permissible because of confidentiality, but the rules were somewhat more flexible at the time, and I did ask Bart for his permission.) I spent most of the visit being berated by the parents for not having cured their daughter of her affliction rather than allowing—even encouraging—her to become "no better than a common lesbian." They threatened lawsuits and the wrath of God, and I left their home rather abruptly, feeling shaken and sad. Bart later called me to apologize for his parents' tirade, and I would continue to see him from time to time for several years, the best way to assure myself that his life had not been harmed by his having known me.

One of my most interesting transsexual clients was a woman living in a man's body. His name was Larry, and he was an attractive young man of 19, rather slight of frame and soft-spoken. He wanted to be the woman he believed he had always been, and he wanted that as soon as possible. I thought it important to try to slow his aspirations down a bit because by then I was more informed about the hurdles that transsexuals had to surmount in order to be considered for medical sex reassignment—not to mention the money. As much as he felt like a girl and had since he was four years old, Larry taught me a lot about being a man. One day when we were talking, I was trying to sort out his inner feelings and experiences that caused him to say he was actually a woman. One of the jobs that therapists typically seem to be assigned with transsexuals, for good reasons and bad, is to push them to "prove" their inner gender identity. Larry was somewhat offended by that strategy, feeling that he shouldn't have to prove to anyone else what he knew to be his true self. He sputtered around a bit but then said to me, "Okay, so how about you telling me how you know you're a man!"

Beyond the usual anatomical features that we assume define our sex/gender, I found myself stumped. I now ask that very question to my students in sexuality classes when we're studying gender. Beyond the anatomy and the lame stereotypical jokes ("I know I'm a man because I hate to go shopping" or "because I like to watch football on TV"), we always seem to come down to something like "I just know." What Larry reminded me was that *just knowing* is good enough; it's all we should ever need. Instead of slowing down his quest to become a woman, Larry sped up. He had the good fortune of having a father in the insurance business who managed to get his procedures paid for over about a year's time. Ignoring my warnings, he found a surgeon in New York City who didn't worry much about fancy psychological testing or other prudent protocols and who would perform the surgeries as long as Larry had the requisite funds. Perhaps that was a mercenary position on the part of the surgeon, or maybe it was an empathic political stand in support of people who were simply asking to allow their genuine genders to emerge. I don't know.

I had the privilege of talking with Larry regularly as he transformed into Tammy, a lithe and attractive woman who liked to wear skirts and blouses, and transferred to a women's floor in the residence halls. Tammy was a wonderful young woman, happy and self-assured. She graduated with honors and moved to a different state where she continued to live, love, and work as a woman until she was tragically killed in an automobile accident about a dozen years later. I received a phone call from her mother, who had happened across my phone number while cleaning out Tammy's apartment following her death. Her mother told me how much my support had meant to her *daughter* (she used that word, which Tammy would have so appreciated) and that the final decade of her life had been her happiest. We both shared memories and wept. Ironic as it might seem, Tammy, who rejected her man body in order to honor her inner experience of being a woman, taught me to own my own inner experience of being a man.

The traditional gender lines can get blurred at times, or maybe they just get pushed a little farther out so they make more sense for particular people. I've talked with more than a few young lads who have got themselves into hot water for stealing girls' underpants or other lingerie, often trying these undergarments on themselves. Usually, this is as close as they're going to get to girls' bodies for the time being, and they use the stimulation to heighten arousal for masturbation. A few of those boys seem to have deeper, almost inexplicable (to them and therefore somewhat to me) reasons for wanting to possess feminine underclothes.

Sam was one of these boys, 11 years old and not quite fully into puberty. His mother had discovered his penchant for wearing girls' panties, and in the marvel that is today's family openness about such things, Sam fully admitted that he preferred this underwear. He wanted his mother to purchase the panties for him and allow him to wear them even to school, something she had resisted out of concern for her son. She didn't want other kids to find out and ridicule the boy. One of the especially interesting players in this family drama was Sam's dad, a burly man who served in the military police on a nearby army base. On the day that I talked with the parents together in my office, it was clear that Sam's father was not comfortable with his son's undergarment preference, but he was not about to tell the boy that he was forbidden to wear girls' underpants. In fact, he believed that if it was what Sam needed to feel whole, he should be allowed to pursue it unimpeded. By the way, I've never seen a case study about girls who have an erotic attachment to wearing boys' underwear, but there are plenty of Internet postings about girls who believe that underpants designed for boys are actually more comfortable.

It was too early in Sam's life to begin pinning him with labels, and even though there was an erotic component to his underwear preference, there were no obvious indications that he was either transgendered or gay. He seemed to have some beginning attractions to girls and showed boy-specific play interests and activities, but it was too early to make many assumptions about his sexual proclivities. He was just a boy who felt best when he wore panties, and he was not ashamed of admitting that in my presence. He didn't care to have his friends know about this, so he agreed that he would not wear the panties on days when he had to change into his gym shorts, but that was his only concession. The most difficult part of this kind of situation is usually a parent who is wholly against a child's behavior, and we need to go through a balancing act to keep everyone somewhat satisfied. This was not the case with this loving, communicative family, so Sam has a good chance of growing into a happy young man, whatever he may be wearing under his trousers.

That is not to say that Sam's undercover transgender preference might not presage some later sexual interest. Cross-dressing among males encompasses a vast spectrum of behaviors, ranging from those gay males who dress in drag or enjoy performing as female impersonators all the way to transvestites who are most often straight males who find dressing in women's clothes to be relaxing and liberating. Transvestism can have roots in behaviors similar to Sam's, coupled with the sexual excitement associated with intimate contact with girls' garments. In many cases, the sexual element wanes over time, leaving only nonerotic cross-dressing as the preferred behavior.

Sam might also turn out to be *autogynephilic*, a boundary-blurring mixture of erotic excitement and quasi gender bending. First identified in the early 1990s by Canadian sex researcher Ray Blanchard, autogynephiles usually grow up with masculine boyhood interests, eventually finding themselves fetishistically sexually interested in female clothes and female bodies. This is in stark contrast to effeminate gay males, who usually show a lot of girl-specific play and mannerisms even as children. As autogynephiles become sexually active, they fantasize about what it would be like to experience sex as a woman, as if their heterosexual attraction becomes erotically preoccupied with knowing the sexual pleasures of a female body from the inside out—the ultimate immersion experience in female sexuality. They may invent masturbatory activities that involve anal penetration as they imagine being female, even though they still enjoy the erotic pleasures that penile stimulation and ejaculation offer. For a long time, sexologists had been aware of "transsexual" men who had been surgically reassigned as women, only to later regret their decision. There is now evidence that some of these men were autogynephiles who had become so obsessed with the idea of having sex as a woman that they thought actually becoming a woman would satisfy their obsession. In the process, though, they gave up the male organs with which they had achieved sexual pleasure and that were, in a sense, the very basis of their heterosexual desires, so they could only regret the loss of the essential physical maleness that made them love women so deeply. Perhaps they never asked themselves the question "How do you know you're a man?" because they might have come face-to-face with that "just knowing." So who knows? Sam might eventually show autogynephilic tendencies, although it is also likely that he will not share these intimacies with his parents.[5]

Or Sam might be happy with more traditional cross-dressing behaviors, as was the case with Alan, a retired aerospace worker whose wife had come home early from grocery shopping one day to find him fully dressed as a woman. She was shocked and upset, and they subsequently consulted a well-known psychiatrist who specialized in sex therapy. The psychiatrist told the wife that

Alan was not going to be able to change his behavior and that she might as well get used to it. This plunged the poor woman into a major depression and terrible doubts about her 38-year marriage that had otherwise been quite happy. After a year of continued treatment without satisfactory results, the couple's therapist referred them to me. Miriam, the wife, expressed the guilt she felt at not having been able to accept Alan's cross-dressing. Alan expressed his guilt at causing such distress for his wife and also shared his long history of transvestism, stemming back to the age of five when he had come across a trunk in the attic filled with women's clothes. He enjoyed putting them on. He was not gay and simply enjoyed adopting a female persona from time to time. It didn't seem to me that their mutual guilt was very constructive to either one of them or to the health of the relationship.

Alan and Miriam wanted to maintain their marriage, but their current impasse seemed intractable to them. He felt the need to cross-dress; she didn't like to see him in that role. As it turned out, the solution was a simple one to negotiate with them. Alan was happy to agree to cross-dressing in the extra bedroom he used for his den, with the door locked and only after informing Miriam that he was not to be disturbed. Miriam was fine with this arrangement, caring only that she not see him in women's clothing. She was relieved to feel that she no longer needed to see this as an inadequacy or failing on her part. The psychiatrist who had in effect created this burden for Miriam was in effect out of line for placing the responsibility for adaptation and adjustment solely on her shoulders. Relationships and all the negotiated resolutions they entail must ultimately be accomplished through mutual sharing and balancing of answers that provide satisfaction and sacrifice for both parties.

My quick Internet search of these issues yielded the following numbers, each in a fraction of a second: *transsexuality:* 432,000 results, the first page of which looked extremely useful; *transvestism:* 794,000 results; *autogynephilia:* 86,200 results; and *boys wearing girls panties:* 1,360,000 results, the first few of which included loads of stories from boys who did and offered mostly encouraging advice for parents whose sons wanted to, and some sites that may well have been pornographic. I didn't dare look at them since this clearly could be kiddie porn territory. In any case, little wonder that few would need a therapist these days to explore these erotic topics!

BOYS TESTING OUT THEIR SEXUAL WIRING AND PLUMBING

Adolescence is a crucial time in sexual development, particularly for males. On average, girls' sexual maturation happens earlier on the physical level but then plays itself out more subtly and gradually, flowering more fully within the relationships that are developed. For boys, their testes start producing testosterone again at puberty for the first time since fetal life, and this resolutely stirs their capabilities and desires for sexual arousal and responsiveness. Nearly all of them begin masturbating during this time in their lives, and the masturbatory patterns established in these young years will continue for most of them without much modification throughout their lives. That is still a fact that a lot of men don't like to admit to and a lot of women find hard to believe, but it seems to be true.[6]

It is during these adolescent years, flush with newly triggered facilities for sexual arousal and persistent efforts to find new ways of exercising the pleasures of that arousal, that some specific sexual interests get crystallized into boys' sexual natures. It is surely the time when sexual orientation becomes more fully consolidated and the vague leanings toward romantic and sexual attractions of childhood become full-fledged sexual desires and targets. That's the easy part. What is far more complicated and far less understood are the particular, sometimes peculiar, sexual proclivities that seem to get put into place during these critical periods of boys' lives. Once these interests and activities have "set," they seem relatively stable and unwavering, for better or for worse. Since I was considered to have some expertise in adolescent sexuality, it was not unusual for colleagues or agencies to send me the cases they found to be baffling or bizarre. It was never until I managed to help an embarrassed and fearful boy feel a bit more comfortable with me and assured that I was not judging or condemning him that I *might*, just occasionally, get some insights into whatever behavior the young man had been sent to me to talk about.

What I began to realize about these boys was that their sexual behavior had emerged from a place deep inside them, perhaps from some of the older, instinctual, nonverbal parts of their brains, craving a sensual pleasure that lay beyond their abilities to understand or interpret it. (Do any of us understand our sexual cravings, really?) It had activated the pleasure–reward centers of their brains, and modifications in this part of our brains usually seem to make an impact on our behavioral lives. Something had called it out of the boys and caused them to act on it, but being asked to talk about it left them tongue-tied and bewildered. This was not entirely out of embarrassment. They were often as baffled by what they had done as the people who referred them to me. The trouble was, I suspect, that they had been discovered—found out—when it probably would have been better all around if their sexual secrets had been able to remain just that.

I found myself in the delicate position of trying to work with such boys as gently as I could, mingling my own befuddlement with theirs, unable to make a whole lot of rational sense out of what had happened while—for lack of anything better to offer—trying to reassure them that sexuality can be a curious and puzzling part of our lives. And then I would try to come up with some further reassuring words for parents or social workers who were mostly anxious to leave the whole thing behind anyway. We try to predict what sexual signs of youth may turn out to represent unsettling patterns to be watched in the future, but more often than not, these quirky youthful sexual exploits do not lead to future sex criminals—just adults with pretty typical sex lives who would prefer not to be reminded of their embarrassing and confusing behavior of the past, just like most of the rest of us. I am inclined to suspect that future sex criminals learn more thoroughly in their early years how not to get caught in their sexual exploits.

Danny was a 14-year-old foster child when he was referred to me by his caseworker. He had, in fact, adapted quite well to the home where he lived. Late one afternoon after most everyone had gone home from school, Danny was discovered by a school custodian in the gym, sitting naked high up on one of the basketball hoops. That was it, just sitting there naked, all by himself. The social worker told me that Danny was always rather quiet and that he had refused to talk with her about the incident or his motivations for it. I could hardly blame him. In my office, he was friendly and polite but quiet. I explained to him the story of his actions as it had been described to me, and he confirmed in his quiet manner that it was indeed accurate. When I tried to probe a bit in order to find some sort of motivation for the nude basketball hoop sitting, Danny politely told me that he didn't really know why he had done it. He also told me, looking me straight in the eye, that he would rather not talk about it.

That was the clincher for me. Why did anyone really need to know why Danny had done what he did? What did it matter? Could there really be a satisfying rational answer anyway? Somehow, being naked in the gym, alone on the basketball hoop, meant something to Danny. It probably felt sexual and free and powerful in such a public place. Something like that. Perhaps it had something to do with basketball or basketball players. Who knows? It was risky to be up so high, but kids take those kinds of risks all the time. That wasn't the point here. So I used the remainder of our time together to talk about sexuality and the many directions it can take in our lives, and I did my duty to mention the dangers of climbing up so high. We shook hands, and I told him that I would suggest to the adults around him that they not bring this incident up again. He seemed grateful. That was it, and as far as I know, Danny never went back on the basketball hoop again. Or, if he did, I'll bet he was much more careful not to get caught.

There are plenty of anecdotes about the neuronal wiring for sexual turn-ons getting tangled with some nonprototypical sexual triggers. One of the most interesting for me was the 18-year-old who was troubled and inconvenienced by the fact that every time he saw a girl hiccup or burp, he would spontaneously ejaculate in his undershorts. It had all started a couple of years before when he had been sexually aroused while watching a movie. A female in the movie did indeed belch, and Greg experienced his first spontaneous ejaculation.

That seemed to have represented a critical learning point that somehow built the stimulus and response into the neurophysiology of his sexual responsiveness. So simple and yet so frustrating. The reason Greg finally sought treatment was the fact that while on an ocean beach during the summer, he had witnessed a young woman drinking a soft drink and burping slightly as we tend to do with carbonated beverages, causing him immediately to come in his shorts. He had to make a hasty retreat to the bathhouse to clean up the mess. Not the best way to impress the girls.

Greg was a rather tense young man, prone to obsessive-compulsive tendencies, and this quirk of orgasmic wiring seemed to fit right in with some of the other things that troubled him. As we worked on the psychological and social complexities of his quirk, I encouraged him to wear some extra padding when he was in public, and he even tried wearing a condom, but it tended to slip off his flaccid penis. Eventually, we were able to extinguish this response for the most part, but it was a good reminder of the separate natures of orgasm and ejaculation in men, even though they most often occur together. It was also a reminder that our sexual arousal cues can get cross-wired without our meaning for that to happen.

Several Internet searches for something to connect sex and nudity with basketball or basketball hoops didn't turn up anything that would have been helpful to Danny, but when I searched "orgasm, hiccups," I did find some information that might have helped Greg and I find some explanations for his unusual predicament. In 1988, Dr. Francis Fesmire commented in the *Annals of Emergency Medicine* about using rectal massage to cure hiccups, and in 2000, Drs. Roni and Aya Peleg published a case study in the *Canadian Family Physician* that described how a man's intractable hiccups had ceased when he had experienced orgasm during sexual intercourse.[7] Both articles described the neurological complexities of hiccups involving the phrenic nerve, vagus nerve, and hypothalamus, all of which are also involved in orgasmic responses. The vagus nerve also connects the brain to the anal sphincter and rectum as well as the genitals.

I also found a website called "The Physics of Sex: Where Science and Intimacy Collide," on which a blogger claims to have tried masturbation to cure hiccups and enthusiastically endorsed the method. The upshot of this is that the hiccup-generating reflexive mechanisms seem to be controlled by a complex set of neurological connections that is not fully understood,[8] in my estimation much like the orgasm/ejaculation-generating reflexive mechanisms. After all, both hiccups and orgasm involve a lack of control and a sudden tightening of the diaphragmatic musculature. Most of the time, the neural "switch" on both mechanisms is in the "off" position and only occasionally gets turned "on." It doesn't seem much of a neurological stretch to me that the two mechanisms might sometimes get cross-wired, and that is apparently what happened in Greg's case. That wouldn't be of much help to him in dealing with the mess, but I found it helpful by way of possible explanation.

Sexual fetishes of various sorts are good examples of this. I'm not sure I would classify Ken's problem as a fetish, but it got him into trouble. He was 15 years old, and his family lived near a college sorority house. He would sometimes go out at night, hide in the shrubberies at the edge of the sorority's backyard, and spy on girls in their upstairs bedrooms, hoping to see them in some stage of undress. This voyeuristic behavior did not strike me as particularly surprising or sinister for a teenage boy, but it surely did constitute an invasion of others' privacy even if they did neglect to close their curtains— enough so that it got Ken arrested and eventually sent to me. He was mortified by the fact that his arrest had been in the newspapers and that his parents were humiliated and horrified. This is one of those difficult situations when a boy engages in fairly normative behavior (wanting to see girls' bodies) in ways that violate our codes of proper social conduct. My own suspicion is that most males have placed themselves in similarly compromised situations, although most don't get caught and have to go through the formalities of contrition that faced Ken. But he got through it all, managed not to get branded as a sex offender, and left town for college as soon as possible. I figured there was no good reason to search for this on the Internet and get a million or more results.

Matthew never got caught acting on his fetish, which was far more intrusive than Ken's and could have led to some serious violence against him, but his own guilt about his fetish plagued him enough to seek me out before any of that happened. After hemming and hawing his way through the first three sessions with me, clearly trying to check out if he could feel comfortable enough with me to divulge his sexual secrets, he told me that he was highly aroused by men's feet. He had no particular attractions to other parts of men's bodies and was not sexually aroused by women, but men's feet did the trick for him. This type of fetish is particularly curious to me because it does not entirely fit for me that if one is turned on by feet, why would it matter which sex the feet are connected to? But it does, and who ever said that sex needs to be rational anyway? It reminds me of the 1992 movie *The Crying Game*, in which the protagonist fell in love with a person he presumed to be a woman, only to be shocked and befuddled later on when he found out that the "woman" came attached to a penis and testicles. Of course, in most states, marriage between two people with penises or two people with vaginas is not yet permitted. If one person in either of those pairings were to have sex reassignment procedures, losing the penis or vagina and replacing it with a surgeon-created other-sex organ look-alike instead, they would then be permitted to marry. For erotic purposes, all parts of the body seem to be imbued with an inherent gender, even if it is only a symbolic gender, that is literally critical to sexual motivation and response. For political and legislative purposes, the genitals can indeed be figuratively detached from the rest of the body, thereby transforming the person's entire gender category. Some interesting social wiring.

In any case, it mattered to Matthew that the feet he loved be attached to a man. As a fraternity member with pretty typical male interests, Matthew had access to lots of men's feet. What troubled him was his typical erotic practice of waiting for one of his frat brothers to pass out from drink so that he could then use the opportunity to remove the guy's shoes and socks and caress his feet. Although he found this sexually arousing, he didn't masturbate on or with the feet; he simply touched them with his hands and lips and later masturbated by himself. Nonetheless, he quite rightly saw this behavior as exploitative and intrusive and wanted to stop doing it. That turned out to be easier wanted than done, but we continued to struggle with impulse control until he reached a point where he felt all right about himself.

These are difficult cases in which to find alternative and legitimate ways of achieving sexual pleasures, especially when the fetish is so specific and exclusive. When I was working with Matthew a decade and a half ago, it was not so easy to search for other men who might want to share foot sex. When I now search the Internet for "foot fetishism, male," I get more than 70,000 results. I clicked on the first few sites to find pictures of men prominently displaying their feet, sometimes with dirty socks, sometimes naked and engaged in sexual activity, sometimes not. I got the distinct impression that male-male foot fetishism had sadomasochistic overtones, with references to "masters" and worshipping. I also realized that men's feet were being portrayed very differently from the delicate and smooth feet of women that "heterosexual" male foot fetishists must lust after. Surely there are women with large, raw-boned feet and men with small, dainty ones, but clearly that misses the gender mark that is such a central part of eroticism. I suspect that the Internet would be the route that Matthew would want to pursue today—and indeed probably has explored by now—to discover that he wasn't as unusual or isolated as he felt at the time. He might even have found some willing and conscious partners. This cyber intertwining of sexual hardwiring has yielded astounding outcomes and represents one of the remarkable developments of our 21st-century sexual transformation, even as fetishes remain largely unexplored by sex research.

THE WOMAN WHO CAME TOO EARLY AND THE MAN WHO COULDN'T COME AT ALL

Once the basic diagnostic categories and protocols of sex therapy were established in the 1970s, it was relatively easy to find the right cubbyholes and diagnoses for most of the problems that were brought to us. It wasn't long, however, before we began to run into presenting problems that didn't quite fit any of the rubrics. It is these exceptions to every rule, I think, that truly challenge any practitioner to reach beyond the standard treatment parameters when they have instead become unhelpful limitations, and this in turn encourages any profession to expand its horizons. The theory and practice of sex therapy have indeed been transformed through this evolutionary process. My own practice saw many such cases, but I'm going to discuss only three.

I had worked with Elizabeth several times as she sorted through her relationship with her husband, a man somewhat older than her 38 years. He was adamantly disinterested in counseling, judging it to be a sign of weakness and lack of will. Elizabeth's concerns had not involved sexuality until she made an appointment with me to discuss what she referred to as her lack of sexual arousal. This is not an uncommon complaint among women, with research showing lack of desire for sex being reported by nearly 40 percent of American women and lack of arousal by more than 25 percent.[9] At first, Elizabeth described her symptoms in ways that I took to indicate a lack of sexual desire, but then I realized that she seemed very interested in having sex with her husband. When I began to ask more specific questions about her patterns of sexual response in order to figure out how to work with her concern, I realized that I had completely misinterpreted her opening comments. In fact, she looked forward to her sexual encounters and quickly became aroused. That was when the trouble started. Within a few seconds of the moment her husband entered her vagina, she would experience orgasm and feel entirely satisfied. In a sense, she felt done. Her husband had spent his sexual lifetime proudly cultivating the capacity to last quite a long time before reaching orgasm, a quality that Elizabeth understood to be desirable for most women and admired by most men.

I could only conclude that Elizabeth was on the short end of the bell curve's fuse when it came to orgasmic reaction time, a less common place for women to be and an analogue of the far more common male premature ejaculation. Lacking any published guidance on the matter, I co-opted the methods used for treating lack of ejaculatory control in men, and we managed to devise some homework exercises for Elizabeth to try out at home. Over a few weeks' time, she gradually became more able to slow down her orgasmic response when having intercourse with her husband. So many women would wish for a quicker response, but Elizabeth's situation reminds us of the sensible caution to be careful what we wish for. Online I found fewer references to this problem but surely enough to have reassured Elizabeth that she wasn't alone with it. Some women online didn't see it as a problem at all and simply accepted that their sexual encounters would be brief but satisfying. One woman commented that many men had been reaching orgasm rapidly forever, so they shouldn't complain, and another added that these men would love to have such women as partners. This seems to be another issue of sexual functioning that remains largely unexplored by researchers.

Joel's problem was a more typically female complaint. He was unable to reach orgasm at all. He consulted me in the early days of my practice, he a 20-year-old who, after experiencing orgasm a few times during masturbation in his teenage years, ceased being able to climax at all. He had a girlfriend with whom he had intercourse regularly, and to her delight, he could keep going for as long as she might like, but he never ejaculated. This was frustrating and depressing to him, causing him to feel disappointed and unsatisfied with his sexual life. This too was unexplored territory in the sex therapy literature and essentially still is, although I published a thorough case study about Joel and his treatment.[10] My dilemma was that all the treatment protocols for what was then crudely termed ejaculatory "incompetence" or "retarded" ejaculation assumed that orgasm in some men simply took undue effort to achieve and asked them to build on the orgasmic capacity they already had. In Joel's case, this was none, so these approaches were essentially useless.

Although I did employ several techniques that offered both Joel and me some clues about the problem, I decided that it might be a valid time to use a little old-fashioned psychologizing, including a bit of the placebo effect. I told Joel that I thought his problem was the result of some psychodynamics that we needed to discover and explore. This may well have been the case, although this is not a model that I have ever embraced with confidence. I do very much believe, however, that people's belief systems can be very powerful and motivating. I had also been exploring the value of guided imagery techniques in my practice, finding them to be interesting and instructive for both myself and my clients.[11] So I led Joel through some relaxation techniques and then created a guided fantasy in which we could both participate. I asked him to imagine himself in an important location for his life, and he eventually saw himself in his family's living room on Long Island, a few hundred miles away from where we were talking. He pictured his father there too, sitting in his easy chair reading the paper. His dad had always been somewhat detached from the family, and Joel often felt distant from him, imagining him to have a vague sense of disapproval over his son's life. Joel imagined himself to be a marionette, under his father's control, and at my suggestion he managed to cut the strings in his fantasy.

This was the point at which I sensed I could make an important move. I asked Joel to visualize another string, attached to his own penis and controlled by his father. This is where the imagery became interesting. In his mind's eye, Joel visualized an enormous, thick rope—the kind used to tie ships to the wharf—emerging from behind his father's newspaper and going down the front of his own pants. The rope was knotted repeatedly around his genitals, and Joel expressed doubt that it could ever be undone. So now we were into the really powerful symbolism, and I could only hope that it was convincing symbolism for Joel. I urged him to persist in working on untying the knots, with his girlfriend's help, and eventually they succeeded in getting the fantasized rope unknotted, and it fell away from his penis. That seemed like an ideal time to end the guided fantasy. I suggested that he take a few relaxing deep breaths and open his eyes. He felt happy and relaxed. The rest of the story turned out with the happy ending you might anticipate. Joel called me at home that night at about 11:30 to tell me that he had reached orgasm during intercourse with his girlfriend. He seemed thrilled. I saw him a few more times for follow-up, and his newly found orgasmic capabilities never again failed him while I knew him. I don't know if the relationship with his stern father really had anything to do with Joel's orgasmic hesitancy, but the important thing was that our little fantasy journey was enough to remove the orgasmic block from his sexual functioning. He was happy, his girlfriend remained happy, and so did I.

Studies on sex therapy and the incidence of sexual dysfunctions continue to grapple with two crucial issues. One involves whether personal distress must accompany some lack of expected sexual function in order for it to be considered a valid problem. If, for example, a woman is perfectly happy to participate in sexual activities without experiencing orgasm, does she really have a problem? Some experts believe she does, as in she doesn't know what she's missing, while others do not. The other issue is that for every person willing to admit they have a sexual problem or to seek help for it, there are probably many others who simply keep it to themselves. So, in a sense, sex therapy is still in its infancy, finding its way among people who would like to have more satisfying sex lives but who are often hesitant to seek professional help to do that.

Data from the National Health and Social Life Survey indicated that about a quarter of women reported that they had difficulties reaching orgasm during their sexual activities.[12] My own data from several years of surveying college students demonstrate that this problem may trouble up to 70 percent of young women![13] Yet sex therapy is still perceived as a rather esoteric branch of the helping professions and not easily accessible to the average person. Indeed, it is not a service that is easy to find, and few medical or psychotherapy professionals yet receive much solid training in the treatment approaches that are most effective. Most physicians continue to neglect to ask their patients about their levels of sexual satisfaction, and that may at least in part be due to the reality that they don't quite know what to do when sexual complaints are voiced. The erection drugs have helped doctors out, although I would maintain that the real effectiveness of these medications in fully resolving erectile disorder remains questionable and veiled in advertising mystique. While America's sexual transformation has opened possibilities for talking about sexual dysfunctions and slightly increased access to some helpful aids, we still have a long way to go.

And then there are the exceptions, the cases that seem to boggle the mind and shatter some of our fundamental understandings about sexual functioning. I worked with one couple for more than 25 years, from the time both were in their 40s until both were close to 70. Their complaints revolved around a variety of relational dynamics that were not very healthy for either one of them, but they doggedly stayed together even through their darkest of times. Their primary issue, although it always seemed to get subsumed by the other complexities of their marriage, was the man's erectile problems. Every time the couple attempted intercourse, he would either lose his erection or not be able to get an erection at all. I assigned all sorts of homework exercises for them, many of which were never carried out because both seemed to lack the motivation to do so. As the pharmaceutical companies began to offer new hope with various medical approaches, they tried everything from vacuum pumps to injections into the penis to two of the erectile drugs available, Viagra and Cialis. None of them proved to help much, and further medical imaging suggested that the man might indeed have some arterial blockage that was the source of the problem. He never did have any surgery.

He came to see me, after I had ceased seeing them as a couple, to report that he was having an affair with a woman, entirely unknown to his wife. They were involved in oral sex, anal sex, and vaginal sexual intercourse, and he was having no erectile problems whatsoever! He was even having more than one sexual experience at a time and more than one orgasm too. Here we have a guy with a nearly 30-year history of impotence, about 70 years old—a time of life when most men are having some erectile difficulties—and he has been "cured" by a hot attraction to a new person in his life. This doesn't make sense in terms of everything we know about sexual arousal and response, and yet it happened. Was a new, exciting stimulus all that was needed? If this works, what does this say about long-term relationships in which a loving couple gradually adjusts to less-than-wonderful sexual responsiveness? Or even no sex at all?

The one thing that I am seeing among college students is their openness and willingness to talk about their sexual lives and sexual functioning. For the most part, they, at least, have come to accept their sexuality as a natural and acceptable part of their lives, worthy of fine-tuning, tweaking, and perfecting. They can find a lot of what they need online, but this does not always substitute adequately for a knowledgeable and helpful person to talk with. One way or another, we need to figure out how to help people find access to uncomplicated, affordable, and unembarrassing ways to improve their sexual satisfaction. Medications alone are not going to accomplish this, nor is Internet surfing. The challenge to sex therapy is evident; how it will rise to the challenge is not.

Chapter 4

ONE FOR THE BOOKS: WHAT MY SEX BOOKS HAVE TAUGHT ME

I've liked to write since I was a child, and the more I wrote, the more I developed some facility for putting words and sentences together in sensible ways. My early publications were mostly about biology, but as my own professional directions shifted, so did the topics that I wrote about. After accomplishing some success in sexuality education and becoming a member of the board of directors of the Sexuality Information and Education Council of the United States (SIECUS), I had formed some solid opinions about what the field should be striving to accomplish. In 1974, Barron's Educational Series contacted Mary Calderone, then executive director of SIECUS, for suggestions of an author for a new book on sexuality for teenagers, and she kindly put my name forward.

Most of my writing at that time was heavily influenced by Carl Rogers's person-centered psychological theory and practice that I studied in graduate school as well as his writing style. I had met Rogers a few times and agreed with him, as I still do, that human beings are essentially good, that they flourish when treated with respect and positive regard, that their feelings should be legitimized with empathy and genuineness, and that they need to be helped to embrace all aspects of their personalities in order to be able to grow and flourish optimally. It was this philosophy that I wanted to use as a foundation for my book on sexuality for teens. I wanted it to be warm, nonthreatening, personal, and—most important—honest and clear. I wanted no lies, exaggerations, or trumped-up scare tactics when it came to sex. Instead, I wanted my

I wanted no lies, exaggerations, or trumped-up scare tactics when it came to sex.

youthful readers to better understand their bodies, their sexual feelings, the sexual behaviors they might eventually choose to engage in, and the ways in which they could prevent some of the negative consequences of sex. I also wanted to help them assess their own readiness for sex in order to be responsible in choosing to share this significant human connection with another.

My preparation for writing the book was mightily influenced by the sex books for young people that had been authored by Eric Johnson and Wardell Pomeroy.[1] Johnson was a much-admired teacher at a Quaker Friends' school in Philadelphia, and I wanted to emulate the warmth, honesty, and sensitivity that he had been able to convey in his writing about love and sex. Pomeroy had been one of Alfred Kinsey's co-researchers, and I admired his ability to transform the rather dry data of that research into terms that would both interest and inform boys and girls about their own bodies and behaviors. His work was more statistics heavy than I cared to be, but it was also a marvelous reminder of the necessity for scientific substance in approaching the subject of sexuality, even for the young.

My writing of *Learning about Sex: The Contemporary Guide for Young Adults*[2] flowed pretty smoothly, using a straightforward and personal style as if I were talking with a teenager. I got married in the middle of the writing process, and Betsy was my best sounding board for how the tone was coming across. In the first chapter, I recalled some of my own confusion and worry about sex as a teen and how I had longed for someone who would just tell me the truth. I disclosed my own perceptions about the power and positivity of sexuality while reminding readers that they would have to make their own choices with careful thought and responsible values. And I took the perhaps bold step at the time of stating that "people differ greatly in their preferences for various forms of sexual behavior," then going on to say that "I cannot judge the 'rightness' or 'wrongness' of any of these behaviors. Instead, I hope that you can find the sexual life-style which is best for your own life—one which will provide great pleasure for everyone involved; lead to happiness and satisfaction; feel natural and spontaneous; and, of special importance, a sexual life-style that helps you to feel good about the person you are." This was a central manifesto for the book and one, I've been told, that opened the widest doors to its criticism and eventual condemnation. It was, after all, a clear declaration of support for one of the more controversial educational movements of the time, values *clarifica-tion*, as opposed to values *inculcation*. This remains a sore subject in sexuality education circles even today.

Subsequent chapters dealt with how the body and sex organs grow and develop, how we understand our own attitudes and sexual responsiveness, how sex did indeed entail "different strokes for different folks," gender realities and stereotypes, problem sex, marriage and other partnerships, birth control (including abortion, which had become legal just six years before), and parenthood. I was particularly proud of the chapters on sharing sexual feelings and communicating about sex, both of which included self-evaluations for exploring how prepared or not the reader might be for sharing sex with someone else. I never troubled over the inclusion of any particular information since I was striving so intensely for honesty. I included sections on masturbation (including how it was done), penile–vaginal intercourse, oral sex, and anal sex, along with extensive discussion of potential reactions, problems, and the need for emotional readiness and individual consent. Most important, my inclusion of these topics was based on my knowledge of the involvement of teenagers in these sexual behaviors. It was the 1970s, after all; the sexual revolution was in full throttle, and for the most part no one was talking to kids openly about the sexual activities many of them were already engaging in.

The first edition of *Learning about Sex* appeared in 1976, a heady time for me professionally. I was heading up a university counseling center and was involved in the founding of a school for talented high school students within the university. I had instituted one of the first graduate courses in sexuality for counselors in training and was serving as guest editor for a special issue of the *Personnel and Guidance Journal* (now the *Journal of Counseling and Development* of the American Counseling Association) on "The Counselor and Human Sexuality."[3] When the special edition was published, it included a full-page, inside-front-cover advertisement for my book. The journal included articles that helped counselors explore their own attitudes about sexuality, understand the multidisciplinary nature of the emerging field of sex therapy (including a paper by Masters and Johnson), and learn about innovative programs that were helping people deal with sexuality and sexual problems. Details about production of the journal were coordinated by Judy Wall, the journal's highly competent production editor, who was also a senior editor at APGA Press, the parent organization's publishing arm.

Somewhere along the way, during one of our many telephone conferences, Judy and I began discussing possible illustrations to highlight various parts of the special issue. It was probably I who suggested that photographs of real people might be in order. This was the decade when even some scholarly tomes about sexuality were illustrated with photographs of people, sometimes including their breasts or genitals. For me, this symbolized a liberation of body and sexuality, the graphic metaphor for the sexual revolution. It may well have represented an over-the-top level of hubris on my part as well, but I was too lost in liberation to recognize that. Judy hired a professional photographer in Washington, D.C., to do some photographs with nude models, and he produced some very tasteful and artistic photos. Judy and I cooperated in picking out five images to use in the special issue, including the cover photo, which consisted of a kissing embrace of the couple. None of the photos actually displayed any suggestive body parts except for one image that showed the woman's nipples. In the end, we congratulated ourselves for the tinge of eroticism we had injected into the normally staid journal.

A couple of months after the issue had gone out to the membership, Judy Wall called to let me know that she was leaving the journal and APGA Press. While she was too professional to divulge any of the details, I was able to glean that some of the brass at the organization had taken offense at the explicit nature of the photography in the special issue, and Judy took the fall for the poor judgment in allowing it to be used. I suspect that my hubris may have created an unfair vulnerability for her. In *Learning about Sex*, I had taken a far more conservative approach, and the publisher had found an artist to do some line drawings and slightly shaded images that I had suggested as illustrations for the subject matter. I never got any negative feedback on them, even though in some ways they were more revealing and erotic than the journal's photographs.

SOBERING BUT TRUE: LESSONS FROM BOOK 1

The first edition of the book did well from the start, garnering enthusiastic reviews and a designation by the American Library Association as a "Best Book for Young Adults." I would find it in bookstores everywhere I went and occasionally saw a boxed counter display holding multiple copies for sale. I was thrilled. Needless to say, this did not put me in the most receptive state of mind for a letter that arrived from Ronald Gold, who worked for what was then called the National Gay Task Force. His letter was 18 full pages long, typed single spaced and with very narrow margins. He was clearly determined to crowd as much onto these pages as he possibly could. It was, in fact, a page-by-page set of suggestions with which I could make the book even more useful for gay teenagers. While the 18 pages overwhelmed and vexed me initially, Ron Gold caught my attention by stating that he found it disappointing that gay kids didn't have anything of similar value for them. He then set about showing how with some tweaking throughout—really in order to eliminate the book's clear heterosexist bias, although he was savvy enough not to put it that crassly—it could be rendered acceptable for gay youth as well. Although I was still steamed about the letter, I had to admit that his suggestions were not particularly difficult or dramatic, for example, changing "sharing sexual intercourse" to "sharing a close sexual encounter" or rewriting "getting married" (which was not under realistic consideration for gays in 1976) as "entering into a lasting, committed relationship." He sent a copy of the letter to Mary Calderone, who had graciously written the introduction for the book.

My first response to Ronald Gold was polite and offered thanks for his careful reading of the book, but I went on about how I wasn't sold on the idea of making so many modifications in its text in order accommodate a single sexual "minority." It made such clear sense to me at the time, and it seems so narrow-minded and thoughtless to me now. The minority sentiment was what Mary Calderone addressed in her response to Gold, which she copied to me, in which she did indeed underscore the need for and appropriateness of bending over backward to accommodate all minorities as equals. And, she suggested, revising my book would be a wonderful way to do just that! After a few more readings of Gold's tightly packed letter and taking a deep breath about the possibility of some hard work ahead, I proposed the revision to my publisher. The sales of the book had been strong enough that they were going to do more printings anyway, so they permitted me to do the revision almost immediately. The revised edition appeared in 1977, just a year after the first edition, with thanks offered to Ronald Gold. I was indeed grateful that he alerted me to my blatant heterosexism, a lesson about which I have needed to be reminded many times over. The new book was recommended by the National Gay Task Force and other national organizations for gay, lesbian, and bisexual youth.

Although it surely got plenty of competition in the market, *Learning about Sex* remained one of the gold standard sex books for teens for about a decade. While it was too detailed and too explicit for most public schools, it was widely used at private schools. They had more autonomy and the luxury of greater realism in making their text choices. As we slipped into the 1980s and HIV/AIDS made their appearance, it was time for a new edition of the text and some new cautions for sexual safety. The third edition was published in 1986. However, I had failed to apprehend the power of the changing tide of opinion about human sexuality in the country. While conservative voices had never been completely silent through the earlier years of the sexual revolution, HIV, the two-decade flaunting of liberal agendas, and a spate of controversial Supreme Court decisions provided the break those voices needed to be heard loud and clear once more. As the 1980s progressed, there was a gelling of these polarized ideologies into two rather strong, opposing, politico-religious camps. This intensified what we now call the culture wars, fraught with wrestling matches that attempt to sway public opinion, elections, and social policy first one way and then the other.

Not fancying myself to be a particularly political animal, I blithely marched on with little heed being paid to the forces building around me. During the first week of December 1986, my office fielded numerous telephone calls from producers of radio and television talk shows in the New York City area, inviting me to go on the air to defend my book. It had been debated on the *Phil Donahue Show*. Various out-of-context passages from the book had been cited by an attorney that the *New York Times* reported worked for the Roman Catholic Archdiocese of New York, even though a spokesman for the archdiocese disavowed any connection with the criticism of the book. Nonetheless, the attorney insisted that the archdiocese was leading an effort to have the book removed from lists of recommended books at both the city and the state level.[4] Wisely, I think, I declined to fan the hysteria by appearing on any of these shows, insisting instead that the book spoke for itself. That was true, of course, but when it comes to sex, any words are clearly open to interpretation and judgment. It was irritating that the criticism revolved around the pre-HIV 1977 edition, even though a 1986 revision was already in print that had taken care of many of the complaints.

Nonetheless, I had indeed stated that both oral sex and anal sex were enjoyed by substantial numbers of people and that "sadomasochism may be very acceptable to sexual partners who agree on what they want from each other." I also said that "it is typical for people to think of sex when they think of marriage . . . [but] many people do not feel this to be true, and accept that sexual intercourse may be all right and meaningful in a loving, committed relationship, even without marriage." These statements were cited in a letter from the Coalition of Concerned Clergy that went to New York State's Commissioner of Education in March 1987, complaining that the book should not have been rated by that agency as "one of the best books out for teens on sex" and demanding an apology to every parent in the state whose child's "values were tarnished by virtue of [the] Department's promotion of sexual promiscuity and adventuring in perversions." The letter did not reveal how the tarnished children might be identified but blamed the book for the proliferation of out-of-wedlock pregnancies and venereal diseases. A friend sent me a news clipping from another part of the state, telling the story of a woman describing herself as an "outraged grandmother" who had come to a local board of education meeting to condemn my book, calling it "ridiculous and obscene," even though the book was not used in the district.

Although I was frustrated by how unfairly quotations from the book were portrayed without their surrounding words of caution, caring, and warning to temper their impact, it was difficult not to wonder if I truly had gone overboard in my honesty and explicitness. The New York Public Library tried to come to my aid by again declaring the book one of the best for young adults, and sales for the book were boosted by all the publicity, but it was a dark and fretful time for me as I sorted through what directions I should be taking as a sexuality educator. Things finally clarified themselves for me when I put together a whole new version of the book that was titled *Sex and Sense*. The essential information and values of the book did not change much because I had again confirmed that teenagers were truly engaged in these sexual behaviors already; they needed the truth, and they needed help figuring out what was right for them individually. So even if the Archdiocese of New York, Cardinal and Archbishop John O'Connor himself, or other "concerned clergy" believed that my book was an example of the instruction in perversion and sodomy that had "been percolating thru and polluting our educational system," I was not about to cease and desist.

Sometime in the 1970s, I signed a petition along with many other sexuality professionals, asking the pope to reconsider the Church's stand on masturbation as a mortal sin, given current empirical data on the frequency and psychological normalcy of the behavior. A fool's errand, to be sure, since theological dogma and science often don't mix well. Needless to say, there was no response from the Vatican. Even though there has been hope among some Roman Catholics that many of the Church's stands on sex and birth control might shift, the traditional prohibitions have only been repeatedly reaffirmed. After being vilified by public health activists in 2009 for telling the citizens of AIDS-ravaged sub-Saharan Africa that it would be a sin if they used condoms, Pope Benedict XVI made a rather garbled and halting statement in a 2010 interview about how use of condoms to prevent disease transmission *might, rarely, in very specific cases*, be okay but that this still didn't justify their use to prevent conception.[5]

This was a huge news story for several days, even though it represented a relatively inconsequential waffle as a statement that could not be considered an official Church "teaching." Some hopeful commentators opined that this was another step in an evolutionary process of liberalizing the Church's stands on sexuality and birth control,[6] but with all due respect, I wouldn't hold my breath. Even as the Church struggles to recover from pervasive international scandals over its lack of intervention with sexually abusive priests, it has been no more articulate in reflecting on contemporary sexual issues with clarity and directness. Not that religious institutions have any obligation to modify their theological positions because of changing mores in popular culture, but followers do deserve clear and unequivocal statements about what is expected of them. I worry that vague pronouncements such as Benedict's condom statement only increase the sexual ambiguity and confusion for the faithful. This is not a time for ambiguity or confusion in matters sexual; it's simply too risky. Perhaps the key lies in the reality that when the adherents to a particular faith don't like the hierarchy's positions on sexual matters, they simply ignore them, or in groups that spring up, such as Condoms4Life, that take out advertisements in international venues on World AIDS Day to provide guidance for the faithful, defiantly declaring, "We believe in God. We believe that sex is sacred" and "Good Catholics use condoms."[7]

SEXUALITY EDUCATION AT ANOTHER LEVEL

It was not by religious fiat that my book for teenagers gradually slipped out of print in the 1990s; it was instead the victim of the refreshed paradigm of sexual fear and abstinence that rather quickly overtook whatever remained of the sexual revolution. I was somewhat sorry to see the book fade away, but by that time, my college text in sexuality was absorbing far more of my time and was proving to be far more successful in every way. It had originally been published in 1980 as a sexuality book for adults by the same publisher that had produced *Learning about Sex*. However, the audience for the book's first version was less clear and the publisher less able to market it well, so commercially it bombed. Yet at a time when only a couple of texts had been published for use in college-level courses on sexuality, a few professors had adopted mine for their classrooms. When Dushkin Publishing Group, a small firm in Connecticut, was looking for a sexuality text to market with their other line of helpful books on sexuality, one of those professors suggested that they try to buy the rights to my book because he was having difficulty using it after it too had gone out of print. In 1988, the first Dushkin edition of *Sexuality Today* was published, and it soon had been adopted for use at a few hundred colleges and universities in the United States and Canada.

Unlike many texts, I would eventually discover, the book turned out to be a survivor. Publishers at the time were in conglomerate-building mode, which seemed to be one way to survive financially. After my book's third edition with Dushkin, the company was acquired by Brown and Benchmark, a textbook company in the Midwest. My text was placed in the company's Health, Physical Education, and Recreation Division, so in its two subsequent editions, it took on a somewhat more health-related tone and focus than I had been used to. This was also the first time I realized that a single publisher often carries several competing texts in the same field, testing out which sold best and eventually allowing weaker ones to fall by the wayside. This made me uncomfortable, but I was assured that each book had its niche and that mine was doing fine. I managed to hold my ground through renegotiations, and sales actually seemed to trend upward quite nicely. Before long, though, the behemoth McGraw-Hill acquired Brown and Benchmark to become one of the largest textbook publishers in the world. *Sexuality Today* seemed like the ugly duckling at McGraw-Hill for two editions, as it bounced from one editorial staff in Boston to another in California, but it managed to outdo a couple of the company's other sexuality texts. Finally, it won its way into the

Psychology Division, where it really belonged and where it has continued to flourish.

Textbooks eventually take on a life of their own, with their authors shepherding them through the changing business climates their publishers must face. Texts are referred to in classrooms by their authors' last names, as in "We'll be covering chapter 10 in Kelly next week." The author and the book become synonymous, and this is about how wedded I feel to my book. I once dreaded the labor of the inevitable revisions every two or three years. Now I look forward to it, ready to embrace the new research that will come my way and then relishing the act of putting it all into terms that my readers can readily understand. As I worked on the official 10th edition of the text (I say "official" because it doesn't count the first version I did or the "updated" seventh edition that took just as much work as the eighth), an editor reminded me that after so many editions, any book needs a lot of housecleaning. On top of that, for the last two editions, the publisher has wanted to shorten the text by a "signature" each time, meaning by 32 printed pages. This is partly a cost-containment issue, I gather, but also may represent preparation for concise e-versions of texts that are beginning to appear. I for one can't wait to work on a nicely hyperlinked e-version of my text. Talk about a brave new world! I have come to value these book-shortening challenges because having to cut topics down to size has helped trim my writing skills and my ego.[8]

SEXUALITY KNOWLEDGE EVOLVES

The most remarkable thing about having to keep up so closely with developments in a special field is observing the speed with which sexuality scholars are constantly replacing old theory with new and widely held hackneyed beliefs with fresh and vital perspectives based on reliable evidence. Bolstered by the legitimacy with which the sexual revolution imbued the pursuit of sex research and by new sources of funding generated by sexual health fears and by pharmaceutical companies hoping for help in finding some post-Viagra sexual wonder drug, the field has flourished. Keeping up with it has become more daunting but no less exciting than it ever was. As I compare some of what I wrote in the early editions of *Sexuality Today* with what I'm writing now, the signposts of progress are clear.

One of the major difficulties I faced in the first five editions of the book was the dearth of reliable data about the frequencies of various forms of sexual behaviors among various segments of the American population. This was exactly the same problem that Alfred Kinsey had faced when he was asked to teach courses on human sexuality, and this led to his subsequent groundbreaking research on male and female sexual behaviors. Even 30 years after Kinsey's data were published, they remained the best—and largely *only*—statistics available. The sexual revolution had been in full swing for quite a while in 1978, and I was using research data published in 1948 and 1953. There had been several popular studies sponsored by publications such as *Playboy* and *Redbook* and a few other surveys by academics, but their scientific reliability was compromised by skewed study populations, questionable methodologies, and poor statistical analysis. I cited the data in the appropriate places, suspecting that there was probably a major discrepancy between the Kinsey figures and the sexually enthusiastic responses of people willing to fill out a survey from *Playboy*.

Others wanted fresh data as well, and in a time when the HIV/AIDS crisis called out for better understanding of current modes of sexual behavior, it was crucial that studies be done. In 1987, the National Institutes of Health called for proposals for a study of sexual practices and attitudes among American adults. Three distinguished sociologists submitted a proposal and then embarked on a four-year battle for funding. In 1991, even after their research had been approved, conservative members of Congress were able to introduce legislation that effectively eliminated any funding for research about sexuality. The scientists managed to attract funding from a number of private sources instead, although only about a quarter of what would have been needed to conduct the more extensive study they had hoped for. Nonetheless, they were able to interview a representative sample of 3,432 individuals, and the first results of the National Health and Social Life Survey (NHSLS) were published in 1994.[9] The new statistics portrayed a less sexually adventurous American populous than the image that magazine surveys and social mythology had created. I was just excited to finally have some current and reliable statistics that I could cite in the book.

As I recently prepared the 10th edition, I was heartened by the data now available on adolescent sexuality, another critical population for which Congress had long been hesitant to fund any study. I was, however, again feeling stifled by what felt like a waning validity of information about adults since the NHSLS data had now been collected nearly 20 years before. Then, in 2010, researchers from Indiana University's Center for Sexual Health Promotion—in cooperation with much of the senior staff of the Kinsey Institute—released a new survey of a representative sample of 5,865 people in the United States ages 14 to 94. It was called the National Survey of Sexual Health and Behavior (NSSHB).[10] I was thrilled.

So what are some of the marked changes that have occurred since I wrote the first version of *Sexuality Today*? Some of them have been dramatic. Even the Kinsey data that I used in the earlier editions of the text[11] were based on a "convenience" sample that was probably not particularly representative of Americans as a whole. In portions of his study, Kinsey also chose to quantify "sexual outlet" on the basis of numbers of orgasms experienced within periods of time or as the result of certain types of sexual interactions. This was based on his belief—still a common misconception—that human beings build up sexual "pressure" like a steam boiler until that pressure is released through orgasm, and then the pressure begins to build again. He also believed that if the mounting sexual tension was not released in one way, such as orgasm during sexual intercourse, it would be released in another, such as masturbatory orgasm. This all makes intuitive sense based on the way a lot of people experience their own "horniness," especially males, but it also fails to take into account sexual activities in which orgasm does not happen or the important understanding we now have that motivations and incentives to share sexual activities like intercourse seem to be quite independent from the incentives to masturbate on one's own. Instead of one sexual outlet compensating for another, as Kinsey believed, we know that the motivations for shared sex and solitary sex are quite separate and different.

Doing the best I could with those primitive and fragmentary statistics, I was able to state early on that at least 92 percent of men and 62 percent of women had masturbated during their lifetimes. The Kinsey data on oral sex were particularly interesting. Among college-educated men, about half reported having stimulated a woman's genitals orally, while just 5 percent of men with only a grade school education reported having done so. Among all women, only about 40 percent had orally stimulated a man's penis, and then this was done infrequently. Simply stated, in the middle of the 20th century, oral sex was not the widely accepted practice it seems to be today, and its popularity seemed to be determined mostly by the enlightenment of attending college, where we might assume that students have always been provided with a greater opportunity to share ideas, suggestions, and sexual encounters with other sexually charged young adults like themselves.

We know that the sexual revolution apparently cleared the way for greater openness about both masturbation and oral sex. The data from the most recent study of American sexual behaviors, the NSSHB,[12] were arranged by age-group and showed that among men, solo masturbation was one of the most widely reported of sexual behaviors. Among men in their late 20s, 94.3 percent indicated having masturbated before, with about 84 percent having masturbated within the past year. In the older age brackets of men surveyed, there were just slight declines in the lifetime masturbation rates reported. Women's solo masturbation rates follow similar trends but with slightly lower numbers than men. Women in their late 20s reported an 84.6 percent lifetime masturbation rate, and 71.5 percent reported having masturbated within the past year. So these figures are not all that different from the Kinsey data, and all studies have indicated a somewhat lower rate of masturbation among women. Unlike any previous studies, the NSSHB also inquired about masturbating with a partner, finding that among adults ages 18 to 59, this is a common behavior for around half the American population, with only slightly greater frequency among men.

Oral sexual behavior clearly has increased in popularity since the Kinsey days. Among men ages 20 to 59, nearly 90 percent have received oral stimulation from a female, well over half within the past year. (Around 10% of males in that age-group have received oral stimulation from another male, slightly more than 5% in the past year.) Among women ages 20 to 59, more than 80 percent have received oral–genital stimulation from a male, with more than 70 percent of those in their 20s and about 55 percent of those in their 30s and 40s having done so in the past year. (Higher proportions of women than men have received oral sex from another of their own gender, with figures ranging from 8.2% to 16.8% in various age-groups during their lifetimes and 1% to 8.5% in the past year.)

When preparing the first few editions of the text, I had almost no reliable information about adolescent sexual behavior. I knew only from talking with young people that they were engaged in a variety of sexual behaviors. There were a few surveys of teens published in the 1970s and 1980s, but their methodologies seemed flawed and their data therefore questionable. This is finally changing, especially as the federal government has seen the wisdom of supporting such studies. The National Longitudinal Study of Adolescent Health follows more than 20,000 teens, with 500 interviewers getting information from them. Both the ongoing National Survey of Family Growth and the Centers for Disease Control's Youth Risk Behavior Surveillance System have finally begun including questions about adolescent sexual behavior and health. The data that continue to emerge from these studies confirm that adolescents and young adults are indeed engaged in a wide range of sexual activities. It doesn't really matter whether we like it or not or approve of it or not; kids are engaging in sexual activity.

Looking back at the first edition of *Sexuality Today*, I find few statistics about the sexual behavior of teens and lots of educated guesswork. In fact, coverage of childhood and adolescent sexuality took up fewer than nine pages in a chapter titled "Sexuality through the Life Cycle." In the ninth edition of the text, I divided that single chapter into two, and in the 10th edition, the chapter on "Sexuality in Infancy, Childhood, and Adolescence" has expanded even more. I am now able to state, with the authority that reliable empirical data can support that of kids ages 14 to 17, the majority of the boys (80%) have masturbated and that less than half the girls (48%) have done so,[13] confirming a gender differential that has shown up in research for more than 60 years. I must admit that I still find myself a bit skeptical about the male statistics indicating that 57.8 percent of the boys reported they had masturbated in the past 90 days given the popular notions about the behavior in teenage males and the data gathered in my own classes indicating that some 98 percent of male students masturbate, most of them quite regularly. I am a little less surprised that only 35.9 of the girls in the study reported masturbating within the past

90 days, although this figure is considerably lower than I have seen elsewhere too. So something seems a bit out of whack here to me, but this may simply mean that I need to readjust some of my assumptions about masturbatory behavior in adolescents.

Less surprising to me is the finding that the proportion of teenagers who report having had penile–vaginal sex increases for each year of age, as does the percentage of teens engaging in oral and anal sex. The frequency of these behaviors does not seem to be startlingly high, but it is encouraging that rates of condom use for penile–vaginal sex was 80 percent for males and 69 percent for females, higher than most previous studies have reported.

Even though we still labor under some negative misconceptions about teenagers' sexual habits, much of the data on adolescent sex in America demonstrate downward trends. Over the past two decades, the National Youth Risk Behavior Survey has shown a marked decrease in rates of teen intercourse, having more than four sexual partners, and use of alcohol or drugs before sex. During the same period, condom use during last intercourse has increased nearly 10 percent.[14] Also contrary to popular opinion, rates of teen pregnancy have declined quite dramatically since 1991, reaching the lowest rates since the National Center for Health Statistics began tracking the numbers in 1940. There was a slight upward blip in 2006 and 2007, but 2008 then brought even lower numbers than before. Likewise, the rates of live births and abortions among teen women have continued to decrease during the same period, with the lowest rates ever in 2009.[15] The reductions in pregnancy and abortions seem to be the result of increased use of various forms of contraception, and they would probably be reduced even further if emergency contraception were prescribed more often for American teens who have had unprotected sex, as it is in other nations.[16]

During the next decade or two, we are finally going to have the most accurate and realistic picture of American sexual behaviors that we've ever had, and I look forward to using the data to reshape the pages of my text. In many ways, I have come to realize that we have allowed our nation's sexual self-image to be shaped by sound bytes and media hype. The bottom line is that we're not a particularly wild population when it comes to our sexual behaviors. On average, we take our time becoming sexually active, and we're relatively cautious about what we do and with whom we do it. There are always some risk takers, and there are always times when some of us take sexual risks we later regret, but on the whole, we're a pretty conventional bunch.

THE NAKED TRUTH

One of the decisions I had to make in the early editions of the text was whether to illustrate it primarily with drawings when it came to body parts and sexual activities or to use photographs. After the rather negative outcome of my use of photos in guest editing the journal mentioned earlier in this chapter, I decided to stick with tasteful drawings. Over the years, more and more sexuality texts have included nude photos, but I have persisted in using artists' renderings, beginning with monochromes but now with colored highlights. Somehow I've never thought that photos were all that necessary, except for illustrating some specific things like sexually transmitted diseases or surgically created genitals in transsexuals. The approach has seemed to work.

That is not to say that there has been no controversy over the drawings in the book. The chapter on sexual behavior has always included what has been called a "veritable Kama Sutra" of various illustrated positions for heterosexual intercourse, and this generated ire from some reviewers about the lack of illustrations depicting same-sex couples. Gradually, I have increased the number of drawings that do just this, and they seem to have enhanced the sections on male–male and female–female sexual activity nicely. The publisher and I have also continued to try to be responsive to calls for greater ethnic and age diversity in the illustrations and even to show more bodies that are overweight or otherwise "less than perfect." Each time the text is revised, I receive a number of anonymous reviews that are arranged by the publisher, and I pay careful attention to them. I usually make changes if more than a single reviewer raises an issue. And, frankly, I typically get the best ideas from the reviews that are the most caustic, even though they always make me fume a bit at first.

SEXUAL ORIENTATION BY THE NUMBERS

Scientific perspectives on sexual orientation represent another area of the text that has undergone tremendous modification since the early days. In the 1970s, like most other sexologists, I assumed that our attraction to women or men or both developed out of the experiences and exposure we had as children and adolescents. I was never sold on the psychoanalytic interpretations involving libido and "arrested" psychosexual development, but neither could I fathom how our genes or hormones might actually shape our erotic and romantic attractions. My original discussion of potential biological shapers of sexual attraction was limited to a single page of the book. Neither did I have any clear or coherent theory of how social forces determined sexual orientation. Gradually, my explanation of possible biological templates of sexual orientation has expanded to several pages, and this is covered in greater detail in chapter 7 of this book.

At the first writing of the text, the American Psychiatric Association had just decided to exclude "homosexuality" as a type of mental disorder. Like others, I was also using some retabulated Kinsey data suggesting that 13.95 percent of males and 4.25 percent of females, or about 10 percent of the total American population, had had either extensive homosexual experience (21 or more same-sex partners or 51 or more experiences) or more-than-incidental homosexual experience (5 to 20 partners or 21 to 50 experiences). We now know that these figures are not applicable to the general American population and represent one of the unfortunate misconceptions that resulted from Kinsey's reliance on a study population that was somewhat overrepresented by prisoners, frat boys, and those who frequented gay bars.

The 10 percent figure was used for many years to support various gay causes, and I was one of many authors who perpetuated it even though it never did quite ring true in terms of what I heard from students and counseling clients anecdotally. More recent studies have demonstrated a far more balanced picture that is also more complicated. People simply do not distribute easily into sexual orientation categories of any sort. Granted there are many people who clearly and proudly define themselves as gay men, lesbian women, or bisexual people. But these terms are simply inadequate and inaccurate for labeling the somewhat ill-defined masses of others who seem to have had some sexual attractions to or experiences with others of their sex, sometimes substantial numbers of them, but do not care to categorize themselves in any particular way. In recent times, this seems less the result of fears of social stigmatization and more because our standard labels are overly limiting and narrow-minded.

Psychologist Fritz Klein was one of the first researchers to remind us that a single label would always be inadequate to describe anyone's sexual orientation, instead saying that we needed to look at past, present, and "ideal" conceptions that people have of their sexual selves and a whole list of other variables, including attractions, behaviors, fantasies, emotional and social preferences, lifestyles, and self-identification, all of which may reflect very individualized leanings.[17] The National Health and Social Life Survey demonstrated that there is actually little congruence among people's desires, behaviors, and self-identification when it comes to their sexual connections with others. So even though we must categorize and label the various phenomena of human sexual experience in order to think and communicate about them in an orderly way, the categories we have developed are largely inadequate and fail to capture the nuances of individual sexual natures.

A LITTLE FUN WITH NAMES AND TITLES

I always tell my students that when it comes to the serious matters of life such as sexuality, it is important that we find the humor within. Beyond the off-color joke, our daily experiences with our sexual nature are filled with funny perspectives. Because sex makes people tense and a little nervous, they like being able to laugh about it too. I treasure the laughs that I have with my students and the editors who help me with each revision of my text. We have a good time with it all.

Of the things that make me chuckle, the names of researchers who have tackled sexual topics and sometimes the titles of their publications really can be a hoot. I want to share some of these here. I always thought it humorous that Dr. Thomas *Wiswell* (*wizz-well*, get it?) was the chief investigator on a study of how lowering rates of male circumcision were leading to increased rates of urinary tract infections and that Trevor *Butt* helped conduct a study showing that kids who got spanked were more likely to integrate spanking into their later sexual activities! I really enjoy it when I notice that a Dr. *Wang* has been a coauthor on several studies relating to erectile dysfunction—who could be better? And urologist Jack *McAninch* was a co-researcher in a famous study that measured flaccid and erect penis lengths. Marc *Breedlove* seems well suited to his work on possible genetic links to sexual orientation in twins, and John *Devine* (let's assume he pronounces it "divine") was a perfect coauthor for an article on "priestly celibacy" in the journal *Sexualities*. I sometimes wish that Evelyn *Hooker* had studied prostitutes instead of gay men, that David *Buss* had examined kissing instead of evolutionary mating strategies, or that Jennifer *Manlove* researched gay men instead of adolescent sexuality, but those are selfish desires.

The scientific journals of late seem to have loosened up in allowing some fun and puns in the titles of articles. The subtitle of an article about how to classify dyspareunia, or painful sexual intercourse, that appeared in the *Archives of Sexual Behavior* was subtitled "A Painful Classification Decision." An article in the *International Journal of Impotence Research* was titled "'Up and Coming' Treatments for Premature Ejaculation." An article in *Sexuality and Culture* about sex-related articles in men's magazines was called "Master Your Johnson."

Yes indeed, we must learn to laugh at sex and ourselves when it seems appropriate. Writing my books has been one of the most interesting and exciting parts of my career in sexology, even when the reactions to them have been less than positive. Yet even those lessons have tempered my ego and the certainty of my judgments in ways that ultimately have clarified my vision of the meanings of sexuality in human life. For me, that adventure continues and gets ever more fascinating all the time.

Chapter 5

COMING OF AGE: BEYOND COMPREHENSIVE SEXUALITY EDUCATION

As I completed my undergraduate degree in biology, my faculty mentors were expecting me to accept one of the graduate school fellowships I'd been offered to pursue a doctorate in physiology. However, I was not sold on that plan for my future, and so with a good deal of guilt and trepidation, I turned down the fellowships. After working in a medical laboratory for a year doing some research on diagnosing genetic disorders and how such findings could be translated into genetic counseling, I was asked to consider a high school job, teaching biology and health education. I decided to give it a shot since I had always been drawn to teaching.

I taught four classes of biology and two of health education during my first year in the school system, thrust into a classroom jammed with teenagers for six class periods in a row. No such thing as "planning periods" in those days. My planning was reserved for evenings and weekends. I found the job as exhilarating as it was exhausting. Being 23 years old, it seemed that some of my older students were almost as mature as I, and from what they confided to me it was clear that some of their sex lives were far more evolved than my own. So while I strived to teach them the concepts of life science and healthy lifestyles, my students taught me about the nuances of power imbalances between people and about how warmth, honesty, and sensitivity in relationships can forge bonds of mutual trust and respect. Before long, I realized that I had found what I had been looking for and what my undergraduate education had failed to provide, even with a minor in psychology: a better understanding of human connection. My high school teaching experience was, in fact, the reason that I ultimately chose to pursue graduate work in counseling and human development.

My health education classes were populated at the time mostly by juniors and seniors who were not on a college track. They were enrolled in health instead of biology because it was the easier, lifestyle-oriented course thought to be better suited for what was perceived as their less academic capabilities and pursuits. I taught one section of health in the morning and one in the afternoon because most of those students attended the regional vocational school for the other half of the school day. New York State had not quite yet mandated health education for all students, so my students were mostly 16 to 19 years old, streetwise, used to not being considered particularly bright (even though they were), and not all that interested in sitting in undersized desks listening to teachers babble on. They had become—either by choice or by classification—"hands-on" learners. Some of the males were grown men, with beard stubble and packs of cigarettes tucked over bulging biceps under the sleeves of their T-shirts. (Cigarettes had not yet been banned, and clouds of smoke would roll out of bathrooms between class periods, even though some intrepid teachers would venture in and try to stop the smoking.) The females were already women too, with their bodies tucked into tight blouses and miniskirts that barely covered them. Those studying cosmetology had sexy hairdos (for the time) and lots of makeup. These "kids" captured my attention and my heart. They were also the ones who participated easily in classroom discussion and were willing to be more open and honest in those discussions than many of the students I have taught since.

By my second year of teaching, I was realizing that for my courses, sex was indeed the elephant in the classroom, ever present but unmentionable. The biology textbook had a brief, innocuous chapter on sexual reproduction—chapter 47—but the teacher whom I replaced made it clear that she had simply skipped it in order to avoid laughter and other unspecified "problems." The publisher of the health textbook had a separate chapter on sexuality that could be purchased as a supplement, but it had never been used at the school. My health students loved to talk about sex, but I always found myself feeling uneasy and ambivalent about these unauthorized detours, unsure of what I should be doing. Yet of all the topics I was dealing with in both courses, it was crystal clear to me that these students wanted—and needed—to know more about sexuality. I began to talk this over with my curriculum supervisor, who had had a successful teaching career himself and had become a caring and helpful mentor to me. He listened carefully to my arguments for the need to deal with sexuality more openly in my courses and eventually told me to proceed but to do so "cautiously." This was hardly the way that the experts would eventually advise school systems to get started with sex education—they would suggest having meetings with parents and staff and getting approvals from the PTA and the board of education—but it suited me just fine. So I did move ahead.

TRIAL BY FLUSHED FACE

There was scant literature to consult at the time regarding the content and philosophy of sexuality education, so I was pretty much on my own. I would soon find many allies and teachers who were experimenting with various methods, but at first I was flying blind. Probably just as well. Here is what I knew. My students were not well informed about their own bodies or how they functioned. Some of them were engaging in a variety of sexual activities, including intercourse, but they seemed largely ignorant about birth control other than condoms, and those were available only by asking for them at a pharmacy. Condoms were still kept behind the counter at the time, and not all clerks were either sensitive or nonjudgmental when they were requested. One of my biology students, a 17-year-old, confided to me that he and his girlfriend were having intercourse, and I reminded him of the importance of using birth control. He agreed but said they would have to wait until he got a ride to another town because he didn't want to obtain them from the local druggist, a good friend of his parents. I sometimes regret that I didn't offer to give him some condoms, but frankly I wasn't that brave. A few months later, his girlfriend was pregnant, and he asked me to serve as best man for his hurriedly arranged wedding. After the ceremony, his heartbroken mother said to me, "If he had only listened to you," and I regretted even more than I had not had the guts to give him some condoms. His life and kids turned out okay, even though the marriage didn't last, but it was another dramatic reminder for me that kids' lives could be forever altered by their sexual decisions and actions.

I knew that my students were not well prepared for the choices they were making. The most explicit message they were getting from their parents and religious leaders was a call for abstinence until marriage, but there was sometimes ambivalence and a wink of the eye embedded with that message. Boys were often told to *just be careful*. Girls were cautioned not to sully their reputations and reminded that presumably because they didn't "need sex" as much as boys, it would be up to them to keep things under control. In any case, these kids didn't seem to be following the advice any more than had many of those offering it. Hypocrisy aside, I realized that the desire to have sex was a powerful one that would not always be resisted no matter what the risks or possible consequences. Therefore, I determined that knowing how to protect oneself from pregnancy and disease transmission seemed like a basic premise for what students should know.

The possibility that sex might have positive outcomes for teenagers was not paid much heed until quite recently, but to me 40 years ago it seemed anecdotally to be quite reasonable.

When I began to get more involved in the broader social dialogue about sex education, there was a lot of talk about respect and responsibility, both fine concepts and worthy of a place at the table but often misapplied, I thought. The need to treat one another respectfully and responsibly can never be overemphasized, but there has always been an undercurrent of belief in this country that teenagers, especially girls, get involved sexually because they lack self-respect; that is, they don't care enough about themselves to avoid having sex, or they dislike themselves enough that they allow themselves to be "used" for sex. These are sobering claims, albeit not based in much empirical evidence, that seemed supportable by at least a few of the kids I knew but certainly not by all of them—even the majority of them. Many of my older students actually seemed quite positively inclined toward their sexual relationships and if anything felt more mature, confident, and satisfied because of them. They seemed to feel more autonomous and self-confident than some of their peers. The possibility that sex might have positive outcomes for teenagers was not paid much heed until quite recently, but to me 40 years ago it seemed anecdotally to be quite reasonable. So in my interactions with students, I wanted to be cautious not to frame sexual interaction only in negatives and in fact worried that this might produce self-fulfilling prophecies. Teachers are, like it or not, mythmakers and perpetuators of social mythologies, and I didn't want the ideas I perpetuated to lead to any more darkness or negativity for youth than they already faced. What possible good could that reap?

The kinds of sexual activities that the sexual revolution was beginning to open up for discussion at the time were hardly typical fare for high school classroom discussions at the time: masturbation, premarital sex (as we called it then), oral sex, and anal sex. Yet again, it was clear that my students were engaging in these behaviors and had no particular avenue for learning about them other than from each other. I recall one young man who asked to talk with me after school, and as we sat together in my empty classroom, he hemmed and hawed until he finally was able to confide to me, red faced, that he masturbated. I've never been entirely certain if my almost reflexive response was appropriate or prudent enough—it probably wasn't—but I laughed a little and said, "So do I." It worked for him at least, and my personal admission filled him with a sense of relief and the knowledge that he wasn't so different after all. And there was no news story with a headline that read "Local Teacher Tells Student He Masturbates!" With all the openness in today's media about masturbation, it is difficult to imagine any young person feeling the same hesitancy and embarrassment today, but this kid's ignorance about the commonplace nature of sexual self-pleasuring was actually quite typical for the time. I knew that my sex education should include solid information about these behaviors.

I also believed that I had a responsibility to help young people feel comfortable in their own skins and in their own sexual orientations and identities. Even though teenagers seldom came out publicly with their sexual proclivities in those times, I knew that at least some proportion of my students must be gay, and I would eventually come to understand that a few were transgendered. How could sexuality education possibly be successful if it did not offer information about these things while helping kids feel at least a little less lonely in any sexual differences they might possess? I understood then, as I do today, that this is delicate territory to explore, fraught with competing social, political, and religious beliefs. But I could still offer the best scientific information that was available and try not to impose my own beliefs on the impressionable young faces that I found before me every day.

I was also convinced that the choice of abstaining from or postponing sex until one has carefully considered one's readiness deserved prominence. I have always been supportive of messages about abstinence in sexuality education because it is clearly a choice that many young people make and feel good about. I do have reservations about across-the-board calls for abstinence until marriage because they call on values that not everyone espouses and because the data on human behavior indicate that the vast majority of people do not abstain until they are in settled relationships. And more and more people are simply not getting married. I do, in fact, believe that many teenagers get sexually entangled prematurely and that the decision to share sex with someone is not something to be taken lightly. But I am convinced that these concepts are not applicable solely to youth. I've observed as much ill-considered and irresponsible sexual decision-making among adults of all ages as I have among teenagers. In fact, since kids often seem to understand the import of their early

I've observed as much ill-considered and irresponsible sexual decision-making among adults of all ages as I have among teenagers.

sexual decisions, I think they sometimes give those decisions more careful consideration than their elders do. Abstaining from sex until you know you're really ready or until you can be assured that you and your intended partner have not been "swept of your feet" by momentary passion is not a bad policy for people of any age.

By gathering books on sexuality and arming myself with as much information as possible, I gradually developed some level of confidence about the sex information I could share with my students. Kinsey's studies were already nearly historical, but Masters and Johnson had just published their two groundbreaking books. A spate of other studies—some based on substantive research and some simply pithy news stories—were beginning to appear. As I ventured not so cautiously along my sex education path, I finally decided to try a sex question-and-answer session in my health classes. I told my students that I was going to tape record the session so that I could try to convince the school's administration that they were mature enough to handle this material. They were. I gave out three-by-five cards and asked everyone to write down a question in block letters (so I wouldn't recognize their writing) that they would like to have answered or thought someone else could benefit from having answered. To counteract the bravado of pretending not to have any questions, I asked everyone to write something on the card, even if they had no questions about sex. As it turned out, everyone did. Here is a small sample of those first questions, all of which I tried to answer as accurately and honestly as I could:

- Is it normal for one of a woman's breasts to be larger than the other?
- What is a hysterectomy? Can a woman still have sex after she has had a hysterectomy?
- Is an erection of the penis caused by the testes or by the mind?
- How can a person overcome a personal shyness toward sex and sexual activities?
- We always hear about boys trying to be seducers. Do girls ever set out to seduce?
- If a boy has lost one testicle, can he still have a normal sex life? (I would discover later that this question had been submitted by a boy who only had one testicle, a fact that every other male student in the room seemed to know already.)
- I'm a girl, and I don't understand how an erect penis can ever fit into a vagina. Isn't the vagina too small?
- Why is it a guy sometimes can't keep his erection during sexual activity, like during a change of positions?
- How long does it take the average person to reach a climax during sex?
- Is it all right for a girl to engage in sex during her period?
- Are there any dangers in giving a boy a blow job?
- Can masturbation cause any damage to physical or mental health?
- If you participate in some homosexual acts at the age of 12 or 13, does it mean that you're going to be homosexual?
- Is there such a thing as Spanish fly or other substances to get people turned on?

These were obviously very specific questions, and one of the things I immediately realized was that they were deserving of respect and honesty. They were loaded with opportunities for offering information about relationships and ethics, quite aside from the factual points. They were pleas for some reliable information; they were signs of trust that I would give them honest answers. I did my best to do just that, realizing that my preparation on the topics was indeed going to pay off. I did my best not to give the impression that I was encouraging anyone to do anything sexual; I was simply encouraging them to think their decisions through carefully and to be armed with solid information. I played the tape recording of my responses and the ensuing discussion for my supervisor, and he played it for the superintendent of schools. They both thought it had gone well and again gave me permission to proceed with my one-man sex education effort. As I think back on this informal agreement, I realize that a few angry phone calls to the school or a nasty article in the local newspaper could have stopped my efforts in their tracks, but for reasons that escape me now, I simply didn't worry about it. I was generally liked by students and their parents, which may have helped, but I also suspect that the sexual revolution was causing everyone to feel more open to—or helpless to oppose—the opening of sexual topics to the young. After I had left the school, I did hear a rumor or two of building unrest about my openness with students, so perhaps I got out of Dodge just in the nick of time. I'll never know. Before I left, the state mandated health education at all levels, and I was asked to serve as coordinator of health education. I repeated the question-and-answer session many times over when I was still there, eventually to the college bound students as well, and the questions were always very specific and explicit.

When it comes right down to it, I think the explicitness that teenagers want is one of the things that intimidates educators and parents. I was once leading a workshop for teachers on sex education when one of the participants described his own attempt at a classroom sex question-and-answer session that had been quickly aborted. He collected the questions from the students, and the first one he looked at read, "If a boy comes in my mouth, should I swallow it or spit it out?" He judged the question to have been deliberately provocative and decided not to proceed. Perhaps a student had been trying to embarrass him, but the question is nonetheless a legitimate one and represents something that young people do indeed wonder about. But he was also wise to understand his own limits. It takes some dedicated preparation to be able to use sexual terminology and discuss the intimate details of genital interactions without uneasiness. It surely took some work for me. The first time I used the terms "penis" and "vagina" in those early classes, I could feel my face flush. I simply held my head high and pretended it wasn't. The fact of the matter is that kids wouldn't really have cared anyway. They only appreciate your willingness to make the attempt to be open with them about some things they are struggling to understand in themselves.

Perhaps most powerful of all the things that we explored in these classes were the discussions about love and relationships and how sex did and didn't fit into the picture. We talked openly about coercion and consent, selfishness, and using others for one's own pleasure. We talked about attractiveness and how everyone felt pressured to keep up with impossible social standards of sex appeal. We discussed ways of resisting sex when we didn't feel ready and ways of making sure we were safe when we did feel ready. My philosophy for effective sexuality education continued to take shape, and I would come to realize that it was consistent with what eventually would be called the *comprehensive* approach.

SOME HISTORICAL PERSPECTIVE

The wave of interest in sexuality education that was spawned by the sexual revolution did not constitute the first time that there were efforts to educate people about sex, and to understand the roots of the movement is to grasp how much things had changed by the 1970s. So some history is in order here.

Colonial America was, by all accounts, a pretty bawdy time in the history of the United States, and despite bundling boards and efforts to protect reputations and conform to social standards, people were having sex with some abandon. About a third of brides came to the altar pregnant. The Victorian period, the influence of which was very much felt in America, pushed sex underground in the name of morality, propriety, and good taste, but under the covers things didn't change all that much. As urbanization brought increased numbers of American youth to cities for vocational training and jobs, concerns began to develop about increasing threats to the traditional family. By the early 20th century, rates of marriage were in decline and rates of divorce soaring, both trends that were attributed to "immoral" influences. Several political and social movements that took root in the late 19th century began to flourish amidst growing fears of moral decay. An Anti-Obscenity Movement was spearheaded by a New York City grocer named Anthony Comstock. With the help of the YMCA and the Women's Christian Temperance Association, Comstock founded the New York Society for the Suppression of Vice and at age 29 was able to persuade Congress in 1873 to pass a law that outlawed the delivery or transportation of "obscene, lewd, or lascivious" material as well as any methods of or information pertaining to birth control. The Post Office even got nervous about transmitting anatomy texts.[1]

Clergymen, once considered the primary arbiters of sexual matters, were supplanted by physicians as the male authorities on the subject, and they became leaders of reforms. The Social Hygiene Movement wanted to curb the scourge of venereal disease and prostitution that they believed stemmed from sexual ignorance and wantonness. A leader of this cause was a moralistic physician by the name of Dr. Prince Morrow, who formed the American Society of Sanity and Moral Prophylaxis in 1905, aimed at "inspiring the youth of both sexes to lead pure lives and . . . minimizing the appeal of the prostitute."[2] With support from the American Purity Alliance and the National Vigilance Committee, a united front emerged intending to use publicity and education to dampen sexual desires and encourage the purity of American youth. This was the beginning of a long period, persisting in some ways today, during which medical and moral issues became confusingly intertwined.[3] Contemporary efforts in sexuality education still get mired in confusion between scientific facts and moral codes. Clearly, they both have some place in various venues for sexuality education, but it is crucial not to lose sight of the differences between the two.

In 1912, the National Education Association called for programs that would prepare teachers to talk about sexual matters in public schools, and debates emerged about how such sensitive and personal subjects might be broached in the classroom. The proposal never gained much traction, although some schools did implement unrefined educational efforts. My father was apparently exposed to one of those early sex education efforts in the small village school that he attended in the early 1920s. After I had later become a sexuality educator and therapist, he—the youngest child of three, raised by a widowed mother—told me about this formal introduction to the subject of sex. The principal of his high school, a corpulent and stuffy man whom they addressed as "Professor," gathered the boys in a room and described for them the reproductive organs of female and male, along with the diseases they could convey. They were soundly admonished to be strong enough to avoid the risks at any cost. The only reaction my father could recall was that it made him feel sick to his stomach. It was an introduction that perhaps explained some of the ambiguity he always held regarding sexual topics. Such uncertainty and embarrassment about sexuality were pretty much de rigueur for his generation. Although attempts to "normalize" sex education limped along, the training of educators was practically nonexistent. The American Social Hygiene Association said in the 1930s that sex educators should be of "good character" and "well versed" in their subject matter and recommended that those who were "embarrassed, abnormal, unhappily married, or pessimistic" should not be allowed to be sex educators.[4] One can only wonder how such qualities of life and personality were to be assessed.

During the decades of the 1940s, 1950s, and 1960s, there was increasing interest in providing sex education for young people, bolstered by the very same social developments and scientific studies that were fueling the emerging sexual revolution. There was also a gradual shift away from moralizing to students and toward the provision of scientifically supportable facts. The American Medical Association collaborated with the National Education Association to produce five pamphlets about the sexuality of young adults that were widely distributed. Professionals who had long touted sexual topics mostly within the context of marriage began to rethink that position and adopt a depathologized perspective that put an emphasis on the positive ways in which sexuality could be integrated into the human experience. The important thing was to deal with values as well as substantive content.[5] In contrast to this significant philosophical shift was the typical pattern for instituting sex education programs in schools. Most often some teachers, parents, and board of education members would become alarmed by a flurry of teen pregnancies and decide that sex education was needed to stem this regrettable tide. Again, the primary motivation was largely preventative in nature, with maybe a touch of moralism mixed in. The only problem was expecting that some relatively brief exposure to sex information and prohibitions would actually get at the complex social mechanisms behind teen pregnancy. Certainly, information about methods of contraception might be of some assistance, even though many schools and parents were uncomfortable with this, but studies tended to show that the most effective programs in preventing unintended pregnancies were those that offered access to contraceptive methods. Not many schools were willing to venture that far.

By the 1970s, the remarkable social openness about sexuality was bolstering formalized efforts in sexuality education, and developments such as legalization of the Pill and abortion, more boldness from the media about sexual topics, and political efforts to underscore the equality of the sexes (such as the effort to pass the Equal Rights Amendment) only seemed to further the cause. However, any momentum toward more liberal goals tends to be met with opposite momentum to reverse course toward more conservative ways. At first, much of this opposition came from conservative voices such as Phyllis Schlafly in her efforts to preserve traditional marriage, Anita Bryant in her crusade against gay rights, and Jerry Falwell of the fundamentalist Christian group The Moral Majority in his opposition to sex education in schools, gay rights, abortion, and pornography.[6] As an organization that valued sex education for the young, including information about birth control and abortion, Planned Parenthood affiliates were frequent targets of the opposition, both locally and nationally. While the right-wing activists were often perceived as fringe figures by the general public, they still crystallized some of the vague moral discomfort that the sexual revolution had stirred in many people, which was certainly understandable given the moralistic roots that we all share. These stirrings were not usually strong enough to motivate full support for the conservative voices, but neither did they stimulate strong advocacy for what were perceived as sexually liberal causes.

As I described in chapter 1, doubts and concerns about the sexual directions that society seemed to be taking were further catalyzed by the HIV/AIDS scare that took shape in the early 1980s. A lot of people began to think, "Maybe we've been going in the wrong direction after all." Ambivalence never powers movements very well or for very long, so as state governments began to pass legislation to mandate HIV/AIDS educational efforts, comprehensive approaches to educating youth about sexuality began to recede once again into the background. Prevention again became the watchword, and this obscured the broader objectives of helping young people integrate a healthy sexuality into their personalities and lifestyles.

THE FEDERAL GOVERNMENT AND THE ABSTINENCE-ONLY CRUSADES

One of the hot-button issues for politicians is single welfare mothers, beginning with unwed teenagers who require public assistance and including women who have had babies and yet continue to require welfare funds because they do not have jobs or partners who offer financial support. In many urban environments, many of these women are black or Hispanic. For a variety of understandable reasons, these cases raise the hackles of the taxpaying public, so politicians are often motivated to make promises about "cleaning up" the problem. When teenagers have babies, it is the welfare specter that rises in the political background, even though some pregnant teens come from financially sound families.

First Lady Nancy Reagan garnered both public approval and ridicule for offering her "Just say no" solution to the country's drug problem, but her husband clearly thought that the same simplistic remedy could be applied to the country's "sex problem" as well. In 1981, Reagan's administration succeeded in getting the Adolescent Family Life Act passed as part of Public Health Law. Dubbed the "Chastity Act," it sought to provide support to adolescents before they became sexually active in order to "promote self-discipline and other prudent approaches to the problem of adolescent sexual relations, including adolescent pregnancy." It included funding of grants for projects to develop educational programs that would encourage sexual abstinence and also included clauses that limited use of the funds by family planning agencies (which could provide birth control) and forbade the funding of any programs that "advocated, promoted, or encouraged" abortion. In other words, the Bill was explicit in drawing conservative political and religious lines of proscription around what its sex education programs could include.

Not surprisingly, a number of sex education programs soon emerged that called for abstinence-only-until-marriage, and by the early 1990s many school districts had adopted them as the basis of their sex education curriculum. The essential difference between the comprehensive approach and the abstinence-only approach is that the former offers information about sexuality, including methods of protection against disease and pregnancy, recognizing the data indicating that most young people will choose to participate in various sexual activities before they settle into a long-term relationship. The abstinence philosophy holds that providing much sex information will only encourage premature sexual activity and affirms a moral position that having sexual relations prior to marriage is simply wrong. Its approach strives to convince youth that they should therefore put their energies into self control, avoiding any sex until they are married.

It was not long before studies began to appear in professional journals demonstrating that the new abstinence-based curricula were fraught with problems. Many of these programs had been designed under the auspices of conservative religious groups that were desperate not only to turn back the sexual revolution's permissive clock but to teach specific religious values as well. They employed inaccurate medical information, ineffective scare tactics, gender stereotypes, and opinions that were stated as facts. In their earlier versions, they sometimes quoted Christian teachings. They were attacked by some citizens for their use in public school settings and led to challenges in the courts that held the Adolescent Family Life Act to be unconstitutional because of its religious leanings. While this eventually led to court judgments about the need for any funded material to be reviewed to ensure medical accuracy and religious neutrality, the game suddenly changed.[7]

In 1996, during the Clinton administration, welfare reform changes to Title V Section 510(b) of the Social Security Act not only provided block grants for states to teach abstinence-only-until-marriage, with marriage being established as the "expected standard of human sexual activity," but it included very specific definitions of what constituted abstinence-only education, developed by a representative of the conservative think tank, the Heritage Foundation.[8] This abstinence-only education provision actually got slipped into the welfare reform legislation while it was undergoing technical revision and therefore became law without any public input or congressional debate. From a legislative point of view, it was, in every sense of the term, an end run around those who were recognizing the inadequacies of abstinence-only-until-marriage sexuality education in favor of state-sanctioned support for a narrow-minded, unscientific, religious-based, moral stand on sexual behavior. What was at least superficially intended to address some very real problems in a relatively small population within the nation's welfare system—problems that remain unresolved today—became the national dogma to be delivered to our nation's youth. I sometimes wonder what would happen if the federal government suddenly incentivized a canon of expectations for social studies education, the teaching of mathematics, or English literature. I would wager that state education departments would rise in united opposition and teachers unions and educational organizations throughout the nation would cry bloody murder. In the case of this imposed approach to sexuality education, nobody said very much at all.

President Clinton, who allegedly was having occasional sexual encounters with Monica Lewinsky at the time, had nothing to say. Ambivalent and nervous schools and parents seemed happy to have something easy and morally unambiguous to grab onto, even if it was out of touch with reality. Conservative politicians and religious leaders were pleased that their righteous point of view had prevailed. And the money to the states was a nice perk too. In 2005, additional monies became available through Community-Based Abstinence Education, which would fund programs for up to $600,000 per year for five years (a $3 million limit per program). Over a relatively short span of years, these three sources funneled $1.5 billion of taxpayer money to states in support of abstinence-only-until-marriage sexuality education. As far as the evidence suggests, the whole plan was a colossal failure that may have caused more problems than it solved.

WHAT SEXUALITY EDUCATION "WORKS," AND HOW DO WE KNOW?

Despite the articles that appeared in professional journals in the early 1990s raising serious concerns about the moral, religious, and scientifically unsupportable biases in the abstinence-based curricula, it would take several more years before really reliable analyses would be published about the efficacy of various approaches to sexuality education. During these years, federal monies continued to be doled out to states for abstinence-only programs. An overarching difficulty in evaluating sexuality education—or any academic curriculum for that matter—is coming to some consensus about what it would mean for any approach to be "effective" or "successful." The preventive, abstinence-only perspective on success would be to see young people stop their sexual involvement, thereby making the "proper" moral choice and also eliminating the possibility of pregnancy and disease transmission. The comprehensive sexuality education perspective also supports the goal of reductions in unintended pregnancies and sexually transmitted diseases (STDs) but additionally wants to see young people able to make well-informed decisions about their readiness for sexual sharing while being well prepared to make choices to be considerate, responsible, and protective if and when they decide to share sex. In that sense, it is more proactive than reactive.

I think it is not stepping out of line to state that most comprehensive sexuality educators also want their students to be able to feel good about their individual sexualities and to integrate sexuality into their lives in positive and satisfying ways. In 2001, Dr. David Satcher, who was serving simultaneously as U.S. surgeon general and assistant secretary of health, brought this broader perspective to the concept of *sexual health*. In the Introduction to his *Call to Action to Promote Sexual Health and Responsible Sexual Behavior*, Satcher wrote,

> Sexual health is not limited to the absence of disease or dysfunction, nor is its importance confined to just the reproductive years. It includes the ability to understand and weigh the risks, responsibilities, outcomes and impacts of sexual actions and to practice abstinence when appropriate. It includes freedom from sexual abuse and discrimination and the ability of individuals to integrate their sexuality into their lives, derive pleasure from it, and to reproduce if they so choose.[9]

The chairman of the American Academy of Family Physicians declared that Satcher's position represented an "overdue paradigm shift" at the national level, although it seemed to have little impact on the national political leadership at the time. Conservative political groups thought the report was too permissive in its stands on homosexuality and condom distribution in schools. Satcher, a Clinton appointee, was gone as surgeon general in the George W. Bush administration within a year of the publication of the *Call to Action*.

By this time, some members of Congress were growing uncomfortable with the constant flow of funds to states for abstinence-only sexuality education when criticisms about the content and effectiveness of the programs continued to mount. Representative Henry Waxman asked for a study to be done on the merits of these curricula. The resulting analysis, appearing in 2004, demonstrated that many of the programs contained medical inaccuracies, blurred lines between religion and science, and stereotypes about gender differences being presented as fact.[10] To investigate whether the abstinence-only programs were indeed preventing teenagers from engaging in sexual intercourse (their stated goal after all), the Department of Health and Human Services funded a study through a respected independent public policy research agency in Princeton, New Jersey, Mathematica Policy Research Group. They studied the actual programs that had been generated with the federal funding. Their findings were startling. Not only were the abstinence-only-until-marriage programs *not* preventing teenagers from engaging in sexual intercourse, but the kids in the programs were just as likely to have sex as those who were not in the programs, and they started having sex at about the same age (on average, just under 15 years) and with the same numbers of sexual partners.[11] In other words, the programs weren't fulfilling the objectives for which they were being funded.

Two other major studies supported these conclusions. One analyzed data on 1,719 students aged 15 to 19 from the National Survey of Family Growth in order to compare those who had participated in abstinence-only, comprehensive, or no sexuality education at all. The other analyzed data on a number of abstinence-only-until-marriage programs that involved nearly 16,000 students.[12] The combined findings of these studies may be summarized as follows:

1. Abstinence-only programs were not significantly associated with a risk reduction for teen pregnancy when compared with no sex education.

2. In comparing abstinence-only programs with comprehensive sex education, comprehensive sex education was associated with a 50 percent lower risk of teen pregnancy.

3. After adjusting for demographics, abstinence-only programs were not significantly associated with a delay in the initiation of vaginal intercourse.

4. Abstinence-only programs were not significantly associated with reduced risk for an STD when compared to no sex education.

States had already begun to opt out of the abstinence-only approach, and by 2009 half of them had refused the federal funding, some indicating that they would gratefully accept funding for comprehensive programs instead but saw no point in proceeding with programs that weren't working. A common practice in some of the abstinence-only curricula was to ask kids to sign "virginity pledges," promising that they would not have sex until they were married. There has been plenty of research showing that teenagers are generally not faithful to these pledges and in fact tend to forget that they even signed them, but a couple of research studies found more troubling outcomes. One study discovered that while the virginity pledges might delay students from having vaginal intercourse for a brief time, the teenagers who had taken the pledges were one-third less likely to use condoms or other forms of birth control when they eventually did have sex. The other study found that those students who had taken virginity pledges had the same rate of STDs as those who had not and were in fact six times more likely to have engaged in oral or anal sex than their nonpledging peers, probably as ways to avoid vaginal intercourse.[13] These findings indicated that the sexuality education programs that were most intended to protect young people from the negative health effects of sex were actually setting them up for even more sexual health risks. These findings were consistent with earlier studies showing that young people who felt ambivalent or negatively about their choices to have sex were less likely to prepare themselves with condoms or other forms of birth control. Going into sexual activities with uncertainties about one's choice is not a good idea; this is why scare or guilt-producing educational approaches may do more harm than good in the long run.

So what about the effectiveness of comprehensive approaches to sexuality education? Douglas Kirby, who had long been an advocate of educational efforts to help young people postpone their sexual involvements and who believed that abstinence was a valid premise for any approach to sexuality education, set out to analyze the outcomes of effectiveness studies of eight abstinence-only programs and 48 comprehensive programs. He and his colleagues at ETR Associates, a private research firm, used robust meta-analytic statistical techniques in the research.[14] What Kirby found was that about half of the comprehensive programs actually did delay the initiation of sexual intercourse for a while, and none of them led to earlier initiation of intercourse. About half of the programs also led to increased condom use when students decided to have sex and increased use of other contraceptives. Some of the programs reduced the number of sexual partners that participants had. Kirby's analysis of abstinence-only programs confirmed what other research had found: they had little effect on reducing sexual behaviors of participants. Slightly more than half the participants in both types of sexuality education remained sexually abstinent while the programs were in progress, potentially reflecting normal developmental patterns that were not altered by educational efforts.

Kirby and his colleagues were able to identify 17 characteristics of sexuality education programs that actually did seem to affect kids' behavior in positive ways, defined as delaying the initiation of intercourse or increasing the use of condoms and other types of contraception once they did have intercourse. While it is beyond the scope of this chapter to list all these characteristics, they were related to how each curriculum was developed, what was included in its contents, and how it was implemented. The significant bottom line here was that the characteristics of effective programs revolved around using many people who had expertise in the field of sexuality to develop a program designed specifically for the young people it would serve, then presenting accurate information in a logical and honest manner. The effective programs made their health goals clear and focused multiple activities around the behaviors that could accomplish those goals (including abstinence and use of condoms) while creating a safe environment for the students. The educators who presented the programs were carefully selected for desirable characteristics and then trained, supported, and supervised during the teaching process. I have elucidated the qualities of good sexuality educators with some detail in another publication.[15] All these qualities are consistent with how comprehensive sexuality education is supposed to be developed and implemented.

In terms of trends at the national level in the United States, there is both good news and bad. The Centers for Disease Control conduct the National Youth Risk Behavior Survey every two years among 9th through 12th graders in public and private schools throughout the country, and the data have been encouraging. During the sexual revolution years, beginning in the 1970s, there was a steady increase in year-to-year rates of sexual intercourse among teenagers that continued through the 1980s. Since 1991, however, there has been a steady decline in the proportion of high school teens having intercourse, with 47.8 percent indicating in 2007 that they had had intercourse compared to 54.1 percent in 1991. The proportions of teens indicating that they had been sexually active in the past three months has also fallen each year, as has the proportion who have had intercourse with four or more partners. Condom use at last intercourse has risen more than 15 percent (to 61.5%) since 1991. Teen birthrates have also been on the decline during most of the same period, falling 6 percent just between 2008 and 2009, the year in which that rate (39.1 births per 1,000 teens) reached an all-time low since the government began tracking the data in 1940.[16] I call this the good news because most experts do consider sexual activity among teens to be risky and to have negative effects, even though not all research data support these assumptions. We'll come back to that issue in the next chapter.

The bad news, perhaps again depending on one's perspective, is that the United States still has one of the highest rates of teen births among industrialized nations of the world. Germany, Canada, and Israel also have double-digit rates ranging from 13 to 32 per 1,000, but we're clearly at the head of this dubious pack. The other potentially disappointing fact is that there is little evidence that the decreasing rates of sexual intercourse among teens, which in fact we must also admit have been rather modest, are attributable to sexuality education efforts, except potentially for the effects of some comprehensive education programs mentioned above. Neither are the decreasing rates of teen births, which, as I mentioned in the preceding chapter, are believed to be mostly the result of the increased accessibility to birth control methods. Again, we could consider this development within a positive framework if we were to so choose.

For me, the most reasonable conclusion to draw from all this is that substantial numbers of adolescents, numbers that increase with every year of age, are engaging in a variety of sexual activities. I believe that this underscores even more vividly the responsibility that we who are adults in this society have to offer the young people of America the best possible information and preparation we can so that they may think through more carefully their personal readiness for sex and make informed choices about how best to protect themselves from any risks if they do decide to share sexual activity. In fact, in terms of sheer numbers, it isn't so much a matter of *if* they make the decision to have partnered sex as it is a matter of *when*.

"AT RISK" YOUNG PEOPLE IN THE SEXUAL TRANSFORMATION

When it comes to sexual behaviors of young people, much of the research in the past half century has framed those behaviors in term of "risks"—risks to physical, psychological, or spiritual well-being. No one would deny that there are risks associated with sex, including pregnancy (intended or unintended), and STDs. These risks exist for all age-groups, even though we tend to place less emphasis on riskiness when addressing the sexual behaviors of adults. This is partly due to our fear that young people are less prepared to anticipate and make plans to avoid the risky parts of sex, although I'm not aware of any studies that show youth to be any less prepared than many adults seem to be. Nonetheless, I agree that teenagers are sometimes at greater risk than anyone else, even though my reasons for believing this may differ from the typical public health assumptions. In fact, I believe that at-risk young people are young people who can be characterized as follows:

- Their parents or other caretakers don't take the time to listen to them and to build relationships of mutual trust and respect with them.

- They are experiencing their own sexual interests and desires, surrounded by the teasing of sex-laden popular media, but have no guidance or direction for channeling their sexual needs in healthful ways.

- They decide to share sex but lack access to condoms or birth control methods or to the information about how to use them properly.

- They are gay or transgendered or ambivalent but receive little affirmation or positive role models for their sexual identities.

- They feel constantly guilty or ashamed because of sexual interests or behaviors that are normal and predictable for their age and developmental stage.

- They have not been helped to develop the sense of autonomy and self-efficacy they will need to make reasonable and responsible sexual choices.

- They are being sexually abused or exploited but do not know how to escape and become empowered.

- Their education about human sexuality has been left, by default, to chance, peer input, personal trial and error, and the Internet (where, in order to find much solid sex information, one must wade through lots of highly explicit pornography).

This final bullet is a reminder of the unavoidable fact that to the degree we neglect to offer the youth of America accurate and useful information about human sexuality in an intentional and well-planned manner, they will fill the gap with online sources of information now available to them. This is a relatively new development in sexuality education and one that must not be ignored. Our kids can now find out just about anything they want about sex with a couple of mouse clicks, and they can see pictures of it all too. If we're not accompanying that with ways of helping them to keep perspective on this deluge of sexual information and images, we have abdicated an important duty, and society will end up paying the price.

COMPREHENSIVE SEXUALITY EDUCATION AND AMERICA'S SEXUAL TRANSFORMATION

With the research evidence showing quite clearly that the abstinence-only-until-marriage approach to sexuality education doesn't work, the Obama administration had sound backing for shifting federal funding in the direction of comprehensive sexuality education. It was, in a sense, a second chance to move in the direction to which the empirical signs had been pointing. Nonetheless, political positions and mythologies can be complicated to change. The public political struggle began when the House of Representatives passed an appropriations bill in July 2009 that eliminated funding for all three of the federal abstinence-only initiatives, diverting more than $114 million instead to programs that "provide medically accurate, age-appropriate, and complete information to youths." Just a month before, the American Medical Association had passed a resolution at its annual meeting promoting comprehensive sex education as the most effective strategy to prevent HIV, STDs, and teen pregnancies and recommending that federal funds be redirected toward this end. The American Medical Association has always been supportive of the comprehensive approach, as has the majority of parents, even those who are Catholics or evangelicals. Surveys have continued to demonstrate that 80 to 90 percent of American parents support comprehensive sexuality programs over abstinence-only-until-marriage programs.[17]

After July 2009, there was considerable political maneuvering in Congress. In late September, the Senate Finance Committee approved two amendments to the health care reform bill that accomplished two interesting things and represented a political compromise: one of these amendments created a funding stream of $75 million for comprehensive sexuality education by states; the other reinstated the Title V annual funding of $50 million for abstinence-only-until-marriage programs for an additional five years, even in the face of evidence that the programs had failed to fulfill their purposes. In 2010, two new programs were established that would promulgate more comprehensive strategies for sexuality education: the Teen Pregnancy Prevention Initiative and the Personal Responsibility Education Program, although by the time that 2011 budget allocations were being made, their funding was in jeopardy. While about 20 states have passed legislation calling for comprehensive sexuality education, the struggle over how funding should be directed continues at the federal level, and sexuality education continues to be muddled in politico-religious ideological wrangling.[18]

We should keep in mind that the most encouraging part of the picture is that excellent comprehensive sexuality programs can be developed and implemented without federal funding! They only require the dedication and energy of sincere people who want to do what seems to be best for the youth of our country. We manage to accomplish such things in many other arenas. Why not this one?

There are two major problems that have represented obstacles for sexuality education, and ultimately these must be addressed or, better yet, overcome. One is that in our present highly polarized political climate, sexuality education has too often been co-opted as a venue for proselytizing various moral and political beliefs and might I even suggest for garnering votes from constituents. This means that, unlike most other school "subjects," sexuality education has lost its focus as an academic enterprise. While I have stated previously that any educator has some responsibility to help young people construct a mature set of moral principles and decision-making skills, *based on widely accepted and*

agreed-on codes of conduct and social interaction, this is not a license to pros-
elytize one's own particular values on the political controversies of the day.[19]
Where else in education would we allow this to happen and not raise strong
concerns and objections?

The other problem rests with educators or educational systems that operate
with a "power-over" mentality, assuming that it is an educator's job to whip
students into line, to convince them of the rightness of particular moral values,
or to impose beliefs on them that are inconsistent with their personal belief
systems or cultural heritages. Since my earliest days as an educator—and not
simply as a sexuality educator—one thing has been clear to me about the quality of the atmosphere in the educational environment. I do not believe that
an authoritarian tenor or a sense of "power over" on the part of the teacher
can ever be consistent with effective education, perhaps especially with sexuality education of the sort I advocate. This, I think, can still be a stumbling
block in education even today, although it may be more subtle than it once
was. Children and adolescents—perhaps all of us—do not learn as well when
being told what to believe or what to do rather than encouraged to figure out
our own beliefs and choices. Neither do any of us respond particularly well to
being coerced into points of view that run counter to our instincts or smack
of propaganda for something we oppose in our hearts. Unfortunately, for an
inexperienced or uneasy educator, it may seem a lot easier to nurture an illu-
sion of control over students than to provide a truly nurturing environment
in which they can grow, be honest, and clarify how they will make their own
decisions in life. Although kids don't generally very much like an authoritarian environment, and it surely doesn't do much for their self-esteem or sense
of self-efficacy, they can become quite adept at learning the games of deception, omission of significant details, and hiding of feelings and behaviors when
these things constitute the best way to get by in a classroom. How much more
difficult it can be—and yet how very satisfying at the same time—to work
with kids in ways that build trust in open communication, openness for the
debate of ethical perspectives, and a willingness to discuss and strategize the
big sexual steps they will take in their lives. This is the best foundation I know
for comprehensive sexuality education.

LOOKING TO EUROPE FOR GUIDANCE

As the government-funded abstinence-only-until-marriage fiasco began to
dominate the sexuality education scene in America, the voices calling for a
more realistic and sensible approach seemed to fade somewhat in the dust
generated by the scramble for money. The work continued, nonetheless, and
yielded some truly wonderful results. By the mid-1990s, a coalition of organizations representing the country's leading experts on adolescent sexuality,

called the National Commission on Adolescent Sexual Health, had formulated a thorough and well-founded matrix of milestones and skills describing what we might hope for in sexually healthy youth.[20] The Sexuality Information and Education Council of the United States made use of the panel of experts to develop well-supported and researched guidelines for the development of comprehensive sexuality education programs.[21] But nobody seemed to be paying much attention.

While the United States was mired in controversy over a fundamental philosophy for sexuality education, Europe forged ahead with a far more holistic approach that could easily serve as a model for us. In 2008, the World Health Organization Regional Office for Europe and the Federal Centre for Health Education called together 19 experts to develop guidelines for sexuality education to be promulgated through the 53 countries in that part of the world. In 2010, their report was published as *Standards for Sexuality Education in Europe: A Framework for Policy Makers, Educational and Health Authorities and Specialists.*[22] It is a remarkably intelligent and thoughtful document that advocates sexuality education for children to begin soon after they are born. It clearly articulates standards for placing sexuality within the broader framework of personal growth and development instead of aiming at prevention and problem solving. It recognizes sexuality as a normal dimension of being human and states openly that "in Western Europe, sexuality is not primarily perceived as a problem and a threat, but as a valuable source of personal enrichment." It offers sensible guidelines for the kinds of information and skills that are needed from infancy to early adulthood.

One of the interesting things about the WHO report is that it bemoans the fact that most of the sexuality education research literature that is available in English comes from the United States and therefore focuses largely on whether programs have been effective in delaying intercourse or reducing the number of sexual partners in young people. They're used to looking to us for educational innovation and in this area find us sorely lacking. In Europe, the focus is on how effectively and responsibly young people have integrated their sexuality into their lives, so our research objectives that grow out of questionable fears and unrealistic hopes of preventing youthful sexual expression are of less value to their efforts. Perhaps it's time we admitted loudly and clearly that our own national efforts to educate American youth about sexuality have been mostly unrealistic, ineffective, and wasteful of time and money. Perhaps it's time we look across the pond to gain fresh perspectives.

Chapter 6

SAVED, SHAVED, AND PRETTY WELL BEHAVED: WHITHER THE MILLENNIAL GENERATION?

In my formative years as a teacher, headmaster of a school-within-a-university for talented and accelerated high school students, and a university student affairs administrator, my mettle was tested in the unforgiving crucible of Gen-Xers. Born and raised in the midst of the antiestablishment days that encompassed much of the sexual revolution, these kids were feisty, free-spirited, savvy, and often fiercely independent. When there was a controversy in the wind, their initial reaction was to blame anybody in charge and become confrontational. In the Clarkson School, we had weekly gatherings of the community, during which the group could raise concerns about the rules or recent problems. There were many evenings when I dragged myself home from those meetings, figuratively still stinging from the barbs and arrows that had been slung my way. But I loved the energy of these kids, their willingness to question the status quo, their openness to new ways of thinking, and, yes, even their gutsiness in challenging me. They were an energizing and inspiring bunch, many loner types who still found courage and comfort in their shared academic community.

THE MILLENNIALS COME OF AGE

Around the turn of the millennium, I became aware of some changes appearing in the young people I was working with. They were very respectful and even deferential. They seemed far more trusting of the judgments of their elders.

As I talked with them about their families and occasionally watched their interactions with those families, it became obvious that they were close to their parents and respected their parents' values. These kids were easy to work with, and they listened to reason. I was concerned about—and sometimes more than a little annoyed by—the fact that when these kids faced problems, they tended to call on their parents to fight their battles. It wasn't long before I became aware that this generation of youth, born since 1982 and coming of age in the new millennium, had been dubbed the "Millennials" by two researchers, Neil Howe and William Strauss, who had studied generational characteristics in detail.[1] Their work confirmed that there had indeed been a marked shift in the fundamental nature of youth and that it was time for educators to recognize and adapt to that shift.

As children, the Millennials had spent more time in daycare than any previous generation. Their daily lives were shaped by the schedules and judgments of adults, and they were encouraged to participate in a variety of sports and other extracurricular activities. In fact, their lives were a whir of activities. They learned to trust that parents and other adults would take care of their needs, they learned to think of themselves as special and eager to change the world for the better, they learned to work in teams and to expect secure and regulated environments, and they became respectful of social norms, conventional thinking, and institutionalized regulations. Howe and Strauss also coined the term "helicopter parents" to characterize the constant hovering that so many of this generation's parents tended to do right through high school, college, and beyond. So these kids have indeed been nice to work with, even though they lack some of the feistiness of the generation before them. That has been supplanted by self-confidence, engagement in the community, dreams of a better future, and their strong sense of self-efficacy.

The Pew Center for Research released an extensive study on the coming of age of Millennials that provides great insights into the things that are important to them.[2] The study found that today's American teens and 20-somethings are forging their futures with confidence and optimism, more educated and less religious than former generations. When asked about the most important things for their lives, the top answer, cited by just over half these young people, was "being a good parent." Some 30 percent said "having a good marriage." Fame, fortune, and McMansions are even less important to this generation, with only 20 percent indicating that owning a home was important to them and only 15 percent saying that having a high-paying career was a high priority. Even though they do indeed respect and get along well with their parents, they also concede that their own work ethic and standards of morality are not as firmly held as those of their elders. They are more supportive of progressive social agendas than any other generation but also disappointed that governments have not made more rapid progress in improving the lot of American citizens. This may reflect a tendency toward impatience and lack of realism on their part that sometimes annoys their employers.

This study, along with another study by the Pew Research Center and *Time* magazine that examined current attitudes toward marriage and family arrangements,[3] remind us that the importance of marriage seems to be waning in American culture. Just over 20 percent of youth in their 20s are married today, compared to over two-thirds in 1960, and nearly 40 percent of all Americans now consider marriage to be an obsolete institution. Younger people in particular are generally very accepting of sex without marriage, having children without marriage, and cohabitation.

TRAPPED IN THE FOUNTAIN OF YOUTH AND MISCONCEPTIONS

All this said, I want to make the point that another quantifiable shift in American youth may be developing. It's too early to tell if this simply represents an evolutionary branch growing on the Millennial generation tree or if we'll eventually be able to discern an entirely new generational cohort, but some things are changing. The Millennials who have been coming of age since the turn of the millennium ranged in age from about 8 to 20 when terrorists brought us temporarily to our knees on September 11, 2001. They watched the twin towers fall on television and sensed the threat as the disaster unfolded. This may help explain why the Pew study on Millennials showed this generation casting a wary eye on human nature and believing that "you can't be too careful" in your interactions with other people. I've certainly seen that wariness reflected in my students' approaches to life, even with their generally optimistic view. But I'm beginning to wonder if their trust in their elders may be beginning to waver as well. After all, it was clearly the greed, ignorance, and lack of fiscal responsibility and attention on the part of the nation's adults that precipitated the economic collapse in 2008, causing family assets to shrink in value and our most trusted financial institutions to be unmasked as the reckless, risk-taking, self-interested organizations they are. The economic crisis has meant greater difficulty in finding jobs after college and a 37 percent unemployment rate among 18- to 29-year-olds. Millennials who graduate from college during this economically compromised time are likely to suffer lingering effects on their careers and earning levels for more than another decade. The timing of the beginning of the disastrous recession correlates with a 2008 shift among Millennials toward discouragement over lack of change in Washington politics and decreasing support for socially conscious causes. As I said, it remains to be seen whether this shift will ultimately represent the beginning of an entirely new bundle of generational traits.

The economic pinch that has resulted in many college graduates having to move back home with their parents is only one of the factors making it increasingly difficult for the youth of America to grow up. Used to overprotective parents who have played an integral role in structuring their lives, committing to extended years of undergraduate and graduate education, and facing a shaky economy, it's not so easy to establish one's autonomy. The trappings of adulthood and the passages to reach them have become increasingly blurred and difficult to achieve. A few decades ago, the milestones that earned adult status were quite clear: a college degree, a place of one's own, marriage, children, and financial independence. When you had reached those goals, you knew you were an adult, and most had earned that status by the time they were 30. Not so any longer. Today only about a third of people have reached these milestones or their equivalent by the time they are 30 or have been able to replace them with other goals that might help them feel mature and autonomous. In fact, a third of young men and women between the ages of 26 and 30 feel ambiguous about defining themselves as *adults*.[4] They're trapped in a kind of limbo that simply makes it difficult for them to grow up.

Even as they face obstacles in establishing themselves as adults, it would be a mistake to revert to a perception of today's youth as the troubled, misguided rebels without a cause that the media invented in the 1950s and 1960s. It was not all that well founded then, and it surely is way off the mark today. Millennials hold on to their respectfulness, conscientiousness, and levelheadedness as they struggle toward seeing themselves as mature and ready for adult status. They roll with the punches and bounce back on their feet. Let's look at two assumptions we tend to make about college students: that once they escape parental supervision at home, they are prone to more risky sexual behavior and that their out-of-control drinking leads to irresponsible sexual decisions. Neither of these perceptions holds up all that well under scrutiny.

This is not to suggest that sexual behaviors do not increase during the college years, because they do. But this is true of all youth whether or not they go to college. It is developmentally normal and expectable for frequencies of shared sexual behaviors to increase with each year of age through the early 20s; this is simply the normal evolution of a mature sexual nature in youthful human beings that has been documented in every longitudinal survey of sexual behaviors. It is also true that alcohol consumption increases in college, partly because young people typically reach the legal drinking age during college but also because underage drinking is very much embedded in the culture of higher education. Yet we cannot ignore the fact that drinking is very much a part of adult culture as well, and so to expect maturing youth to wait until they're 21 to imbibe alcohol may simply be unrealistic. Forcing the states to raise the national drinking age to 21 through threats of losing federal funds was as much a counterrevolutionary political response to the perception of unruly, out-of-control youth as it was a move to make the country safer. It remains a topic of controversy and debate.

What is especially interesting is that recent research simply does not support some of these long-held perceptions about college students. Research has shown that students' previous patterns of sexual behavior and their personal levels of impulsivity seem to play a far more significant role in leading them toward casual sexual encounters or lower condom use than does their alcohol use.[5] Similar results were found in another study that followed the sexual behaviors of more than 800 young adults for six months after they left high school.[6] This study found that the young people who went to college were actually less likely than their noncollege peers to participate in any sex or in risky sexual behaviors. College students were also more likely to use condoms consistently during their sexual activities. Living at home instead of living in college residences didn't provide these young people any special protections against sexual risks either. In general, college youth do not seem to be the hard-drinking, sexually uncontrolled people we have sometimes imagined them to be.

GROWING UP SEXUALLY

Mostly unmarried and quite likely to cohabit during their 20s, the majority of young adults in America seem to have active sex lives. The findings of the National Survey of Sexual Health and Behavior (NSSHB) tell us that women and men ages 18 to 24 and 25 to 29 are among the most sexually active of the age-groups, with those 25 to 29 years old being the most sexually active of all. Up to 60 percent of all the women studied in these age-groups and 77 percent of the men reported that they had masturbated in the previous 90 days (depending on relationship status), with those who were single and dating masturbating the most (94% of women and 97% of men). The NSSHB is the first major study to inquire about masturbation with a partner, finding this to be more common in women in these younger age-groups than in younger men or in the older age cohorts. About a third of all women and men in the 25–29 age-group had done this in the previous 90 days, but up to 65 percent of the women who were single and dating had done so, while 28 percent of the men who were single and dating had.[7]

The majority of women and men with sexual partners said they had participated in oral sex during the previous 90 days, either having given or received fellatio or cunnilingus or both. For partnered people, the figures ranged from about two-thirds to over 70 percent involved in oral–genital sexual activities. Of the women and men in relationships, between 70 and 92 percent had experienced penile–vaginal intercourse in the previous 90 days, with the majority of all young adults in these age cohorts indicating that they had had intercourse as well. Anal intercourse never emerges as one of the most frequent sexual behaviors but instead as a behavior that some couples try experimentally and that a few practice as a regular part of their sex lives. The NSSHB found a gender difference between the 18- to 24-year-old and the 25- to 29-year-old cohorts.

More women (15%) than men (6%) had experienced anal intercourse in the previous 90 days among the 18- to 24-year-olds, while more men (16%) than women (10%) had had anal intercourse in the previous 90 days among the 25- to 29-year-olds.

Analyses of data from the National Longitudinal Study of Adolescent Health and the National Survey of Adolescent Males have given us more reliable information on typical sexual behaviors among 6,421 18- to 26-year-olds who had been involved in a sexual relationship for at least three months.[8] Fifty-eight percent of them had engaged in vaginal intercourse, cunnilingus, and fellatio, with an additional 22 percent adding anal intercourse to that combination, accounting for 80 percent of the youth studied. Close to another 19 percent had shared only vaginal intercourse in combination with either fellatio or cunnilingus but not both. The remaining few couples had other combinations of sexual activities. This squares with the information I obtain each year in the survey that I conduct with my students in a human sexuality course. They are mostly upper-division students and so usually in their early 20s. Most of them have very active sexual lives that they seem to perceive as a matter of course for youth of their age. They seem to find their sex lives satisfying for the most part, although they do encounter some of the same problems with differences in levels of sexual interest, keeping erections, and reaching orgasm that are found in couples of all ages.

FINDING MATURITY IN SEX

When I was between the ages of 18 and 24, what little sex life I had was surrounded in shame and secrecy. It was not something I was about to share very openly with many others. Today's youth seem far more willing to admit to, even discuss, their sexual interactions, again tending to perceive their sexuality to be an expected and normal part of their lives. Many can even be quite open about these things with their parents, although there is still a cadre of parents out there who kind of know what's going on with their kids' sex lives but prefer not to talk about it openly. That seems to make it too real for them.

When we look at the vague signposts we now seem to have for reaching adulthood and the many practical obstacles that stand in the way of youth achieving many of the milestones before they are 30, it seems obvious to me that an active and satisfying sexual life is one of the few adult domains that is easily accessible. It is in their sex lives that the youth of America can find success, autonomy, and satisfaction. They can take pride in their sexual

An active and satisfying sexual life is one of the few adult domains that is easily accessible. It is in their sex lives that the youth of America can find success, autonomy, and satisfaction.

prowess and expertise. They can enter this one corner of the adult world in which they can excel and feel good about it.

This isn't to say that every young adult is having sex or that everything is rosy in the sexual lives of American young adults. Some young men and women choose not to engage in shared sexual activity because they consider themselves too young or simply not ready, believing it to be immoral or believing that their parents would disapprove.[9] Some college students end up having some regrets about their sexual experiences because they felt they were inconsistent with their values, felt pressured, realized that they wanted something different from their partner, or neglected to use condoms.[10] In one study of more than 1,000 college students, about 12 percent had decided to revert to "secondary abstinence," or not having intercourse again until they felt more ready. Interestingly, the choice of secondary abstinence was significantly less likely among those who had participated in abstinence-only sexuality education when they were younger.[11] So some of the youth of America also struggle with sexual issues that have been around since before the sexual revolution and probably always will do so. Nevertheless, as I've noted in earlier chapters, the rates of sexual intercourse, unintended pregnancy, births, and abortions among adolescents have all decreased during the past two decades, so even the younger members of our youthful population seem to be making sexual decisions more carefully and with a more sophisticated awareness of how to protect themselves from unwanted consequences. This too demonstrates an increased level of maturity.

YOUTH, RELIGION, AND SEX

The Pew Research Center study of Millennials found that a quarter of young people under age 30 report not being affiliated with any religious tradition or denomination. Two-thirds of young people indicate they are members of a Christian denomination, with 43 percent saying they are Protestants, considerably lower numbers than are found among those over the age of 30.

Among young adults who report a religious affiliation, over a third indicate a strong loyalty to their faiths. This division between the religiously faithful and unfaithful is nothing new, although the Millennials are clearly more skeptical about religion than previous generations. They are also more likely to believe that society should be accepting of homosexuality (63%) than their elders. More than half (52%) say that abortion should be legal and available in all or most cases, a slightly more permissive view than those who are somewhat older. They are also more tolerant of pornography, with only about one in five (21%) saying it should be illegal for everyone. However, there is evidence that people become increasingly opposed to pornography as they age. It will be interesting to see if this happens with the Internet-savvy Millennials.

The most startling chasm in belief systems among America's youth is evident in the differences that exist between religious conservatives (Evangelicals, Pentecostals, Mormons, some Roman Catholics, and Jehovah's Witnesses) and the more mainstream denominations. While we must always be careful not to overgeneralize about religious groups, there is good reason to group together those that tend toward more conservative religious and usually political values as compared to those that have less dogmatic religious views and more liberal political leanings. In recent times, the links between religious views and political persuasions have become even more pronounced. Before pursuing this topic further, I want to share a couple of anecdotes with you that capture some of what I'm talking about here.

A few months ago, I received an email from a mother who said her daughter was a psychology major at another (unnamed) college and was using the ninth edition of my textbook, *Sexuality Today*. The woman said that she had looked up "spirituality" in the index, and when she went to the page listed, she said there was "no mention of the Christian (specifically, Catholic) view of sexuality." She went on to offer a couple of websites about Catholic teachings from which I might learn more about those views, specifically about natural family planning and abortion. I politely responded to her with an explanation of why I found it inappropriate in a general text to refer to the teachings of specific religious groups. Although this mom was probably a perfect example of a helicopter parent, I found no fault with the interest she was taking in her daughter's education, especially as it related to the family's religious beliefs. She in turn sent a polite response to me, discussing the Catholic Church's view of the many dimensions of a sexual relationship, including the spiritual. She went on to offer the view that being a Christian today is particularly counter-cultural and that "many people do not find the strength to suffer the loss and persecution that goes along with practicing their faith." She regretted their forfeiting of long-term gain for short-term pleasure. She also argued against the idea of relative truth and morality being popularized over concepts of objective (absolute) good and evil. She extolled the virtue of suffering in order to be true to one's religious beliefs.

I think this communication really captures the essence of one of the core differences between those faithful to what I've been calling conservative religious values and those who take a more relativist position. I'm not so sure I buy that a great many young people who are striving to be chaste because of their religions are necessarily suffering many slings and arrows from their peers because of their beliefs, but I know from talking to them that our sex-saturated society makes sex difficult to ignore or turn away from. They may indeed have to wrestle with their sexual urges. Or do they? This is where my next story comes in.

Jeff was a junior when he enrolled in my human sexuality course. He was a good student and was always very attentive in class. Eventually, he asked to consult with me privately, saying that he thought his own story would be interesting to me. It soon became clear in our talks together that he was struggling to clarify an ever-widening gap between his beliefs and his actions. Growing up in an evangelical family that was extremely devout and that expected appropriate behavior on the part of the children, Jeff's faith was central to his life. Yet his sexuality had become central in his life as well. Forced to have anal intercourse by an older brother when he was about 12 and then subsequently abusing a younger brother himself in the same manner, Jeff lived with some sexual guilt. He masturbated regularly and when he was 17 began having a sexual relationship with a woman several years his senior. After coming to college, he had continued to have a very active heterosexual life, consisting mostly of one-night stands. During the period he was talking with me, he was invited by two women to have sex with them at the same time, and he obliged. Yet Jeff continued to maintain that his intention for the future was to settle down in marriage and return fully to the fundamentals of his evangelical faith. The only problem was that he didn't really know how he was going to be able to carry this off. He felt torn between religious teachings that he considered important to him and the pleasures of his extremely active sexual life, all of which were considered immoral within his faith. He had no idea how to bridge that gap.

I don't think Jeff is alone with that conflict, although the gap between what he wanted and what he was doing was greater than that faced by many youth of his generation. At the beginning of my sexuality course, I ask my students to write about who they are as a sexual person at this point in their lives, sharing as little or as much as they feel comfortable. I am always startled by how much they are willing to share. It is not at all unusual for them to write something like this: "Even though I am a Christian (or Catholic) and originally thought I would not have sex until I was married, that changed during (high school/ first year in college/ etc.)." Unlike Jeff, they've usually managed to find ways to square their religious beliefs with their sexual behaviors. Sometimes they've decided that the teachings of their religion were misguided, and sometimes they just decided to violate those teachings in the interest of some positive outcomes. In a sense, they've done what I essentially told Jeff he was going to have to do: either cease his sexual practices, find a way to justify them within the framework of his religious roots, or find another religion with which he could continue his sexual activities and feel okay about them. So far, he has not managed to do any of those things, and he clearly is not alone with this conundrum.

SAVED: SEX AND THE CONSERVATIVE RELIGIOUS YOUTH OF AMERICA

It seems evident to me that many young adults find themselves with some degree of cognitive dissonance between what they have been taught by their religions and parents and the sexual desires and/or behaviors they experience. In some ways, that conflict has probably existed since religions came into existence in human culture. Perhaps it represents one of the archetypal confrontations between spirit and flesh, good and evil. Even in the most ancient Eastern religious traditions where sexual energies are considered to be intertwined with spiritual energies, cautions and proscriptions about sexual activity persist. And today, as always, prevailing belief systems become entangled with politics and social policy.

Sex researchers and legal scholars are beginning to clarify how these seemingly intractable religious obstacles are being navigated by American youth, and they are revealing an intriguing story of religion, socioeconomic class, and political persuasion. Mark Regnerus is a sociologist at the University of Texas at Austin and a research associate at the university's Population Research Center. In his book *Forbidden Fruit: Sex and Religion in the Lives of American Teenagers,*[12] Regnerus points out that although religious affiliation among young people can be a good predictor of their attitudes toward sex, it is not a very reliable indicator of their sexual behaviors. Drawing on results of a national survey he conducted with his colleagues of about 3,400 13- to 17-year-olds, Regnerus found that three-quarters of white evangelical teens believe in sexual abstinence until marriage, as compared to half of mainline Protestants and a quarter of Jewish kids. In contrast to their stated attitude, however, other data showed that evangelical Christian youth are actually more sexually active than Mormons, mainline Protestants, and Jews and that they tend on average to have their first sexual intercourse earlier than any other youthful religious group except for black Protestants. Confirming the findings of previous studies, Regnerus found that when evangelical young people start having sex, they are less likely to use condoms, rendering them more vulnerable to pregnancy and sexually transmitted diseases (STDs). It has been speculated that this could result from their exposure to the abstinence-only movement's mistaken claim that condoms aren't reliable for protection, but it probably also reflects an ambivalence about intentionally preparing to have sexual behavior that they already perceive to be wrong.

It is critical to clarify a point here. There are numerous studies that have shown that high levels of religiosity—quantified by rating how often young people attend religious services, how often they pray, and how involved they are with their religious institutions along with being involved with a close-knit and understanding family—are indeed associated with a somewhat later start for sexual intercourse, although usually not with abstinence until marriage. However, as with all religious groups, there are many Americans who identify themselves as evangelicals but are not necessarily deeply observant of their faiths. In other words, even though they hold conservative religious beliefs, their levels of religiosity are not all that high. Mark Regnerus comments on how difficult it is for youthful evangelicals to resist the constant bombardment of sexual messages from the media: "In such an atmosphere, attitudes about sex may *formally* remain unchanged (and restrictive) while sexual activity becomes increasingly common. This clash of cultures and norms is felt most poignantly in the so-called Bible Belt." These factors may explain some of the seeming contradiction here. But it's deeper than that.

This is where politics comes into the picture. It should be no surprise to anyone that religion and politics are often bedfellows. Every national election brings that reality into clearer focus. Two distinguished family law scholars, Naomi Cahn of George Washington University Law School and June Carbone of the University of Missouri at Kansas City, have identified what they call "red families" and "blue families" who seem to live very different lives in terms of their "moral imperatives."[13] While a predominance of red or blue families may be found respectively in the red states (more politically conservative) and blue states (more politically liberal), Cahn and Carbone don't believe that the divide between Republican and Democrat is as significant as the high proportion of "moral values voters" in the red states.

This is where their findings get really interesting. We might intuitively assume that liberal blue states (i.e., sexually permissive), such as California and Massachusetts, would be rife with divorce and teen pregnancy, while conservative red states (i.e., sexually restrictive), such as Texas and Nebraska, would be havens of sexually abstinent teens and stable marriages. The reality is exactly the opposite. The majority of blue states have lower rates of divorce and teenage pregnancy than the red states have. Married people tend to have babies earlier in the red states as well, probably reflecting the inclination to marry when there is an unintended pregnancy rather than seek an abortion. In two books, Cahn and Carbone's *Red Families v. Blue Families: Legal Polarization and the Creation of Culture* and Mark Regnerus's more recent *Premarital Sex in America: How Young Americans Meet, Mate, and Think about Marrying,*[14] the authors see a new "middle-class morality" taking shape among economically and socially advantaged families who are not social conservatives. In these families, the advantages of higher education for women have been realized and are emphasized. The youth in these families are more inclined to be accepting of sexual involvement without marriage, but the possibilities of pregnancy or STDs simply render sexual intercourse, at least without appropriate protection, too risky for many of them. They don't want to interfere with their goals of college, graduate degrees, career, and an eventual family. So they are more likely to start their shared sexual lives by substituting oral sex and other forms of fooling around for sexual intercourse. Consequently, the rates of teen births are low, rates of abortion are higher, and their rates of divorce are setting record lows. Kids in these families have no intentions of serious relationships or marriage until much later in their lives and are far more likely to wait until their late 20s or early 30s to take that step. In the interim, they are well equipped to use birth control—and are encouraged to do so by their parents—when they do start having sexual relationships. So this "blue" family paradigm constitutes the prevailing morality in urban areas and on the coasts, where many blue states are located.

In the red heartland, things are quite different. Families operating with the "red" family paradigm continue to advocate sexual abstinence until marriage, not allowing teenagers to have birth control, banning abortion, and acting "responsibly" in cases of unintended pregnancy by giving birth and perhaps getting married. As we've already seen, the attitudes about sexual abstinence more often than not do not translate into abstinent behaviors. And couples who marry young because of a pregnancy not only may compromise their hopes of an education and promising career but may have a higher rate of divorce as well. Husbands who are limited by lack of a college education in their capacities to provide well for their families, along with other economic hardships, often force these more conservative women, who may have hoped to remain housewives during their marriages, to take jobs outside the home, leading to dissatisfaction and increased chances of divorce. The economic recession is believed to have worsened this scenario. It is in these respects that the emphasis on the virtues of abstinence and of women staying home to care for their families has been at odds with the realities many ultimately face.

It has been suggested that as proponents of evangelical moral ideals try to explain their reasoning to youth, they sometimes create contradictions that some young people find hard to reconcile. They represent sexual intercourse (without marriage) on the one hand as a base, immoral act with little more than a flash of pleasure to offer anyone and on the other as an ethereal form of spiritual communion between souls (in marriage). They emphasize the virtues of virginity and may also discourage masturbation and use of pornography because they may only tempt further exercising of lust, surely a risky thing to play around with. Ultimately, young people are left with no legitimate form of sensual pleasure and the only approved option of combating the temptations of sexual pleasure that they constantly face. What kind of negativism does this mean they will take with them to their eventual sexual interactions? Mark Regnerus has said that waiting to have sex until the age of 25 or 30 is unreasonable, and he has encouraged evangelical religious groups to consider support for younger marriages and families.[15] That could clearly help reconcile the contradiction between the moral values and sexual behaviors of youthful evangelicals but, in my estimation, does little to improve their longer-term social situation or hopes for a better lifestyle.

What are we to conclude about the influences of religion—conservative or otherwise—on the sexual lives of American kids? It is neither a particularly clear picture nor a pretty one. But here goes. Young people who are really involved and engaged in their religious groups and who also have close families with parents who spend time with them, talk with them, and understand them are more likely to postpone having sex for the first time by maybe a year or so. Socially conservative evangelical Christians are actually more likely to start having sex earlier and more likely to have an unintended pregnancy than other Protestant groups. Sex-negative sexual values do not translate into avoidance of sexual behaviors but may increase the risks of not being prepared with birth control or protection from STDs when the decision to have sex is made. Regardless of religious persuasion, most young adults are having sex by their mid-20s, mostly without marriage. Kids from middle- to upper-class socially liberal families are more likely to start having sex a bit later and to use birth control when they do, and they also tend to delay marriage until they have completed educational and career plans. Kids from lower- to middle-class socially and religiously conservative families are more likely to have sex earlier, not use birth control, experience an unintended pregnancy, and get married earlier, and they have a higher likelihood of the marriage ending in divorce. Finally, it seems to me that religious institutions in American society have done a pretty poor job of helping to shape healthy and responsible sexual lives for our youth. That is a shame in every sense of that word.

RELIGIOUSLY CONSERVATIVE GAY YOUTH

Over my many years of talking with college youth, I have encountered lots of young men and women who were struggling to reconcile their religious beliefs with their gay sexual orientation. Whether or not same-gender sexual contact is considered in a negative light by the Bible has been a matter of debate among theologians for a long time, and many Christian denominations have adopted a very welcoming stance for gay men and lesbian women as well.

A few denominations perform holy union ceremonies to sanctify same-gender relationships in lieu of marriage. The same controversy exists within various Jewish and Islamic sects as well, with varying degrees of tolerance or acceptance being expressed. This is again a sticking point for the more conservative Christian groups. A common position among them is that while God's love extends to everyone, regardless of sexual *orientation*, involvement in a sexual act with someone of the same sex would not be considered permissible. To be fair, these denominations judge heterosexual acts outside marriage to be immoral as well, but for gay youth there is no point at which acting on their sexual proclivities will become acceptable within their faiths.

These are many young people who have grown up with strong religious convictions that they value but who also find themselves attracted to members of their own sex. Some have enrolled in religiously sponsored "reparative therapies" that claim to be able to reroute one's sexual desires in heterosexual directions. Their methods amount to using prayer and support in order to resist homosexual temptation, and some do succeed in making sexual choices considered more appropriate, at least for a time. There is no evidence that there is any actual change in sexual orientation,[16] and some recent research suggests that many of these "ex-gays" tend to resume their same-gender sexual contacts eventually.[17] An additional complication here is that at the same time these kids have been growing up grappling with such fundamental conflicts between their beliefs and identities, they have also been witnessing the dramatic changes in attitudes toward gays coming out and same-gender relationships in our society. This doesn't necessarily change their religious convictions, but it does make for an even more confusing jumble of feelings regarding where they stand in American life.

A recent article in the *New York Times* explores the complications that some gay students are facing at Bible colleges and Christian universities throughout the country when they want to be more open about their sexual orientations. A few of the more liberal institutions have allowed gay student groups to be formed on campus, but for the most part, these colleges and universities have resisted any requests for greater openness or discussion on campus regarding sexual orientation. Baylor University, the largest Baptist university in the country, has refused to allow a sexuality forum, affirming instead that it expects its students not to participate "in advocacy groups promoting an understanding of sexuality that is contrary to biblical teaching." It seems that at these colleges in general, including Abilene Christian University in Texas, most students are ready to open these discussions, but administrators and trustees from another generation are anything but interested in doing so. In fact, they are quick to punish students who disobey their prohibitions, even to the point of withdrawing scholarships or expelling the student. The stated prohibitions against "homosexual behavior" at these colleges can be rather vague so that students are not even certain if holding hands would constitute a violation.[18]

Again, it seems to me that these conservative Christian colleges and universities are at a crossroads, attempting to enforce standards that are not in keeping with the beliefs held by the generation they serve. I am not suggesting that they have any obligation to change their interpretation of scriptural teachings, although that seems to me a valid discussion at any institution of higher learning, but to disallow even the open discussion of the meaning of nonheterosexual orientations and lifestyles seems shortsighted and destructive. Surely, many students want the freedom to have such discussion and debate as part of their searches for personal understanding and sexual identity. It doesn't mean that sexual behavior outside marriage must be accepted, but it does suggest that college should indeed be a time for consolidating one's beliefs and bringing them into line with one's behaviors. Ignoring anyone's need to accomplish this or prohibiting the means for doing so will not make the issues go away. Instead, it may only mean that sincere and well-meaning young people who are trying hard to find bridges between their sexuality and their faith will be driven away from the very religious foundations on which they have built their lives.

SHAVED: THE DISAPPEARANCE OF PUBIC HAIR FROM AMERICAN YOUTH

I want to shift now to a lighter topic and surely one that has received little attention by sex researchers or the media, but it represents a pervasive and little-known trend among our youth. Again, let me begin with a story. A few years back, when I was showing pictures of female and male genitals on the big screen in the front of the lecture hall, there was a rustle of noise, especially when showing the female photos. The noise consisted of some laughter mixed with groans, an uncharacteristic response on the part of my typically sophisticated upper-division students. I interpreted it as a somewhat immature response on the part of a few students, made some dismissive comments, and then forgot about it. Later in the day, a young woman from the class visited my office to tell me that the reason some students had reacted as they did was the fact that the men and women portrayed in my photos had so much pubic hair. In fact, the photos were of people who had what I judged to be normal amounts of pubic hair and certainly weren't unusually hirsute. The young woman went on to say that since nearly everyone in her generation tends to shave or clip their pubic hair, the photographs were bound to seem especially hairy to my students. I wasn't entirely ready to buy this, but I did find the suggestion intriguing.

I posted a question about removal of genital hair on the course's online discussion site, where postings are anonymous, and received an unusually high number of responses. Those who identified themselves as women said things like this:

> I myself am fully shaved and my boyfriend trims up. If I miss a spot or have some stubble, I feel very self conscious when he is down there. I know that I wouldn't want a mouthful of hair when I'm down on my boyfriend.

> I keep it trimmed, but I don't really have a preference for guys. It doesn't really make a difference to me, but I think I'm in the minority in that way.

> I used to keep myself fully shaved, but my boyfriend's pubic area would get irritated as the hair started to grow back in. Now I shave most of it but leave a little landing strip. As for guys, I don't really care either way.

The men tended to be more decisive:

> I prefer girls who are fully shaved and I prefer myself to be fully shaved or trimmed close as well. Skin on skin just feels better and it seems to be the way personal hygiene is headed.

> I like a girl who is fully trimmed or well managed because I don't like the feeling of excess hair. I try to keep myself managed, but I think a fully shaved man looks a little awkward.

> I keep it trimmed and I prefer women who are shaved or trimmed. I had an unusual experience last week when I performed cunnilingus on a girl who was trimmed pretty short and I myself had a five o'clock shadow on my face. The interaction was uncomfortable as it was like rubbing two Brillo pads together.

I've tried to find any information about this youth phenomenon that I could but haven't come up with much that seems particularly reliable. On the website of the Palo Alto Medical Foundation, a nonprofit community health organization that has both educational and research arms, I did find some historical perspective. It indicated that in ancient Egypt and Greece, female prostitutes shaved for hygienic reasons and as a clear badge of their profession. Removal of female underarm and leg hair apparently became established as a norm in the United States between 1915 and 1945, but as bikini bathing suits became popular in the 1970s and 1980s, there was more pressure to remove potentially visible pubic hair. It is not uncommon to hear about bikini waxes or "Brazilians" today.

How pubic hair removal spread to males remains a mystery so far as I can tell. The Palo Alto Medical Foundation site mentions that as pornography became more mainstream, women may have mimicked the well-shorn female porn stars they saw. I wonder if their male partners may have been the primary movers here. Perhaps this is where males began to get the idea for themselves as well, combined with the "metrosexual" trend of paying attention to male grooming, fitness, and sexual attractiveness. When I searched these topics online, most of the sites offered how-to advice for either women or men or both.

Writing on a site called Express Milwaukee, Laura Anne Stuart, MPH, who says she is a sexuality educator and owner of an erotic boutique on the East Side of Milwaukee, reminds readers that having a partner do the pubic hair trimming can be a highly erotic experience. She cites an episode of "Sex and the City" in which Samantha used an electric shaver to trim her man's pubic hair. I'm sure that show got a lot of young women's attention as well. Ms. Stuart goes on to report that many salons now offer a "back, crack, and sack" waxing package for male customers (ouch).[19]

I noted that online sites designed for men talk about this issue in what they consider to be guy-appropriate ways. Here's a sample from AskMen, a website claiming to have 15 million readers: "The hair down there: How do you deal with it? . . . Regardless of the approach—and there should be an approach—trimming your pubes is a highly beneficial move. First of all, it reduces the cloudy bush than can minimize the appearance of your favorite appendage, and secondly it increases the sensuality and fluidity of make-out sessions with your lady." The site says that "the informed manscaper, who wants nothing more than an alluring pubic area, should be acquainted with all his options of pubic hair removal" and then goes on to describe the pros and cons of those methods. These sentiments are echoed in most of the other sites I examined, although I checked out only a tiny fraction of the more than 400,000 sites that came up with the search. Pubic hair trimming is now part of the body grooming routines of our young people.

However this trend evolved, it does seem that pubic hair is now generally seen as gross, unsightly, and a hindrance to many sexual activities by the youth of America. It seems obvious that the increasing popularity of oral–genital sex may have played a role in this. I haven't been able to find any data about its popularity. Three years ago, I did add a question to the survey that I conduct annually with my human sexuality students toward the end of the course, so I do have data on more than 300 students, most of whom are 19 or in their early 20s. I must admit, the figures surprised me. They had a choice of four responses to the question of whether they ever shaved or trimmed their genital and pubic hair. None of the women and less than 2 percent of the men said they would never do that. Fifty-eight percent of the men and about 90 percent of the women reported *regularly* grooming this hair, and another 41 percent of the men and 9 percent of the women indicated that they had done so *occasionally* but not on a regular basis. About 2 percent of both sexes said that they did not groom their pubic hair but would do so if they had a regular sexual partner. Now this is not at all a representative sample of the young adult population, but I was startled by the popularity of the practice in this group.

So for what it's worth, the youth of America seem to think that the escutcheon is a part of their bodies that deserves attention. That word—*escutcheon*—is a term I learned for the first time when investigating pubic hair trimming. The dictionary definition will tell you that it refers to a shield or shieldlike area on a coat of arms. It also is the name of the metal plate with a keyhole that helps to support a doorknob. If you search a little further, you'll find that the medical definition of the term refers to the arrangement of the pubic hair in females and males. Our young people have become escutcheon conscious, and it seems to be quite important and vital to them. In fact, the grooming and shaping of the escutcheon has become a shield of honor and sexual availability.

KEEPING IT CASUAL

In the 1970s and 1980s, I worked with a few couples who were trying to have sexually open relationships. Some of them were married and some were not, but the fundamental goal was the same: preserving the primary relationship while being open to the excitement of occasional fresh sexual experiences with other partners. It was given several names: mate swapping, swinging, open marriage, and consensual adultery. I was working only with couples who had sought therapy, so that may explain why the couples I saw were generally having difficulties making these open arrangements work. It did seem that the motivations behind these "experiments" came mostly from the men, but many of the women seemed anxious to make things work as well. There were two undergirding philosophies that served as beacons for these early rebels. One was the conviction that human beings are essentially nonmonogamous and that we should therefore try to be true to the beckoning of our wandering eyes and reject the strictures of the overly binding, unnatural and unrealistic social convention of monogamy. The other philosophical stance seemed to be an outgrowth of Erich Segal's popular 1970 novel *Love Story*, which perpetuated the nonsensical and entirely inaccurate aphorism "Love means never having to say you're sorry." This was closely aligned with a kind of pop psychology concept that true love would be characterized by a selfless desire to want to see your partner happy and pleased, even if it meant sharing her or him sexually with another. Yeah sure!

What began to evolve out of this bumpy side road of the sexual revolution was an increasing awareness that human beings are indeed pretty territorial when it comes to their loving and passionate relationships and that they don't do particularly well with the idea of a sexual partner sharing the goods with someone else. As the principles of evolutionary psychology have been clarified and researched, we have instead begun to realize that the emotional motivation systems of lust, attraction, and attachment are built-in mechanisms that draw us to a particular person and motivate us to stay with that person at least for a time.[20] In this sense, monogamy is, to an extent, programmed into our genes and neurophysiology. That doesn't mean, especially in societies where sex is a central theme, that our eyes or behaviors won't sometimes stray, but neither does it mean that we could ever be particularly tolerant of knowingly allowing our sexual partners to have sex with others.

So experimenting with no-strings sex is nothing new, especially among the young. In one study of more than 1,300 of today's young adults with a mean age of 20.5 years, one-fifth indicated that their most recent sexual partner had been a casual one. The study went on to explore the psychological well-being of the young women and men who had participated in casual sex, finding no differences between them and those who had not been so inclined.[21] On the survey I give to my students, about 30 percent indicate that they have cheated on a primary sexual partner. Some interesting casual sexual arrangements have been formalized by today's youth. When my own kids went off to college more than a decade ago, they began using the term *hooking up* to describe casual connections, although it was unclear to me how much sex was implied by the term. I began to ask my students and after getting input from hundreds of them, I can only conclude that hooking up means many different things to many people but that it usually means having some kind of sexual contact (most typically not intercourse) without much emotional commitment.

Friends with benefits (FWB) constitutes another arrangement that may have been tried by as many as half of young adults at some point. FWB seems attractive to many because it includes some of the same qualities of any good relationship: trust, mutual acceptance, shared activities, and enjoyment of one another's company. Because women often have more trouble feeling comfortable having sex with veritable strangers, whether because of innate biological imperatives or social inequities, they tend to find FWB to be the most pleasurable of the casual sexual options.[22] *Booty calls*, which are placed more often to women by men, imply less of a relationship than FWB but do reflect at least some previous social interaction and mutual attraction. They may represent a compromise between the really casual sexual hookup with someone just met, which seems more okay with men, and the longer-term commitment that seems to be preferred by women.[23]

The wrinkle with all of these casual sexual connections is the likelihood that one of the partners—and it really can be either one—will begin to develop some romantic feelings and a stronger sense of attachment than the other. Most often, couples in these casual arrangements don't talk much about their feelings for one another and in fact may avoid doing so. This means that things can get strained in a hurry, everyone begins to feel guilty, and somebody gets hurt.[24] From what my students write and tell me, I sense a real skepticism about these tenuous relationships. They seem to know, even when they give them a try, that the hopes of negotiating their emotional intricacies without some stress and collateral damage are slim. As part of a classroom assignment, several of my students recently reviewed the film *No Strings Attached*, which portrays a man and woman who were longtime friends attempting the "with benefits" dimension, and all my student reviewers said they knew that ultimately it couldn't be maintained as such. They were right, of course.

Many young people know from the start that casual sex could never be for them, and others give it a try because its lack of emotional entanglements seems ideal. "No drama," the guys say hopefully, reflecting their reluctance to venture into the emotional discussions that they generally prefer to avoid, only to find that emotions and the vulnerability they create are simply a part of life's drama that accompanies love and sex. No way around it. For the most part, though, the youth of America seem to believe that sex is better within the context of a relationship, and that is what most of them are striving for. They don't all have success in their early connections, but they usually know what they're looking for.

BEING SEXUALLY DIFFERENT ISN'T WHAT IT USED TO BE

I was talking with a first-year student recently who is quite representative of this younger generation's attitudes about sexual orientation and all that goes with it. He told me that about midway through high school, he decided that he was sick of pretending to be something that didn't really fit him. He decided that he was simply going to try to be true to himself. When I asked him what he meant by that—who he was, in a sense—he offered a reply that I would not have heard from a young adult 20 years ago. He said that he was very much in touch with feelings and sensitivities that are more typically feminine than masculine but that he liked being male and felt that he was for the most part "androphilic" (sexually attracted to males). He went on to say that heterosexual interaction didn't strike him as negative or even out of the question but that when he decided to have sex with someone—something he had not yet experienced—it most likely would be with another man. He made it clear that he didn't like to be classified as "gay" and in fact believed that the term was outdated and imprecise.

Ritch Savin-Williams, professor and chair of human development and director of the Sex and Gender Lab at Cornell, agrees with him. In his book *The New Gay Teenager*,[25] Savin-Williams counters the outmoded view of gay young people as necessarily troubled, depressed, isolated, and at heightened risk for suicide. He insists instead that teenagers today are moving beyond the either–or sexual orientation dichotomies that social science researchers seem to be struggling to hang onto. "Rather," he writes, "teenagers are increasingly redefining, reinterpreting, and renegotiating their sexuality such that possessing a gay, lesbian, or bisexual identity is practically meaningless." In research conducted with his graduate student Geoffrey Mean, now an assistant professor of social work at Adelphi University, Savin-Williams has shown that with some 8 percent of people who have had some sexual experience with someone of their own gender since puberty but who often don't consider themselves to be "gay," our standard categories and labels simply break down in terms of meaning and value.

The youth of America are simply not as obsessed with issues of sexual orientation as even the early sexual revolutionaries were. They've grown up with an Internet that has provided them with access to all manner of "variant" sexual activities, and while they usually can tell you what appeals to them and what doesn't, they don't feel so compelled to judge or label the sexual proclivities of others. In fact, they tend to be quite accepting. There are still bullies in schools, and it doesn't take much searching to find evidence of homophobia around us, but many young people are no longer allowing themselves to be intimidated or swayed by such intolerance. Perhaps this is one of the most powerful legacies of the sexual revolution and the subsequent increase in acceptance for consensual sexual activities between people whose interests and choices lie outside the former norms and whose own sexual lives do not lend themselves all that well to simplistic classification schemes.

In a study of about 8,000 college students in the United States and Canada, more than 97 percent self-identified as straight, with about 3 percent of the men and 2 percent of the women saying that they were gay or bisexual. Yet 10 percent of both genders said that at least half of their sexual fantasies involved same-gender partners. In addition to self-identification and sexual fantasies, the researchers asked about the students' behaviors and attractions, finding an "unsettling" number of inconsistencies and contradictions.[26] This has been true of most recent studies that have looked at various dimensions of people's sexual natures rather than focusing simply on actual sexual behaviors. The results are unsettling to researchers because they don't fit snugly into the cubbyholes and paradigms we've been using to understand them.

While it seems valid to assume that throughout human history some people have had sex with members of their own sex, the actual concept of "homosexuality" to classify the behavior or the people is a relatively new one. Beginning in the mid-1800s and for about a century after, it was viewed mostly within a context of pathology. If you were found having sex with someone of your gender, you could be arrested in some places, and you surely could be treated for a mental disorder. When in 1973 the American Psychiatric Association released homosexuality from its "official" classification as a disorder, clearly a result of the research and openness engendered by the sexual revolution, all that changed. But it all has taken time to sink in, to become part of American values and cultural beliefs. It is still sinking in, but the youth of America are now setting the new standard. They are refusing to be hamstrung by sexual labels or behavioral boxes. They want to be free to explore and exercise their sexualities in the ways they see fit, understanding that this demands a level of responsibility and consideration. They possess those qualities. It is not yet entirely clear what new paradigms of sexuality will emerge, but the process has begun, and the outmoded categories of classification are beginning to fracture.

QUIET REBELS TRANSFORMING AMERICAN SEXUAL VALUES

The recent revolutions against autocratic rule in the Middle East and northern Africa have been spearheaded by the youth of these nations, comprising the majority population. Their wildfire impetus and energy spread with the aid of the tools of the world's youth: social networks, quick-messaging sites such as Twitter, and the handheld messaging devices that make instant communication possible. The goals of these revolutions have been clear: freedom from dictatorships and the constraints on individual liberties they perpetuate, greater autonomy and civil rights, an end to human rights violations, and a greater democratic voice in the affairs of state and society. The young people of these global regions have been far from quiet, and in many cases they have been willing to sacrifice their lives for their cause. Youthful rebellion is all around us.

In the United States, the image of rebellious youth has been popular but not particularly objective. In the 1950s, Hollywood popularized a dark, brooding image of a younger generation that was angry at the adult world, always on the verge of violence, distrustful of authority, and bursting with sensuality. Popular psychology seemed to pick up on the theme with advice for parents and teachers on handling the rebellious nature of adolescents. The only trouble was that this image of teenagers was not particularly representative of average young people of the time, who were mostly trying to make it in the world and live up to their parents' expectations. The rebel image probably became some self-fulfilling fuel for the antiestablishment sentiments of the 1960s and 1970s, including the sexual revolution, as youthful baby boomers became the dominant segment of American society and adults became afraid that the younger generation was getting out of control, sexually and otherwise. The kids flexed their muscles while the conservative federal administrations of the time flexed back, but most young adults never did stray very far from the relative comfort that our society affords them.

The cooperative and respectful nature of the Millennials is not all that surprising when we consider how much parents have built their lives around their children in recent times. It doesn't really give youth much to rebel against, even as their relative proportion in the American demographic has shrunk again to a minority. And these kids in general are close to their parents and talk with them about their lives. However, with some exceptions, there is one area that young people and their parents still don't talk about very much, and that is sex. Today's youth indicate that their parents have not done an adequate job of providing information about sexuality, leaving them to get their information from their friends and the Internet.[27] Even though half of adolescent boys and over 70 percent of adolescent girls in fifth or sixth grade say they would consult their mothers if they had questions about sex, by the time they are in grades 10 through 12, those percentages drop to 35 percent and 46 percent, respectively. As young people age, they become more likely to seek sex information from their peers, and parents lose their chances for input.[28]

There is plenty of evidence that parents who are willing to communicate openly and honestly about sexuality, regardless of where they stand personally on sexual issues, can have an impact on their kids' sexual decision making. However, this doesn't work well in the form of the one-time "big sex talk" and seems far more effective as ongoing, repetitive conversations over time.[29] And all this works most effectively within the context of families that share activities together regularly, avoid hostility and negativism with the kids, and have parents who set good examples for their kids in relating to others. While mothers are often seen as the go-to parent for sex information, fathers and stepfathers of sons can play an important role in helping the boys understand their development and how to be responsible in their sexual choices.[30]

Even though the opportunities are there for parents who want to have open communication with their kids about sex, most often parents do not take full advantage of the time window available to them, waiting until their kids are too embarrassed or too cool to listen very carefully. The reason the kids feel that way is most typically because they are already well on their way to establishing what they see as a mature and active sexual life, and they assume they already know more about sex than their parents do (which could be true). So my contention is that the youth of America are channeling whatever flickers of rebelliousness they may have into quietly establishing their sex lives, quite independently from their parents and usually without their full knowledge. In this way, they are shaping the sexual transformation. They not only believe that it is natural and normal for them to behave sexually the way they are but also will be likely to carry these attitudes into the parenting of their own children.

There was some controversy over the title of this chapter. My original proposal for the main chapter title was "Saved, Shaved, and Well Behaved." A couple of early reviewers, coming from the perspective that being sexually active was not a mark of good behavior, suggested that I should change that part of the title to "Not So Well Behaved." At first, I caved to that viewpoint. However, the more I wrote and the more I thought about it, I returned to a position close to my original perspective. Here is that position.

I've seen my share of young people make mistakes in their sexual choices, but I return to my previously stated observation that I've seen similar judgment gaps and stupidities in adults. My experience with youth over the past 40 years of my work generally supports a view that they are trying hard to figure out how sexuality fits into their lives. It is the one part of their lives in which their parents have not been very involved and toward which their educational institutions have mostly turned a blind eye. Given this lack of guidance, coupled with the constant exposure to media that scream sex at them all the time, I think they've turned out pretty darn well! For the most part, our youth are cautious about their sexual interactions and try to be considerate of their sexual partners. They care about what kind of people they are and hope to be good partners and parents in the future. So, yes, I do think that when it comes to their sexual decisions and behaviors, they are pretty well behaved. Not perfect—who is? Not entirely sure of themselves—who is? But putting thought, energy, and feeling into figuring out what kind of sexual people they want to be. They understand that the relationship between sex and love is complex and confusing. They know that sex can have an impact on their health and well-being. And they know that it can be one of the most pleasurable and moving aspects of their lives.

I respect and admire the young adults of America a great deal. I only wish that American culture would begin to step up and offer the kind of sexuality information and education that they deserve and want.

Chapter 7

IS NURTURE TAKING A BACKSEAT TO NATURE? A NEW GUIDE TO UNDERSTANDING SEXUAL INDIVIDUALITY

Our first daughter was born in 1978, and we were determined not to allow our female child to be hampered in her life choices by gender stereotypes or prejudices that we believed had created clear-cut inequities for girls and women. We also had come to accept the prevailing supposition that any personality or skill-set differences existing between males and females were strictly the result of outdated, gender-biased approaches to socializing girls and boys. We felt that it would be in the best interests of our child for us to provide gentle counterbalances to any of the stereotypical female-typed skills and behaviors that would surely be imposed on her by society. We deliberately avoided color coding her gender by decorating the nursery in yellow and dressing her in outfits of varied colors. During her early years, we gave her a mix of toys that were gender neutral or stereotypically boyish, including toy cars and trucks, along with dolls and tea sets and an *Easy Bake* oven (we didn't ever withhold the more girl-typical trappings). At home, out of our own sense of the need for balance in our own relationship, we did our best to share household duties and child care responsibilities, and both of us had careers, thereby exposing our daughter to gender equality. I was thrilled when, on her own, she called me "Mah-dy" for about a year, a name I took to be a contraction of Mommy and Daddy. Four and a half years later, when our second daughter was born, we were a bit less enthusiastic about our gender de-stereotyping efforts, but we persisted to a degree with her as well.

As I've explained in earlier chapters, these were times when gender theory was based largely in concepts of social construction. The prevailing belief was that beyond the clear anatomical differences between boy and girl, it was how children were raised and socialized that determined not only the personality nuances of their masculinity or femininity and their gender identities as male or female but also the differences in their interests, play behaviors, eventual occupational choices, and probably their sexual orientation. Among the major proponents of this approach were researchers such as John Money, who directed the Johns Hopkins Gender Identity Clinic.[1] He and his staff routinely recommended to parents of children born with genitals of ambiguous appearance that the children's genitals be surgically modified to look like those that would be easiest to "build" surgically. This meant they would usually be modified to look female since penises and testicles were far more complicated to mimic surgically than folding tissues into a "vulva" and "vaginal" canal. The further recommendation was to raise the children according to the gender-appropriate guidelines that matched the genitals, again most often as girls. If necessary, the child's physical development was aided by administration of appropriate sex hormones over the course of their adolescence. Money even made the point that once children had been socialized into their gender identity and role for two or three years, any attempt to turn them in the other gender direction would be psychologically catastrophic.

Money was a researcher for whom I had great respect (see chapter 3), and his theories and practices provided ample backing for the social construction of gender. Additionally, there was research indicating that people who showed comfort with high frequencies of both traditional "masculine" and "feminine" qualities actually seemed better adjusted in their lives. So my wife and I felt as though we were on solid ground by encouraging our daughters in more androgenous directions that we thought would ultimately help them to be more whole and more adaptable while protecting them from all manner of inequity and unfairness.

As Betsy and I now reflect on these early child-rearing efforts, we laugh at our naïveté about the vast power of social nurture, and our adult daughters laugh with us. Even while they were still very young, it didn't take long for us to begin thinking that we had failed in our attempts to prevent them from being overly persuaded by lopsided gender stereotypes. The trucks and cars we gave them as toys were cast aside in favor of dolls and frilly dresses, and our daughters persisted in growing up "all girl." They were independent and assertive, to be sure, but also boy crazy, math phobic (yet competent), and fussy about their feminine appearance. Of course, we now understand that regardless of whether we were to believe that gender is shaped by socialization, biological templates, or a combination of both, those influences would be more pervasive than any one household could ever hope to counter. Our intentions may have

Developmental neurobiology continues to amass clues to the genetic, hormonal, and neurological building blocks of female–male, masculine– feminine, and transgender, but the more we learn, the more questions and complexities are unearthed.

been noble enough, if naive, and at least our daughters have remained alert to the snags and seductions of gender they prefer to avoid.

As a sexologist, I accept that the environmental sociocultural brew exerts a potent influence on learned values and behaviors and even on the very foundations of organizational behavior within a culture. Nonetheless, accepting this position still begs the question of whether there are innate biological roots for any of the differences we might see between male and female, another issue that became pivotal during the sexual revolution and has gained some empirical perspective since. Developmental neurobiology continues to amass clues to the genetic, hormonal, and neurological building blocks of female–male, masculine– feminine, and transgender, but the more we learn, the more questions and complexities are unearthed.

THE *DIS*-SIMILARITIES OF WOMEN AND MEN

As I open this can of worms, I want to reaffirm the view that I continue to hold about the dangers of recognizing the existence of gender-specific characteristics, especially because they have so often been used to stifle, marginalize, or discriminate. It is surely clear to me that when it came to educational opportunity, occupational choice, roles in relationships, and sexuality, gender differences were horribly overemphasized in mid-20th-century America. This was largely to the detriment of girls and women but, perhaps in the larger scheme of things, no less warping in a complementary manner for boys and men. When females are compromised in their options, males cannot avoid being influenced by the adjustments and concessions they must make in response and vice versa. Everyone ends up being less genuine and less in touch with the inner identification of gender that best fits her or him. However, in our attempts to rectify that state of affairs in order to play fair with girls and boys and level the playing fields of their futures, we may have gone overboard in putting the spotlight on gender similarities, but that is the sometimes overenergetic compensating effect of activism. The pendulum has now swung back and forth again as America's sexual transformation attempts to make sense of the roots of gender. Let me describe these two dramatic swings.

Even as John Money and gender theorists from the social sciences were upholding the idea of the social inculcation of gender during child rearing, Money was, ironically it would seem, also elucidating theories of how predispositions for feminine and masculine behaviors are established during prenatal development. This has been called *brain organization theory*. In a nutshell, this theory posits that the genetic pairing of sex chromosomes from Mom and Dad, XX for female or XY for male, sets into motion a complex developmental program that will determine not only what genital organs and internal reproductive structures eventually develop in the fetus but also how the brain will become "organized" as essentially masculine or feminine—yes, even before the child is born. There is a gene on the Y chromosome that will, through a chain of gene activations, cause the undifferentiated sex glands of the fetus to become testes. When that gene is lacking—or perhaps because of another set of genes found on the two X chromosomes—the undifferentiated fetal gonads turn into ovaries.

The real kicker here, though, is the fact that as early as the sixth week into pregnancy, a male fetus's newly formed testes secrete testosterone and another hormone that inhibits the development of female structures! These secretions are also believed to establish some brain templates that wire in a greater likelihood for male-specific traits and behaviors later on. A female fetus does not seem to experience any such secretion of sex hormones, and the theory suggests that this leads to a wiring in of a greater likelihood for female-specific traits and behaviors. When we begin to study the complexities of this developmental gender map, things get really interesting, especially when anatomical males or anatomical females are exposed to hormonal influences during fetal life that lead to incongruities between anatomy and anticipated gender behavior.[2]

Popularized accounts of brain organization theory have been impressively convincing and widely read and quoted. They tout evidence showing that females and males process things cognitively in somewhat different ways, and brain imaging studies demonstrating that they use different regions of their brains for that processing. Louann Brizendine, a psychiatrist and former faculty member at Harvard and Yale medical schools and now codirector of the Program in Sexual Medicine at the University of California, San Francisco, has written two books explaining how hormones and neurotransmitters interact with various centers of the human brain to organize moods, emotions, and behaviors.[3] The books are persuasive in describing how the brain differences between female and male brains are manifested in behavioral ways, and Brizendine also brings together data that can help explain the brain differences that lead to predictable patterns of female and male sexual longings and behaviors.

Even in the face of the biological evidence, there has been widespread acceptance of the idea that brain organization by hormones cannot be the only determining factor for what gender-typed characteristics are manifested by a person. Nonetheless, as most children approach middle childhood, they play predominantly with members of their own gender, and their toys and play behavior reflect what is called *sex-dimorphic behavior*, patterns we consider predictable for girls and boys. This is called *gender conformity*. Well of course, you might say, that's the way they've been trained to behave as girls and boys. But that explanation doesn't help us understand why some children don't seem to fit neatly into the gender segregated behavior patterns or why identical twins (with the same genetic makeup) are both likely to follow the same pattern of gender conformity or nonconformity. For example, a Dutch study of 22,500 7- and 10-year-old twins found that among identical twins, if one behaved in a cross-gendered, nonconforming way, the other was highly likely to do so as well, a correlation that was much less typical for fraternal twins, who would not have identical genes.[4] Neither does it explain why, when parents have raised their children in highly gender-conforming ways, some of those children still develop nonconforming behaviors so early in their lives. Gender-nonconforming little boys even go out of their way to hide their behaviors when adults are around because they have learned that "sissies" are subjected to more ridicule by others than "tomboys" are.[5] I have been increasingly persuaded by the evidence that these gender-specific qualities and, sometimes, nonconforming gender qualities reflect inborn influences of nature that do indeed organize the human brain, hardwiring some sex differences into it, if not always along the lines of biological sex. So how much of a role does nurture play?

As I explained above, it was typical for gender specialists of the 1970s to recommend that children with ambiguous genitalia be raised as girls, even if they were chromosomally male, and that their gender identity would then be socially molded toward the feminine by the ways in which they were raised. Even though there were some who believed this represented faulty thinking, it wasn't until the late 1990s that a striking case study flew in the face of the theory. The poster child for a whole new paradigm was an identical twin boy who as a baby had lost his penis through a botched circumcision and had been surgically modified and raised as a girl, while his twin was raised as a boy. After years of fighting his assigned female gender and insisting that he was really a boy, the twin who had been raised as a girl was told the truth about his male origins and allowed to reestablish a male identity. There were many red faces in the clinical community, and the social-constructionist belief system about gender suffered a major blow.[6] The pendulum swung in the direction of innate biological influences for gender, and brain organization theory became an even more widely accepted model.

AND BACK TO SIMILARITIES AGAIN

There has been some momentum building for swinging the pendulum back to emphasize gender similarities and away from models of built-in, or essential, masculinity or femininity. Janet Shibley Hyde, professor of psychology, gender, and women's studies at the University of Wisconsin, Madison, who coincidentally has a college sexuality text with the same publisher as my own text, continues to assert that we are making too much of male–female differences in certain aptitudes and skills and that we should instead be reaffirming the similarities between the two genders.[7] The work of Hyde and her colleagues has now extended to analyses of the studies on gender differences in sexual attitudes and behaviors as well, concluding that any differences that exist between women and men in terms of frequencies of engaging in sexual intercourse, masturbation, or extramarital sex; numbers of sexual partners; age at first intercourse, and attitudes about these things are essentially not nearly as disparate as the authors think is commonly believed.[8] They are probably right, although I'm personally not as convinced as they are that women and men really are perceived to be all that different in terms of abilities, sexual behaviors, and sexual attitudes. It seems to me that women today are typically recognized to be competent in most anything they wish to pursue and to want satisfying sexual lives in which they will share equally in sexual pleasures.

Nevertheless, for purposes of social equality and organizational fair play, I surely understand that gender stereotypes sometimes get in the way of opportunities for individuals, and it is most often women who get the short end of the stick. I also agree that any measurable average gender differences in specific academic aptitudes and motor skills, such as verbal fluency and visual spatial relations, are largely negligible. However, since aptitudes and skills do indeed cross gender boundaries and may help shape our lives to a degree, I'm not so sure that any differences do not or ought not play a role in the academic and occupational choices of boys and girls, men and women. Isn't it reasonable that we optimize our strengths in making such choices as long as we're not being co-opted in some direction for political reasons? This is, of course, where the discourse becomes politically complex, but I still think it is a discussion worth having.

Hyde and her colleagues have done a good job of giving the various biological, evolutionary, and psychosocial theories their due when it comes to trying to understand the impact and significance of perceived gender differences. They also believe that to recognize and emphasize gender *similarities* over gender *differences* is essential to challenging sexual double standards and creating equal opportunities for sexual expression by women and men. In fact, they believe that if society becomes more sexually "liberal," emphasis on gender differences will narrow, allowing this greater equality for sexual expression.[9] This is built on a common political assumption that to be liberal is to be more open about sexuality and sexual activity *and to see women and men as essentially the same.* This view also operates under the premise that if a society treats its girls and boys and men and women equally, the more similar they will be and the more similarly they will behave.

This is where we run into an as-yet-unresolved puzzle in the psychological literature. In actuality, gender differences in personality tend to be the greatest in North American and western European societies that already provide the two sexes with relatively egalitarian treatment and opportunity. In some Asian and African societies that are noted for perpetuating inequalities between the sexes, male–female personality differences are actually less visible.[10] Several psychosocial hypotheses have been proposed to explain this phenomenon,[11] although we could speculate that perhaps they have been raised to counter any suggestion that some differences between women and men might be innate. Yet I cannot help but wonder if the possibility exists that when people are allowed to be more individualistic, women and men simply appreciate and enjoy being different from one another.[12] So even as proposals for putting the emphasis on gender similarities may seem the right thing to do in terms of social and political realities, they may not always fit the ways in which many women (or men for that matter) would like to live their lives. This is a brambled path to explore, to be sure, but one that we cannot entirely avoid.

Two other authors have done extensive analysis of the research that supports brain organization theory and the ways in which evidence from neuroscience has been used to create what they believe are false or exaggerated dichotomies between female and male. Rebecca Jordan-Young, a sociomedical scientist and assistant professor of women's studies at Barnard College, Columbia University, recently published an exhaustive analysis of much of the existing research behind the theory that fetal hormones—or the lack of them—help set up the brain's gender wiring.[13] She calls into question the methods, assumptions, ambiguities, and overly broad conclusions of such work, claiming that the evidence used to support the notions of a biological gender template resembles a "hodgepodge pile" more than it does a theoretical structure supportable by good science. She rightly believes that this critical topic deserves more sophisticated science and that we must clear away the junk science before we can really understand how sex and gender differences arise in human development.

Cordelia Fine, a research associate at the Centre for Agency, Values, and Ethics in the Department of Philosophy at Australia's Macquarie University and a research fellow at the University of Melbourne, goes so far as to claim that we have all become victims of "neurosexism."[14] She believes that we have bought so thoroughly into the findings about the neurohormonal organization of gender in the human brain that we have become persuaded by our "delusions of gender" differences when in fact the evidence to back up such differences is incomplete. She makes a good case for how our current thinking about gender has become lost to premature conclusions of gender difference, that we've become stuck there and unable to focus more clearly on the similarities of female and male.

THE GENDER CHALLENGE FOR AMERICA'S SEXUAL TRANSFORMATION

So there we are, caught in an ever-shifting quagmire of beliefs and data about whether there are any very meaningful innate differences in the natures of girls and boys, women and men. Jordan-Young found that when she interviewed scientists about the question, many of them had simply accepted such differences as obvious and self-evident, not the most objective perspective from which to design research and interpret data. Fine insists that science's obsession with biologically essential differences between female and male brains has caused us to lose sight of the extent to which social context shapes femininity and masculinity. As careful, systematic researchers, they make excellent points. But I fear we must be just as cautious about riding the gender pendulum too far back to the gender similarity—or minimization of gender differences—direction. To be fair, both of these authors allow that there may be quantifiable and predictable average differences between male and female that might indeed be hardwired into our neurophysiology; they simply don't believe that the science is strong enough to yet support such ideas in the form of broad theory, and they advocate for a more measured approach to drawing conclusions from what evidence is now available. It is reasonable advice.

What must also be faced in this discussion is a long-standing academic debate that continues to play out in scholarly circles, based in an old and outmoded dichotomy between science and the humanities. Probably the most widely known critique of this split was delivered more than 60 years ago by novelist and scientist C. P. Snow,[15] who called attention to the gap. The basic position of many in the humanities is that all concepts are culturally constructed and that in fact since science itself is embedded in culture and its language, it is therefore impossibly lost to subjective biases. Those in the sciences believe that its methods can indeed enable clear and objective observations that are not always culturally skewed. As his own life demonstrated, Snow thought that each discipline should inform the other and that they should work toward a united culture of shared knowledge. While that bridging of the gap has happened in some cases, the fundamental hostility and lack of mutual comprehension between the two domains persist to this day. There are still scientists who insist that human identity and personality, everything from our emotions and gender characteristics to our ambitions and illusions of free will, are nothing more than a complex assemblage of genes, hormones, and neurons that determine everything about us. And there are still college gender courses from which students emerge with the impression that the language and the media in which they are immersed have entirely created their personalities, emotions, gender identities, and roles. This is the ultimate declaration of disunion between nature and nurture that is so clearly displayed in the academic gender wars of the present day.

As Rebecca Jordan-Young and Cordelia Fine pointed out, scientific methods can be flawed and interpretations of data biased or exaggerated. Working this all out is, in fact, built into the very dynamic fabric of scientific discourse. Yet humanities and literary theory can be equally dogmatic and narrow-minded in not being able to see that human nature is more complex than culture and context and that biological organization predated language and culture by hundreds of millions of years.[16]

If we look more carefully at the biological science of gender differences, and move beyond lopsided agendas that sometimes attempt to use such research to support arguments for things such as separate educational systems for boys and girls or to exclude one sex or the other from pursuing some line of education or work, we can also see that beyond the shakier science is some very persuasive evidence of sex differences. Recent studies that collected data from more than 200,000 women and men found medium to large gender differences across 53 countries.[17] Other high-quality studies have found sex differences in brains during every stage of human development,[18] influences on emotions and memory by sex differences in the brain,[19] and effects of sex hormones, such as estrogen, on neural development.[20] Even the vast hodgepodge pile of data from the less substantive or long-term studies undoubtedly holds nuggets of genetic and neurohormonal realities that will eventually gel into more comprehensive theories. That is indeed how theories are created.[21]

In debating these socially and politically charged matters, it can be difficult for us to separate our objective selves from our political and activist selves. Little of the work on either side of the debate ever makes it into forms fit for popular consumption, so the young people who could benefit from a clearer and more balanced discussion of all perspectives lose out entirely.[22] That, I believe, is the real challenge for the sexual transformation that is under way. Ultimately, there needs to be a meeting of the minds to clear away the biases that are muddling the issues and an acceptance of whatever truths emerge, even if they are complicated. In arriving at my own conclusions about gender, I have tried to stay mindful of the fact that I am a man who has benefited from and taken advantage of male privilege all of his life, feminist ideology or not. It is not entirely comfortable for me to presume to question women who have so often been on the other side of this social equation having to fight and defend in order to win rightful recognition and respect. Ultimately, I believe that we all have to do the best we can to muster our powers of objectivity while trying to maintain the momentum for social causes that we know in our hearts to be right. The gender findings of science ultimately may prove irrelevant and pale by comparison, but that doesn't mean we shouldn't pay attention to them for other reasons.

In this spirit, I maintain that any innate dichotomies between female and male brains and skills, any essential roots of the feminine and the masculine—which at times surely cross the biological sex borders of male and female—are worthy of celebration in themselves. The two sexes clearly evaluate sexual cues quite differently and may even use differing brain circuitry for processing sexual information and feelings.[23] There is nothing wrong with taking pride in the fullness of being female or male or in touting the special qualities that make you a woman or make you a man—regardless of your physical body and its sex organs! It is only when our dualistic thinking patterns turn such differences into the foolish fuel of conflict or foolhardy competition that we run into trouble.

Deemphasizing gender differences has generally been the more politically progressive approach because it serves progressive causes well. Likewise, calling attention to gender differences has been the clarion call of those on the far right who support traditional roles for women and men in the home and workplace and oppose same-gender marriage and parenting, claiming instead that having a man and a woman as spouses and as parents is the only way to go. This is where I believe the youth of America are ahead of the game. They are able to accept that stereotypical gender roles can be stifling and that gender equality in the workplace is the only fair way. Many, probably the majority, believe that gender should not be the fundamental determining factor for relationships, sex, or even marriage. These things are not huge revelations or stumbling blocks for our youth but instead values that have gradually achieved general acceptance among them—transformative values that transcend bigotry and political fervor.

GENDER STRUGGLES AT THE MOLECULAR AND GENETIC LEVELS

In nature, we know that during displays of mating behavior among mammals and many other vertebrates, males often must compete for female mates. The competition can take the form of colorful feathers and fins, the delivery of pollen from one insect to a much-admired girlfriend some distance away, the sonorous croak of a bullfrog intended to impress the lady across the pond, fancy racks of horns that are crowning glories of maleness, and sometimes fierce aggression.[24] We could draw all sorts of apt comparisons with the preening, strutting, and posturing of human courting behavior, but let's just say that competition for mates in the human community is often more subtle and complex, layered with all sorts of socially shaped nuances and judgments.

When we look at male rivalries at a more microscopic level, we find some fascinating things. In nonhuman animals, we've often assumed that whichever male succeeds in mating with the female has won the mating competition, but in actuality, that may only be the first step in winning the larger battle of whose genes will be passed along to the offspring. In the animal kingdom, it is not unusual for a female to mate with more than one male in quick succession so that more than one male's sperm then must compete to fertilize the available eggs in the female's reproductive tract. And what a competition this can be. Scientists have labeled sperm from different male fruit flies with fluorescent substances and then watched their combative journey through the seminal receptacle of a female. The sperm jostle one another about as they jockey for the best position for fertilizing eggs in a fierce, if microscopic, battle for genetic triumph. The same competitiveness in sperm from different males has been observed in several other species, believed to result from some as-yet-unidentified component of semen that recognizes the sperm from a rival male and attempts to thwart them. We don't know yet if a similar mechanism exists in humans, but at the very least these findings demonstrate reproductive competition at a very fundamental level, and they have been heralded as revolutionary for the field of reproductive biology.[25]

GENETIC STOWAWAYS

There is now another intriguing ingredient in the inheritance mix that adds a whole new dimension to the intertwining of genes and environment. It needs a little historical perspective. Before Darwin's evolutionary theory and Mendel's early studies that gave us some basic principles of genetics, a French naturalist by the name of Jean Baptiste de Lamarck (1744–1829) posited a theory that various characteristics acquired by animals, including humans, during their lifetimes could be passed on to the next generation. This was probably a reflection of folk wisdom at the time and essentially meant that if a carpenter accidentally cut off a finger, it was possible that the absence of a similarly placed finger or the underdevelopment of the digit could occur in the carpenter's progeny. It didn't take very complex scientific experiments to show that this was not the case, and as our knowledge of genes and DNA became more complete, science became quite comfortable with the assertion that only the genetic material derived from the sperm and the egg is passed along from generation to generation. Characteristics acquired in a living thing's environment would not be passed on. Only genes could be inherited.

Around 1950, some scientists began to realize that while it was true that gross changes in the body were not passed along in genetic material, there did seem to be some environmentally acquired auxiliary mechanisms that could be attached to genes. A gene is formed by a particular sequence of bases that join together in a DNA molecule. However, there can be molecular changes to the DNA that do not alter the sequencing of bases, so the basic structure of the genes is likewise not altered, but the molecular changes can modify the expression of those genes. We now know that some of these environmentally acquired regulatory changes in the DNA *actually can be passed along with genes to the next generation!* The branch of science that studies these genetic stowaways is called epigenetics, and it is revolutionizing our understandings of heredity.[26]

To go into great detail about epigenetics is beyond the scope of this book, and, besides, it is still a very young field. There is still debate over its definitions and terminologies. What we can state with some certainty is that not only do social information and other environmental factors affect whether genes are expressed or not, but they can also cause epigenetic changes in the individual's genome that alter gene function, changes that can even be passed on to the next generation. Chemicals in the body, for example, whether natural compounds such as hormones or substances that enter our bodies from the environment, can change brain structures and behaviors in permanent ways, and these behavioral modifications may then be inherited along with the offspring's genome. We will eventually get smarter at factoring these epigenetic possibilities into our understandings of the formation of gender identity, sexual orientation, the coupling process, and each person's unique qualities of sexual individuality. This is the ultimate melding of nature and nurture since genes determine so many qualities, epigenetic modifications are created by the environment, and both are heritable!

Figuring out how epigenetic influences create subtleties of sexual expression will very much be part of America's sexual transformation. Most people have not even heard of epigenetics, let alone understand its significance, and yet it is being recognized as one of the significant determinants of human personality traits and may well unravel some of the mysterious quirks of inheritance that classical genetic theory has never quite been able to explain. Not only is it transforming our understandings of human reproduction and inheritance, it is helping to explain how and why each of us constitutes a uniquely complex individual—sexually and otherwise.

Epigenetics is providing us with clues about another type of gender competition among animals that may well apply to humans. Remember that we get two sets of chromosomes carrying two sets of genes, one set from our father and one from our mother. Essentially, that means that we have a pair of genes that controls some particular function in our cells. It has been assumed until recently that it didn't really matter whether the gene from the mother or from the father happened to be the one that ultimately got expressed or activated in our cells, and in fact this was assumed to be largely a random happenstance, mediated by rather vaguely defined concepts of dominance and recessiveness. Epigenetic studies have changed all this. It has been discovered that sometimes when sperm or eggs are being formed, they are "imprinted" with modifications that ultimately will determine whether, in the offspring, the gene from the father or the gene from the mother will be expressed in the determination of some trait. New research has shown that this mechanism can have profound influences on whether certain brain functions are influenced mostly by genes from the father or mostly by genes from the mother. This is a remarkable finding, demonstrating how environmental influences can cause these epigenetic changes to play out in genetic competition between the mother's genes and the father's genes to be more involved in how an offspring's brain develops and ultimately functions. There are several theories about how all this might affect human cognition and behavior, but we first have to investigate the degree to which this genome competition applies in human development.[27] This is cutting-edge research that will enhance our capacity to understand some of the most fundamental facts about gender and sexuality as our sexual transformation unfolds.

THE UMBILICAL CORD: SOURCE OF ANOTHER BRAIN ORGANIZER

Just when things are getting complicated at the molecular, genetic, and epigenetic levels, another astounding finding has emerged about the shaping of the fetal brain that has surprised even the experts in the field. We know, of course, that the umbilical cord connects the fetus to the placenta, which develops during pregnancy alongside the fetus in the uterus. Up until now, we have thought that the sole purpose of the placenta is to provide a place where a network of blood vessels from the fetus comes into close proximity with a network of blood vessels from the mother. This permits oxygen and digested nutrients in the mother's bloodstream to diffuse into the fetus's blood and waste products of the fetus's metabolism to diffuse into the mother's bloodstream to be removed through her body. The umbilical cord is the delivery tube for these substances to and from the fetus, a wonderfully efficient system of fetal support as it grows and develops. But now we know that this system too is far more complex than we have thought.

In animal models and in humans, it has been known for a while that development of the embryonic frontal cortex of the brain is regulated by the chemical serotonin, a neurotransmitter that later regulates emotions, mood, anger, aggressiveness, and a variety of other personality characteristics. Serotonin is crucial for the wiring of this part of the early fetal brain. The unresolved question was where the serotonin for this early brain wiring came from, the assumption always being that it was produced in some part of the fetus. The newest research has found something that startled everyone. Early on, the serotonin that helps wire the developing brain is actually produced by the placenta and transported to the fetus through the umbilical cord. It is essentially produced by the mother's body! It is in these early stages of brain development that many fundamental characteristics of personality are probably established, including whether the developing child will ultimately be predisposed to mental health or to certain compromisers of mental well-being, such as depression, autism, or schizophrenia.[28]

We can now only wonder what new understandings about predispositions of gender or sexual orientation may emerge from this entirely new line of developmental research, but I will wager that it will be critical to a full understanding of both.

THE NATURE—AND NURTURE—OF SEXUAL ORIENTATION

We're just beginning to find that the brains of some gay men operate similarly to those of straight women and that the brains of some lesbian women operate similarly to those of straight men: another piece of the still puzzling and much debated associations among biological sex, gender conformity/nonconformity, and sexual orientation. These studies lend weight to the long-held psychological belief that males are more lateralized in their brain functions, meaning that they tend to localize particular brain functions in one cerebral hemisphere over the other. This may help explain why boys and men generally tend to have an edge in processing very specific spatial relations and analytic problem solving, while girls and women do better with the more pervasive emotional processing that benefits from using both cerebral hemispheres simultaneously. Newer studies have shown that the right cerebral hemisphere of straight men and lesbian women tends to be larger than the left hemisphere, while in straight women and gay men, the two hemispheres are nearly symmetrical, suggesting a biological link between gender-specific brain characteristics and sexual orientation.[29]

If we compare the prevailing beliefs about the origins of sexual orientation in the late 1970s, which emphasized the influences of parenting styles and social experience, with today's theories that emphasize essential biological factors, the contrasts are stark. For this topic as well, there is another enormous pile of correlations and other data suggesting that sexual orientation—whether we're sexually and romantically attracted to the other gender, our own, or both—is to an extent hardwired into us. However, the extent to which the wiring of sexual orientation is associated with the wiring of masculinity and femininity is another topic of controversy. When I was writing and teaching about gay men and lesbian women in the midst of the sexual revolution, it was not considered appropriate—perhaps it was an early form of "political correctness"—to draw an association between people's outward gender characteristics and their sexual orientation. There was a little research, though not very substantial, suggesting that there was no particular correlation between the two. So I dutifully perpetuated the idea that people's characteristic speech patterns, gaits (ways of walking), and mannerisms were not reflective of their sexual orientations. Just because a man spoke with a "sibilant S," had an "effeminate" gait, or showed stereotypical "limp-wristed" mannerisms was not to suggest that he was likely gay. Just because a woman was gruff in speech, had a somewhat wide-legged "manly" gait, and sat with her legs apart and hands on her knees did not mean she was likely lesbian. The only trouble was, nobody—including me—really believed all of that because knowing many openly gay men and lesbian women had suggested that these characteristics actually were at least somewhat reliable indicators of sexual orientation. Of course, there were exceptions but really not all that many.

The exceptions lie on the other side of the equation: the men who display characteristics of athleticism and macho manliness who are gay and the women who are dainty and sweetly feminine who are lesbian. These are the fascinating variabilities of gender conformity and sexual orientation that confound so much of current sex research. It is difficult to make sense of the many combinations of these factors that can be identified. There is again the social reality that associating gender nonconformity with sexual orientation provides succor for stereotypes that are often used in mocking and discriminatory ways and raise people's hackles. Legitimately so when they are used in such ways, but it doesn't mean that there is no validity to the correlations.

Actually, research continues to yield some pretty convincing evidence that whatever biological mechanisms are involved in the formation of gender conformity/nonconformity may well be closely related to the mechanisms involved in the formation of straight or gay sexual orientation. For example, there is a fair amount of evidence that gender-nonconforming children have a higher likelihood of identifying as gay when they are adults.[30] A small study conducted at Harvard correlated the size ratios of the first and fourth fingers (a ratio that usually differs in males and females) with gender traits in a group of men. It found that gay males who had a finger size ratio similar to that of women tended to report that they had been rather effeminate as boys and preferred feminine-identified occupations.[31] Those who participated in anal intercourse were also more likely to report they preferred the receptive or bottom role. Canadian researchers conducted acoustic analyses that found significant differences in how vowel sounds were pronounced between gay men and women and straight men and women. One possibility the researchers proposed was that these quantifiable differences emerged from the biological processes associated with the development of gender roles and sexual orientation.[32]

In an analysis of data from eight separate studies on differences in personality traits between men and women and between gay/lesbian people and straight people, psychologist Richard Lippa found that gay men tend to exhibit characteristics more typical for females and that lesbian women tend to show characteristics more typical for males. Interestingly, people who self-identify as bisexuals tend to fall in intermediate zones between male-typical and female-typical characteristics.[33] So there is a body of evidence that supports a connection in at least some gay men and lesbian women between sexual orientation and their cross-typical gender behaviors.

That brings us to another scholarly imbroglio that complicates things even more. Even though many gay men and lesbian women may have histories of gender-nonconforming behavior extending back to their childhoods, most of them have gender identities consistent with the sex of their bodies. In other words, they're happy being males or females and have no interest in changing their bodies. So they are not transsexuals or perhaps even transgendered, even though some of their mannerisms and behaviors may seem to cross gender lines. Another complicating issue is the reality that some gay men seem occasionally to dress in drag (I haven't found evidence of anything entirely comparable among lesbian women), but most of them don't consider themselves transgendered either. They might, however, say that they enjoy being in touch with and exercising their feminine sides. The big question—and the most controversial one—is whether their same-gender sexual orientation, that is, their attraction to members of their own sex, represents one of those cross-gendered behaviors. This remains an unresolved issue and may belong more to scholarly theory than it matters in real life.

There is common ground on which those in the sciences and the humanities can stand on these nature–nurture issues. Even though we know that some human characteristics, such as eye color, are nearly 100 percent determined by genetic combinations, we also know that this is not the case for many physical characteristics and most personality traits. A person's height is about 90 percent dependent on inherited genes, but the rest is determined by things such as nutrition and general health. This concept of *heritability* has long played a crucial role in both biology and psychology, and there is quite strong agreement that personality traits—including sexual orientation—are somewhere between 40 and 70 percent heritable, or, in other words, genetically determined. At this point, we cannot support a more precise proportionality than that. There is also strong agreement that regardless of the genetic template that may predispose us to a particular sexual orientation, the expression of that orientation and the sexual choices we ultimately make are also partly shaped by social and cultural influences. The question of whether one's sexual orientation is represented mainly by genetic predisposition, the inner experience of sexual attraction and desire, and/or the practical choices of sexual partners and activities we make remains a matter of conjecture that is answered only through the lens of one's own socially constructed biases.

MATTERS OF THE HEART OR INTERACTIONS OF HORMONES AND NEUROTRANSMITTERS?

The coupling of human beings in loving and sexual relationships—something that behaviorists rather coldly call pair bonding or mating—has always captured the human imagination, probably because it represents one of the most powerful emotional experiences that we as a species encounter in life. We write poems and songs about it. We cry over it. We build entire lifestyles around it. This is powerful stuff. We associate love and sex with the figurative and literary "heart," probably because it is in that region of the chest and abdomen that we get in touch with the unsettling tickles, leaps, slumps, and flutters that characterize the wonders and wounds of loving another. Social scientists have studied and theorized about these phenomena at the macro, person-to-person level, trying to figure out what attracts us together as friends or lovers and what mediates the differences. At this level, we have made great strides in generating theories about how these connections are guided by social and sexual scripts that help us know how to behave, how to make behavioral choices based on the economics of cost–benefit analyses of personal resources such as attractiveness and personality traits, and how to draw our partners from the social networks of which we are part.[34]

Now, for the first time in human history, we are beginning to make sense of these inner longings and pairings at the micro level. As two neuroscientists wrote recently in the journal *Science*, "Neuroscientists once considered social behavior to be too hopelessly complex to understand at a mechanistic level, but advances in animal models of social cognition and bonding, as well as applications of new technologies in human research have demonstrated that the

For the first time in human history, we are beginning to make sense of these inner longings and pairings at the micro level.

molecular basis of social behavior is not beyond the realm of our understanding."[35] It is not an unusual reaction for people to recoil at the possibility of understanding such things as love and sexual desire at the level of molecules and neurons, but this will indeed be part of the language of sexual transformation. Young people who have studied phenomena at both macro and micro levels since the beginning of their educations are not as intimidated by such truths, nor do they assume that these truths will destroy any charming, romantic mysteries of the human heart. They appreciate understanding the complex interactions of the human experience at all levels of organization and know that things are never as simple as our flimsy, superficial fictions would have us believe.

WHAT MAKES LIFE EXPERIENCES SEXUAL?

Many neuron firings, splashes of neurotransmitters across synapses in the brain, and hormones coursing through our bloodstreams are associated with the emotional mechanisms of being attracted to one another, pairing up, and becoming sexually involved. We tend to perceive and talk about these intimacies in terms such as sexual desire or horniness, excitement, pleasure, and satisfaction, but the underlying execution of these pleasant emotional states is only beginning to be understood, as are its genetic foundations. As philosophers and psychologists have been telling us for a long time, situations that we encounter in life are not, in and of themselves, *sexual*. Instead, they become sexualized as a result of what we feel and do in the situation, how we have learned to perceive the situation and our feelings, and what previous knowledge we have to make associations with. Once we can experience sexual arousal and the various stages of sexual response and then make an association between those physical responses and some situation, the sexual meaning for that situation is thereby constructed. That connection then continues to be made with other analogous situations.[36]

Underlying these macro-level learning processes are all sorts of intriguing molecular and neurological things going on. They trigger specific genes to produce particular protein messengers, cause tissues in some glands and parts of the brain to secrete specific hormonal messengers, and then result in stimulation of parts of the brain, spinal cord, and peripheral nervous system to respond with changes in blood flow to sex organs. They also elicit a variety of other physical and emotional reactions. It is at this micro level that the interaction of genes and environment have become so obvious that their interaction is no longer really a matter of conjecture; it is a reality.

The interaction between biology and environment is a two-way street. Let's look at one vector, or street direction, first. Social information is experienced by our sensory organs that then transform these stimuli into neuronal signals and neurochemical messages that the brain will be able to interpret and respond to. Along the way, social influences also produce profound changes in genes that can then alter metabolic states and synaptic connections in neural networks. This is the "hardwiring" that programs certain responses and perceptions into us, for better or for worse. So for this sequence of connections, variations in both the environment and the genes influence how social information is received and sent along to the brain and also influence how the two interact. Now, for the other direction or vector of the two-way street. Our genes and their epigenetic attachments carry the programs of variability that make us uniquely ourselves. Through being "turned on," or expressed, or by being "turned off," or blocked from expression, genes either create or do not create various chemical messengers (RNAs and proteins) that affect brain development and the physiology of the body, and these effects in turn prod our cells and organ systems into functioning and responding in particular ways. Lo and behold, it is these functions and responses that determine our patterns of social behavior. So this setup is sensitive to both genetic and environmental variations and how they interact.[37]

In other words, things cannot be constructed socially without genes, epigenetic components, hormones, neurons, and brain parts being changed in some way, and our biologically innate capabilities and propensities cannot be expressed and exercised without social experience shaping some context of meaning within which they can function. So how we act and perceive ourselves as male, female, or transgendered; who or what turns us on and motivates us to behave sexually; and the people to whom we are drawn as lovers are all results of our biological templates and processes and how they are sculpted by our interactions with the world and other human beings. It's a lovely symphony, really, beautiful because of its elegant and systematic complexity as much as its occasional atonalities and missed notes.

Things cannot be constructed socially without genes, epigenetic components, hormones, neurons, and brain parts being changed in some way, and our biologically innate capabilities and propensities cannot be expressed and exercised without social experience shaping some context of meaning within which they can function.

HORMONES AND TOGETHERNESS

There are a few chemical secretions that are intimately associated with the development of our reproductive capabilities and secondary sex characteristics, namely, testosterone, estrogen, progesterone, and all their molecular precursors and derivatives. There is a growing body of research about the roles that hormones play in pair bonding and sexual behavior. Early on, most of this research was done with nonhuman animals, but now human hormone research is showing that many of the early animal findings do indeed have correlates in human activities. One of the most common misconceptions about what we loosely call "sex hormones" is that they are directly involved in things such as lust and "sex drive." People often assume that when men are feeling especially horny, their testosterone levels must be through the roof. In fact, beyond the reality that testosterone seems to activate the human ability to become sexually aroused, a trigger that is cocked during puberty in both boys and girls, hormone levels do not seem necessarily to be directly associated with levels of sexual interest or desire. When we're feeling the horniest of all, our sex hormone levels may actually be at their lowest ebb.[38] No, the role that hormones play in our love lives is far more subtle and enchanting.

The *sex steroids*, the more scientific term for this group of hormones produced by the adrenal glands, testes, and ovaries, are very much involved in the processes of attraction, partnering, falling in love, and developing commitment. Men with higher levels of testosterone in their bloodstreams and women with higher levels of estrogen are seen by those of the other gender to be respectively more attractively masculine or more attractively feminine. When they are in the early stages of falling in love, men's testosterone levels fall and women's levels rise. Both sexes have an increase of the stress hormone cortisol since love activates all the alerting systems of the body, turning up the intensity of everything. However, higher levels of testosterone in men do not bode all that well for long-term happiness and satisfaction in a relationship and are in fact associated with significantly higher levels of marital disruption. This may be linked to traits and behaviors that make them less satisfactory partners for women, such as irritability, aggressiveness, and a tendency toward philandering. The key point here is that the sex steroids modulate neural activity in the brain and thus are involved in mediating behaviors that may be either conducive or constraining to partnering.[39]

There is another group of hormones, called the *neuropeptide hormones*, that also play important roles in social behavior and sexual relationships. These short chains of amino acids, similar to protein molecules but not as long, are synthesized in the hypothalamus of the brain and then travel to other brain structures or circulate throughout the bloodstream to work their romantic magic. The two that are closely tied to pair bonding are oxytocin and vasopressin, and they seem to operate differently in females and males. Oxytocin, which has

*To understand the underlying mechanics of love,
lust, and lechery neither demeans their meaning
in human experience nor belittles the wonder they
create when they spring from the human "heart."*

been called the "cuddle chemical," seems to play the biggest role in females and is associated with feelings of trust, contentment, togetherness, and sexual attraction when the woman is in a relationship that provides lots of support, hugs, and physical closeness. When a woman falls literally into a partner's arms or bed and nestles away in sexual vulnerability, she is most likely flush with oxytocin. It is the same hormone that makes nipple stimulation from breast feeding or sex so pleasantly satisfying for many women.[40]

Although both neuropeptide hormones are present in both sexes, vasopressin probably plays the major pair bonding role in males. Less is known about its actions than those of oxytocin, but it appears to stimulate the desire to be with a particular partner, stir feelings of rivalry toward potentially competitive partners, and cause men to melt with feelings of intimacy that they may not be so prone to show in other circumstances. His rush of vasopressin renders a man putty in his partner's arms.

Human cultures interpret the behaviors resulting from these neurochemical phenomena within contexts that will render them understandable for us and reflective of the need for responsible human conduct. We see flirting or showing off instead of increased levels of testosterone. We write songs about starry-eyed girls instead of a brain infused with oxytocin. Culture also builds the models and social structures that lend romantic and sexual context to human situations, thus triggering the neurochemical reactions that make it all feel so good. To understand the underlying mechanics of love, lust, and lechery neither demeans their meaning in human experience nor belittles the wonder they create when they spring from the human "heart." To understand these things at all levels of our being simply means that we can regulate our emotions with insight and be answerable for the control of our behaviors. If anything, that renders us even more deeply human.

TRANSFORMING OUR VIEW OF THE SEXUAL DIMENSION OF HUMAN NATURE

We are indeed a complex amalgam of cellular components, held together by bone and sinew, programmed by genes and neural networks, set into motion by environmental stimuli and hormones, and motivated by primordial imperatives to pass along our collective genetic instructions for human nature through the propagation of our species. How fortunate we are that all of this is brought together in bags of skin, as some Buddhists call our bodies, that have sexual emotions and sexual organs capable of generating such ecstasy and bonds of human connection that we cannot ignore them. How fortunate that we, as humans, understand that we must also be good stewards of these powerful gifts and the heritage they represent, usually trying the best we can to exercise them responsibly and with consideration toward others. This is not always an easy balance to maintain, but the knowledge we take with us into these transformative times makes it all the more possible and likely that we can do a better job at it.

Ronald Cole-Turner, professor of theology and ethics at Pittsburgh Theological Seminary, admits that when he is asked what it means to be human, he becomes less clear all the time about the answer. As we gain precision in our knowledge about the human genome, he says, we ironically lose conceptual clarity of what being human is all about. As we realize that we share so many genes with other species and compare the human genome to that of other primates, we realize that "the boundary of our much-vaunted human 'uniqueness' is thin indeed." But Cole-Turner also maintains that the Human Genome Project "hints at a new vision of humanity. We are less clearly defined than we once thought, less set apart from the rest of life, but uniquely able to probe the data and ponder the questions. And, being humans, we let our discomfort give way to wonder. Who are we, and where will we go next?"[41]

In fact, we are finally beginning to understand the dynamic underlying workings of love and sex that have stood for millennia as mysteries, beyond human ken. Formerly, we had only the bewildering longings for sexual connection, the volatile pleasures and frustrations of sexual response, and the spoils of unrequited love and uncouplings that barely had any time to find their glue. There was little else we could do but write and sing and grieve about it all. But now sex research, coupled with scientific inquiry about all aspects of the human experience, is yielding real answers. Things are finally making some sense. I can now tell my students what happens in their bodies when they have sex, but best of all I can also offer theories of what love and longing are all about at the psychological, social, *and* biological levels. Theories are fitting things together so that we no longer are left with guesswork, myth, and hyperbole. Even sex can make sense.

NOTES

CHAPTER 1

1. Zimmer, C. (2008). Isolated tribe gives clues to the origins of syphilis. *Science, 319*, 272.

2. Alan Soble teaches in the Department of English-Philosophy at a sister technological institution to mine, Drexel University, in Philadelphia. I am indebted to his wonderful article for enriching my understanding and discussion of the philosophical and theological dimensions of sexuality: Soble, A. (2009). A history of erotic philosophy. *Journal of Sex Research, 46*(2–3), 104–120.

3. For more about Krafft-Ebing's effects on medical views of sexuality, see: Oosterhuis, H. (2001). *Stepchildren of nature: Krafft-Ebing, psychiatry, and the making of sexual identity.* Chicago: University of Chicago Press.

4. Kinsey, A. C., Pomeroy, W. B., & Martin, C. E. (1948). *Sexual behavior in the human male.* Philadelphia: W. B. Saunders; Kinsey, A. C., Pomeroy, W. B., Martin, C. E., & Gebhard, P. H. (1953). *Sexual behavior in the human female.* Philadelphia: W. B. Saunders.

5. Masters, W. H., & Johnson, V. E. (1966). *Human sexual response.* Boston: Little, Brown; Masters, W. H., & Johnson, V. E. (1970). *Human sexual inadequacy.* Boston: Little, Brown.

6. See Nancy Gibbs's fine essay on the 50th anniversary of the pill and its meaning: Love, sex, freedom and the paradox of the Pill. *Time*, May 1, 2010, 40–47.

7. The data of the National Health and Social Life Survey, and their analysis, are detailed in: Laumann, E. O., Gagnon, J. H., Michael, R. T., & Michaels, S. (1994). *The social organization of sexuality.* Chicago: University of Chicago Press.

8. These HIV data were taken from the following sources: Centers for Disease Control and Prevention. (2008). *STD surveillance 2007.* Atlanta, GA: Author; Centers for Disease Control and Prevention. (2008). *National youth risk behavior survey: 1991–2007.* Atlanta,

GA: Author; Centers for Disease Control and Prevention. (2008). Youth risk behavior surveillance-United States, 2007. *Morbidity and Mortality Weekly Report, 57*(SS-4), 1–131; Hall, H. I., et al. (2008). Estimation of HIV incidence in the United States. *Journal of the American Medical Association, 300*(5), 520–529; Mitsch, A., et al. (2008). Trends in HIV/AIDS diagnoses among men who have sex with men—33 states, 2001–2006. *Morbidity and Mortality Weekly Report, 57*(25), 681–686.

9. Howard, H. (2011, April 21). Vibrators carry the conversation. *New York Times,* E1, 9.

10. Hans, J. D., Gillen, M., & Akande, K. (2010). Sex redefined: The reclassification of oral-genital contact. *Perspectives on Sexual and Reproductive Health, 42*(2), 74–78.

11. Hembree, W. C., et al. (2009). Endocrine treatments of transsexual persons: An Endocrine Society clinical practice guideline. *Journal of Clinical Endocrinology and Metabolism, 94*(9), 3132–3154.

12. See the following for data from these studies: Cubbin, C., Santelli, J., Brindis, C. D., & Braveman, P. (2005). Neighborhood context and sexual behaviors among adolescents: Findings from the National Longitudinal Study of Adolescent Health. *Perspectives on Sexual and Reproductive Health, 37*(3), 125–134; National Center for Health Statistics. (2006). *Advance data from vital and health statistics. Sexual behavior and selected health measures: Men and women 15–44 years of age, United States, 2002.* Washington, DC: Author; Ross, J., Godeau, E., Dias, S., Vignes, C., & Gross, L. (2004, Fall). Setting politics aside to collect cross-national data of sexual health of adolescents. *SIECUS Report, 32*(4), 28–34; Shafii, T., et al. (2004). Is condom use habit forming? Condom use at sexual debut and subsequent condom use. *Sexually Transmitted Diseases, 31*(6), 366–372.

13. Halpern, C. T. (2010). Reframing research on adolescent sexuality: Healthy sexual development as part of the life course. *Perspectives on Sexual and Reproductive Health, 42*(1), 6–7. The quoted passage is on page 6.

14. Douglas Kirby and his colleagues at the private research firm ETR Associates have been contracted to do some of the most extensive research on the effectiveness of various approaches to sexuality education. The results very briefly summarized in this paragraph may be explored in more detail in: Kirby, D. (2001). *Emerging answers: Research findings on programs to reduce teen pregnancy.* Washington, DC: National Campaign to Prevent Teen Pregnancy; Kirby, D., Laris, B. A., & Rolleri, L. (2006). *The impact of sex and HIV education programs in schools and communities on sexual behavior among young adults.* Research Triangle Park, NC: Family Health International.

15. Thanks to Matthew Elser, one of my honors students, for these creative ideas.

CHAPTER 2

1. Hofstede, G. (1998). *Masculinity and femininity: The taboo of national culture.* Thousand Oaks, CA: Sage; Hofstede, G. (2001). *Culture's consequences: Comparing values, behaviors, institutions, and organizations across nations.* Thousand Oaks, CA: Sage.

2. Sanger, M. (1938). *Margaret Sanger: An autobiography.* New York: Norton.

3. Gibbs, N. (2010). Love, sex, freedom and the paradox of the Pill. *Time,* May 1, 40–47.

4. These excerpts were taken from the Preface of Anais Nin's collection titled *Delta of Venus: Erotica by Anais Nin.* Orlando: Harcourt, Harvest Books, 1977.

5. See chapter 1 of Friedan, B. (1963). *The feminine mystique.* New York: Norton.

6. Read more at http://www.notablebiographies.com/Fi-Gi/Friedan-Betty.html#ixzz 0neCzSEDa.

7. From McCormick, N. B. (1996). Our feminist future: Women affirming sexuality research in the late twentieth century. *Journal of Sex Research, 33*(2). Copyright © 1996 by the Society for the Scientific Study of Sexuality.

8. From the introduction of Calderone, M. S. (1974). *Sexuality and human values: The personal dimension of sexual experience.* New York: Association Press.

9. As quoted in Bush, H. (2010). Announcing the Patricia Schiller Founding Plenary. *Contemporary Sexuality, 44*(5), 3.

10. Haffner, D. (1995). Facing facts: Sexual health for America's adolescents: The report of the National Commission on Adolescent Sexual Health. *SIECUS Report, 23*(6). Copyright © 1995 by The Sexuality Information and Education Council of the United States, Inc.

11. These personal recollections of Evelyn Hooker were taken from an article adapted from her address to the 100th annual convention of the American Psychological Association, published as Hooker, E. (1993). Reflections on a 40-year exploration: A scientific view of homosexuality. *American Psychologist, 48*(4), 450–453.

12. Some of Evelyn Hooker's most significant publications: Hooker, E. (1965). Male homosexuals and their "worlds." In J. Marmor (Ed.), *Sexual inversion.* New York: Basic Books; Hooker, E. (1967). The homosexual community. In J. Gagnon & W. Simon (Eds.), *Sexual deviance.* New York: Harper and Row; Hooker, E. (1975). Facts that liberated the gay community. *Psychology Today, 9*(7), 52–55.

13. Kaplan, H. S. (1974). *The new sex therapy.* New York: Brunner/Mazel.

14. Heiman, J. R. (1977). A psychophysiological exploration of sexual arousal patterns in females and males. *Psychophysiology, 14*(13), 266–274.

15. Barbach, L. G. (1975). *For yourself: The fulfillment of female sexuality.* New York: Doubleday. (Newer, updated editions of this book are now available.) It is an excellent and reassuring guide that I frequently recommend to women who are trying to be orgasmic in their sexual activities.

16. Some interesting sources to explore Leonore Tiefer's ideas: Tiefer, L. (1991). Historical, scientific, clinical, and feminist criticisms of "the human sexual response cycle" model. *Annual Review of Sex Research, 2,* 1–23; Tiefer, L. (1994). *Sex is not a natural act and other essays.* Boulder, CO: Westview Press; Tiefer, L. (2006). Female sexual dysfunction: A case study of disease mongering and activist resistance. *PLoS Med 3*(4), e178. doi:10.1371/journal.pmed.0030178

17. The essence of Rosemary Basson's work is well described in these three sources: Basson, R. (2001). Human sex response cycles. *Journal of Sex and Marital Therapy, 27*(1), 33–43; Basson, R., et al. (2003). Definitions of women's sexual dysfunction reconsidered: Advocating expansion and revision. *Journal of Psychosomatic Obstetrics and Gynecology, 24,* 221–229; Basson, R. (2007). Sexual desire/arousal disorders in women. In S. R. Leiblum (Ed.), *Principles and practice of sex therapy* (pp. 25–53). New York: Guilford Press.

18. The literature on queer theory is vast and quite complicated. These sources can offer an overview of the concepts in the early stages of their development: A collection of Teresa de Lauretis's essays has been published by one of her former graduate students, Patty White, as de Lauretis, T., & White, P. (Eds.). (2007). *Figures of resistance: Essays in feminist theory.* Urbana: University of Illinois Press; Butler, J. P. (1990). *Gender trouble: Feminism and the subversion of identity.* New York: Routledge; Butler, J. P. (1993). *Bodies that matter: On the discursive limits of "sex."* New York: Routledge.

19. See Rogoff, B. (2003). *The cultural nature of human development.* New York: Oxford University Press.

20. This is Roy Baumeister's best-known publication about erotic plasticity: Baumeister, R. (2000). Gender differences in erotic plasticity: The female sex drive as socially flexible and responsive. *Psychological Bulletin, 126,* 247–374.

21. Diamond, L. M. (2008). *Sexual fluidity: Understanding women's love and desire.* Cambridge, MA: Harvard University Press. The quote is from page 243.

CHAPTER 3

1. From the Preface to Sacks, O. (1985). *The man who mistook his wife for a hat and other clinical tales.* New York: Touchstone.

2. Leiblum, S. R. (2007). Sex therapy today: Current issues and future perspectives. In Leiblum, S. R. (Ed.). *Principles and practices of sex therapy* (4th ed., pp. 3–21). New York: Guilford Press. The quote is from page 3.

3. These are the articles that are referenced in this section, and they are worth reading today as examples of the conflicting ideas at the time: Nelson, J. (1989). Intergenerational sexual contact: A continuum model of participants and experiences. *Journal of Sex Education and Therapy, 15*(1), 3–12; Maltz, W. (1989). Counterpoints: Intergenerational sexual contact: A continuum model of participants and experiences. *Journal of Sex Education and Therapy, 15*(1), 13–15.

4. Rind, B., & Tromovitch, P. (1997). A meta-analytic review of findings from national samples on psychological correlates of child sexual abuse. *Journal of Sex Research, 34,* 237–255; Rind, B., Tromovitch, P., & Bauserman, R. (1998). A meta-analytic examination of assumed properties of child sexual abuse using college samples. *Psychological Bulletin, 124*(1), 22–53; Rind, B. (2003). Adolescent sexual experiences with adults: Pathological or functional? *Journal of Psychology and Human Sexuality, 15*(1), 5–22.

5. For more information about autogynephilia, see: Bailey, J. M. (2003). The man who would be queen: The science of gender-bending and transsexualism. Washington, DC: Joseph Henry Press; Blanchard, R. (1991). Clinical observations and systematic studies of autogynephilia. *Journal of Sex and Marital Therapy, 17*(4), 235–251; Blanchard, R. (2005). Early history of the concept of autogynephilia. *Archives of Sexual Behavior, 34*(4), 439–446.

6. For data on masturbation, see: Das, A. (2007). Masturbation in the United States. *Journal of Sex and Marital Therapy, 33*(4), 301–317; Dekker, A., & Schmidt, G. (2002). Patterns of masturbatory behaviour: Changes between the sixties and the nineties. *Journal of Psychology and Human Sexuality, 14*(2/3), 35–48; Gerressu, M., Mercer, C. H., Graham, C. A., Wellings, K., & Johnson, A.M. (2008). Prevalence of masturbation and associated factors in a British national probability survey. *Archives of Sexual Behavior, 37,* 266–278; Herbenick, D., Reece, M., Schick, V., Sanders, S. A., Dodge, B., & Fortenberry, J. D. (2010). Sexual behavior in the United States: Results from a national probability sample of men and women ages 14–94. *Journal of Sexual Medicine, 7*(Suppl. 5), 255–265; Janssen, D. F. (2007). First stirrings: Cultural notes on orgasm, ejaculation, and wet dreams. *Journal of Sex Research, 44*(2), 122–134; Halpern, C. T., Udry, J. R., Suchindran, C., & Campbell, B. (2000). Adolescent males' willingness to report masturbation. *Journal of Sex Research, 37*(4), 327–332; Kontula, O., & Haavio-Mannila, E. (2002). Masturbation in a generational perspective. *Journal of Psychology and Human Sexuality, 14*(2/3), 49–83.

7. Fesmire, F. M. (1988). Termination of intractable hiccups with digital rectal massage. *Annals of Emergency Medicine,17*(8), 872; Peleg, R., & Peleg, A. (2000). Case report: Sexual intercourse as potential treatment for intractable hiccups. *Canadian Family Physician, 46,* 1631–1632.

8. Whitelaw, W. A., Derenne, J.-P., & Cabane, J. (1995). Hiccups as a dynamical disease. *Chaos, 5,* 14. doi: 10.1063/1.166097

9. Shifren, J. L., Monz, B. U., Russo, P. A., Segretti, A., & Johannes, C. B. (2008). Sexual problems and distress in United States women. *Obstetrics and Gynecology, 112,* 970–978.

10. Kelly, G. F. (1976). Multiphasic therapy for a severe sexual dysfunction. *Psychotherapy: Theory, Research, and Practice, 13*(1), 40–43.

11. Here is some of the writing on mental imagery techniques I did then and more recently: Kelly, G. F. (1972). Guided fantasy as a counseling technique with youth. *Journal of Counseling Psychology, 19*(5), 355–361; Kelly, G. F. (1974). Mental imagery in counseling. *Personnel and Guidance Journal, 53*(2), 111–116; Kelly, G. F. (1996). Using meditative techniques in psychotherapy. *Journal of Humanistic Psychology, 36*(3), 49–66; Kelly, G. F. (1997). Spiritual knowing in psychotherapy: A holistic perspective. In T. Hart, P. L. Nelson, & K. Puhakka (Eds.), *Spiritual knowing: Alternative epistemic perspectives* (pp. 142–159). Carrollton: State University of West Georgia Press.

12. Laumann, E. O., Gagnon, J. H., Michael, R. T., & Michaels, S. (1994). *The social organization of sexuality.* Chicago: University of Chicago Press.

13. I have eight years of survey data from undergraduate students in human sexuality, a total of about 1,000 people. Some of the data have been analyzed by one of my honors students, Alexandria Barr, under the supervision of my colleague Dr. Tina Norton. While this is surely not a representative sample of the general population, I believe that the students took the survey with serious intent and willingness to give accurate responses. In many ways, I believe these data to be more representative of college students today than anything I've yet seen published.

CHAPTER 4

1. These were the books that became models of tone and topic for my first efforts in writing about human sexuality for teenagers: Johnson, E. (1973). *Love and sex in plain language.* Philadelphia: J. B. Lippincott; Pomeroy, W. (1968). *Boys and sex.* New York: Delacorte Press; Pomeroy, W. (1969). *Girls and sex.* New York: Delacorte Press.

2. Kelly, G. F. (1976, 1977, 1986). *Learning about sex: The contemporary guide for young adults.* Woodbury, NY: Barron's Educational Series. In 1993, a revised and updated edition of the book appeared titled *Sex and sense: A contemporary guide for teenagers.*

3. *The Personnel and Guidance Journal* (March 1976). Volume 54, No. 7. Published by the American Personnel and Guidance Association, Washington, D.C.

4. Perlez, J. (1986, December 3). Phrase deleted from textbook, publisher says. *New York Times.*

5. Seewald, P., & Pope Benedict XVI. (2010). *Light of the world: The pope, The Church, and the signs of the times.* San Francisco: Ignatius Press.

6. Marquand, R. (2010, November 22). Europe greets Pope Benedict's condom remarks as "evolution, not revolution." *Christian Science Monitor.* doi: http://www.csmonitor. com/World/Europe/2010/1122/Europe-greets-Pope-Benedict-s-condom-remarks-as-evolution-not-revolution. This is the actual translation of the pope's statement, as discussed in *The Catholic World Report* at http://www.catholicworldreport.com/index.php?option=com_ content&view=article&id=222:did-the-pope-justify-condom-use-in-some-circumstances &catid=53:cwr2010&Itemid=70. "There may be a basis in the case of some individuals, as perhaps when a male prostitute uses a condom, where this can be a first step in the direction of a moralization, a first assumption of responsibility, on the way toward recovering an awareness that not everything is allowed and that one cannot do whatever one wants.

But it is not really the way to deal with the evil of HIV infection. That can really lie only in a humanization of sexuality." *My additional comment:* You might see why I shudder to think of the varied interpretations that laypersons might make of this convolution of words and meanings, not to mention the conflicting analyses that Catholic theologians have already offered in German, Italian, and English.

7. One of this group's advertisements appeared on December 1, 2010, in the *New York Times* on page A17. Their website may be found at http://www.condoms4life.org.

8. Kelly, G. F. (2011). *Sexuality today* (10th ed.). New York: McGraw-Hill Higher Education.

9. Laumann, E. O., Gagnon, J. H., Michael, R. T., & Michaels, S. (1994). *The social organization of sexuality.* Chicago: University of Chicago Press. This was the full version of the NHSLS, although its data continue to be analyzed to this day. A report about the battle for funding of the study may be found in: Laumann, E. O., Michael, R. T., & Gagnon, J. H. (1994). A political history of the national sex survey of adults. *Family Planning Perspectives, 26*(1), 34–38.

10. The findings of the NSSHB were released free of charge on the Internet in a set of commentaries and nine articles discussing the research from: *Journal of Sexual Medicine, 7*(Suppl. 5), 243–373.

11. Kinsey, A. C., Pomeroy, W. B., & Martin, C. E. (1948). *Sexual behavior in the human male.* Philadelphia: W. B. Saunders; Kinsey, A. C., Pomeroy, W. B., Martin, C. E., & Gebhard, P. H. (1953). *Sexual behavior in the human female.* Philadelphia: W. B. Saunders.

12. Herbenick, D., et al. (2010). Sexual behavior in the United States: Results from a national probability sample of men and women ages 14–94. *Journal of Sexual Medicine, 7*(Suppl. 5), 255–265.

13. The new data cited in this paragraph are taken from: Fortenberry, J. D., et al. (2010). Sexual behaviors and condom use at last vaginal intercourse: A national sample of adolescents ages 14 to 17 years. *Journal of Sexual Medicine, 7*(Suppl. 5), 305–314.

14. Centers for Disease Control. (2008). Trends in the prevalence of sexual behaviors. *National Youth Risk Behavior Survey: 1991–2007.* Atlanta: Author.

15. Martin, J. A., et al. (2009). National Center for Health Statistics. Births: Final data for 2006. *National Vital Statistics Report, 57*(7). Associated Press and CDC press releases of December 21, 2010, offer the data for 2009.

16. Sable, M. R., Schwartz, L. R., Kelly, P. J., Lisbon, E., & Hall, M. A. (2006). Using the theory of reasoned action to explain physician intention to prescribe emergency contraception. *Perspectives on Sexual and Reproductive Health, 38*(1), 20–27.

17. Klein, F. (1990). The need to view sexual orientation as a multivariable dynamic process: A theoretical perspective. In D. P. McWhirter, S. A. Sanders, & J. M. Reinisch (Eds.), *Homosexuality/heterosexuality: Concepts of sexual orientation* (pp. 277–282). New York: Oxford University Press.

CHAPTER 5

1. Elia, J. P. (2009). School-based sexuality education: A century of sexual and social control. In E. Schroeder & J. Kuriansky (Eds.), *Sexuality education: Past, present, and future* (Vol. 1, pp. 33–57). Westport, CT: Praeger.

2. American Society of Sanitary and Moral Prophylaxis. (1910, January 7). *Journal of Social Diseases, 1,* 4–7.

3. Goldfarb, E. S. (2009). A crisis of identity in sexuality education in America: How did we get here and where are we going? In E. Schroeder & J. Kuriansky (Eds.), *Sexuality education: Past, present, and future* (Vol. 1, pp. 8–30). Westport, CT: Praeger.

4. Bigelow, M. (1936). *Sex-education.* New York: American Social Hygiene Association.

5. Somerville, R. M. (2009). *Family life and sex education in the turbulent sixties.* In E. Schroeder & J. Kuriansky (Eds.), *Sexuality education: Past, present, and future* (Vol. 1, pp. 58–95). Westport, CT: Praeger.

6. McCaffree, K., & Levitan, J. (2009). Sexuality education in the ongoing sexual revolution of the 1970s. In E. Schroeder & J. Kuriansky (Eds.), *Sexuality education: Past, present, and future* (Vol. 1, pp. 96–122). Westport, CT: Praeger.

7. I found these chapters from E. Schroeder & J. Kuriansky (Eds.), *Sexuality education: Past, present, and future* (Vol. 1). Westport, CT: Praeger, to be particularly helpful in investigating the historical material in this section: Young, M. (2009). Federal involvement in abstinence-only education: Has the buck been passed too far? (pp. 136–149); Kempner, M. E. (2009). Bitter battles: Lessons from decades of controversy over sexuality education in schools (pp. 150–173).

8. Office of State and Community Health, Maternal and Child Health Bureau, Department of Health and Human Services. (1997). *Block grant application guidance for the abstinence education provisions of the 1996 Welfare Reform Law, P.L.* Rockville, MD: Department of Health and Human Services. (pp. 104–193).

9. Office of the Surgeon General. (2001). *The Surgeon General's call to action to promote sexual health and responsible sexual behavior 2001.* Rockville, MD: Author, page 1.

10. U.S. House of Representatives Committee on Government Reform, Special Investigations Committee. (2004). *The content of federally-funded abstinence-only education programs.* http://oversight.house.gov/documents/20041201102153–50247.pdf

11. Trenholm, C., Devaney, B., Fortson, K., Quay, L., Wheeler, J., & Clark, M. (2007). *Impacts of four Title V, Section 510 abstinence education programs: Final report.* Princeton, NJ: Mathematica Policy Research Group.

12. Kohler, P., et al. (2008). Abstinence-only and comprehensive sex education and the initiation of sexual activity and teen pregnancy. *Journal of Adolescent Health, 42*(4), 344–351; Underhill, K., Montgomery, P., & Operario, D. (2007). Sexual abstinence only programmes to prevent HIV infection in high income countries: Systematic review. *British Medical Journal.* http://bjm.com/cgi/content/full/335/7613/248

13. Bearman, P., & Bruckner, H. (2001). Promising the future: Virginity pledges and the transition to first intercourse. *American Journal of Sociology, 106*(4), 859–912; Bearman, P., & Bruckner, H. (2005). After the promise: The STD consequences of adolescent virginity pledges. *Journal of Adolescent Health, 36*(4), 271–278.

14. Kirby, D. (2007). *Emerging answers 2007: Research findings on programs to reduce teen pregnancy.* Washington, DC: National Campaign to Prevent Teen Pregnancy; Kirby, D. (2008). The impact of abstinence and comprehensive sex and STD/HIV education programs on adolescent sexual behavior. *Journal of Sexuality Research and Social Policy, 5*(2).

15. Kelly, G. F. (2009). Will the good sexuality educators please stand up? In E. Schroeder & J. Kuriansky (Eds.), *Sexuality education: Past, present, and future* (Vol. 1, pp. 207–227). Westport, CT: Praeger.

16. These statistics are from: Centers for Disease Control. (2008). Trends in the prevalence of sexual behaviors. *National Youth Risk Behavior Survey: 1991–2007.* Atlanta: Author and the Associated Press and Centers for Disease Control press releases of December 21, 2010.

17. The following studies show the vast majority of parents in support of comprehensive sexuality education, the third one indicating religious affiliations: Bleakley, A., et al. (2006). Public opinion on sex education in U.S. schools. *Archives of Pediatric and Adolescent Medicine, 160,* 1151–1156; National Public Radio, Kaiser Family Foundation, Kennedy School of Government. (2004). *Sex education in America: General public/parents survey.*

Washington, DC: Author; Peter D. Hart Research Associates. (2007, July 12). *Memorandum: Application of research findings.* Washington, DC: Planned Parenthood Federation of America and National Women's Law Center. http://www.nwlc.org/pdf/7–12–07interest edpartiesmemo.pdf

18. The information on legislation discussed in this section of the chapter was gathered from several monthly policy reports that are made available by the Sexuality Information and Education Council of the United States at http://www.siecus.com. I also want to thank Patrick Malone, public information officer at Sexuality Information and Education Council of the United States, for helping me to understand some of the complexities of this legislation.

19. Kelly, G. F. (2005). Re-visioning sexuality education: A challenge for the future. *American Journal of Sexuality Education, 1*(1), 5–21.

20. Haffner, D. W. (1995). Facing facts: Sexual health for America's adolescents. *SIECUS Report, 23*(6), 2–8.

21. National Guidelines Task Force. (2004). *Guidelines for comprehensive sexuality education* (3rd ed.). New York: Sexuality Information and Education Council of the United States.

22. The WHO report may be accessed at http://www.bzga-whocc.de/pdf.php?id=061 a863a0fdf28218e4fe9e1b3f463b3.

CHAPTER 6

1. Howe, N., & Strauss, W. (2000). *Millennials rising: The next great generation.* New York: Random House; Howe, N., & Strauss, W. (2003). *Millennials go to college.* Washington, DC: American Association of Collegiate Registrars and Admissions Officers, and LifeCourse Associates.

2. Pew Research Center. (2010). *Millennials: Portrait of generation next: Confident. Connected. Open to change.* Available at: http://www.pewresearch.org/millennials

3. Pew Research Center. (2010). *The decline of marriage and rise of new families.* Available at: http://pewsocialtrends.org/files/2010/11/pew-social-trends-2010-families.pdf The more popularized version of the study: Luscombe, B. (2010, November 29). Marriage: What's it good for? *Time,* 48–56.

4. Arnett, J. J. (2004). *Emerging adulthood: The winding road from late teens to twenties.* New York: Oxford University Press; Melby, T. (2008, June). The new twenties. *Contemporary Sexuality, 42*(6), 1–4.

5. Velez-Blasini, C. J. (2008). Evidence against alcohol as a proximal cause of sexual risk taking among college students. *Journal of Sex Research, 45*(2), 118–128.

6. Bailey, J. A., et al. (2008). Sexual risk behavior 6 months post-high school: Associations with college attendance, living with a parent, and prior risk behavior. *Journal of Adolescent Health, 42*(6), 573–579.

7. Herbenick, D., et al. (2010). Sexual behaviors, relationships, and perceived health status among adult women in the United States: Results from a national probability sample. *Journal of Sexual Medicine, 7*(Suppl. 5), 277–290; Reece, M., et al. (2010). Sexual behaviors, relationships, and perceived health among adult men in the United States: Results from a national probability sample. *Journal of Sexual Medicine, 7*(Suppl. 5), 291–304.

8. Kaestle, C. E., & Halpern, C. T. (2007). What's love got to do with it? Sexual behaviors of opposite-sex couples through emerging adulthood. *Perspectives on Sexual and Reproductive Health, 39*(3), 134–140.

9. Patrick, M. E., Maggs, J. L., & Abar, C. C. (2007). Reasons to have sex, personal goals, and sexual behavior during the transition to college. *Journal of Sex Research, 44*(3), 240–249.

10. Lefkowitz, E. S., et al. (2004). Religiosity, sexual behaviors, and sexual attitudes during emerging adulthood. *Journal of Sex Research, 41*(2), 150–159; Oswalt, S. B., Cameron, K. A., & Koob, J. J. (2005). Sexual regret in college students. *Archives of Sexual Behavior, 34*(6), 663–669.

11. Rasberry, C. N., & Goodson, P. (2009). Predictors of secondary abstinence in U.S. college undergraduates. *Archives of Sexual Behavior, 38,* 74–86.

12. Regnerus, M. (2007). *Forbidden fruit: Sex and religion in the lives of American teenagers.* New York: Oxford University Press.

13. Cahn, N., & Carbone, J. (2010). *Red families v. blue families: Legal polarization and the creation of culture.* New York: Oxford University Press.

14. Regnerus, M. (2011). *Premarital sex in America: How young Americans meet, mate, and think about marrying.* New York: Oxford University Press.

15. I found this article to be particularly helpful in writing this section of the chapter: Talbot, M. (2008, November 3). Red sex, blue sex: Why do so many evangelical teen-agers become pregnant? *The New Yorker.* Available at: http://www.newyorker.com/reporting/2008/11/03/081103fa_fact_talbot

16. Zucker, K. J. (2003). The politics and science of "reparative therapy." *Archives of Sexual Behavior, 32*(5), 399–402.

17. Grace, P. (2008). The charisma and deception of reparative therapies: When medical science beds religion. *Journal of Homosexuality, 55*(4), 545–580; Serovich, J. M., et al. (2008). A systematic review of the research base on sexual reorientation therapies. *Journal of Marital and Family Therapy, 34*(2), 227–238.

18. Eckholm, E. (2011, April 19). Even on religious campuses, students fight for gay identity. *New York Times,* pp. A1, A3.

19. Stuart, L. A. (2010, July 10). Trimming pubic hair. expressmilwaukee.com. Available at: http://www.expressmilwaukee.com/article-11522-trimming-pubic-hair.html

20. Aron, A., Fisher, H., Mashek, D. J., Strong, G., Haifang, L., & Brown, L. (2005). Reward, motivation, and emotion systems associated with early-stage intense romantic love. *Journal of Neurophysiology, 94,* 327–337; Fisher, H., Aron, A., Mashek, D., Li, H., & Brown, L. L. (2002). Defining the brain systems of lust, romantic attraction, and attachment. *Archives of Sexual Behavior, 31*(5), 413–419; Fisher, H., Aron, A., Mashek, D., Li, H., Strong, G., & Brown, L. L. (2002). The neural mechanisms of mate choice: A hypothesis. *Neuroendocrinology Letters, 23*(4), 92–97.

21. Eisenberg, M. E., et al. (2009). Casual sex and psychological health among young adults: Is having "friends with benefits" emotionally damaging? *Perspectives on Sexual and Reproductive Health, 41*(4), 231–237.

22. Bisson, M. A., & Levine, T. R. (2009). Negotiating a friends with benefits relationship. *Archives of Sexual Behavior, 38,* 66–73.

23. Jonason, P. K., Li, N. P., & Cason, M. J. (2009). The "booty call": A compromise between men's and women's ideal mating strategies. *Journal of Sex Research, 46*(5), 460–470.

24. Bay-Cheng, L. Y., et al. (2009). Behavioral and relational context of sexual desire, wanting, and pleasure: Undergraduate women's retrospective accounts. *Journal of Sex Research, 46*(5), 511–524,

25. Savin-Williams, R. C. (2005). *The new gay teenager.* Cambridge, MA: Harvard University Press.

26. Ellis, L., Robb, B., & Burke, D. (2005). Sexual orientation in United States and Canadian college students. *Archives of Sexual Behavior, 34*(5), 569–581.

27. Angera, J. J., Brookins-Fisher, J., & Inungu, J. N. (2008). An investigation of parent/child communication about sexuality. *American Journal of Sexuality Education, 3*(2), 165–181.

28. Ackard, D. M., & Neumark-Stainer, D. (2001). Health care information sources for adolescents: Age and gender differences on use, concerns, and needs. *Journal of Adolescent Health, 29*(3), 170–176.

29. Martino, S. C., et al. (2008). Beyond the "big talk:" The roles of breadth and repetition in parent-adolescent communication about sexual topics. *Pediatrics, 121*(3), e612–e618; Miller, B.C. (2002). Family influences on adolescent sexual and contraceptive behavior. *Journal of Sex Research, 39*(1), 22–26; Zamboni, B. D., & Silver, R. (2009). Family sex communication and the sexual desire, attitudes, and behavior of late adolescents. *American Journal of Sexuality Education, 4,* 58–78.

30. Coley, R. L., Medeiros, B. L., & Schindler, H. S. (2008). Using sibling differences to estimate effects of parenting on adolescent sexual risk behaviors. *Journal of Adolescent Health, 43*(2), 133–140; Lehr, S. T., Demi, A. S., DiLorio, C., & Facteau, J. (2005). Predictors of father-son communication about sexuality. *Journal of Sex Research, 42*(2), 119–129; Menning, C., Holtzman, M., & Kapinus, C. (2007). Stepfather involvement and adolescents' disposition toward having sex. *Perspectives on Sexual and Reproductive Health, 39*(2), 82–89.

CHAPTER 7

1. Money, J., & Ehrhardt, A. (1972). *Man and woman, boy and girl.* Baltimore: Johns Hopkins University Press.

2. It is difficult to capture some of the nuances of such developmental patterns in such a short space. For a more detailed and carefully substantiated discussion of these biological processes and their interaction with social processes, I recommend chapter 5, "Developmental and Social Perspectives on Gender," in my own textbook, *Sexuality Today* (10 ed.), New York: McGraw-Hill, 2011. Another good reference is: Becker, J. B., et al. (Eds.). (2008). *Sex differences in the brain: From genes to behavior.* New York: Oxford University Press.

3. Brizendine, L. (2006). *The female brain.* New York: Broadway Books; Brizendine, L. (2010). *The male brain.* New York: Broadway Books.

4. Beijsterveldt, V., Hudziak, J. J., & Boomsma, D. I. (2006). Genetic and environmental influences on cross-gender behavior and relation to behavior problems: A study of Dutch twins at ages 7 and 10 years. *Archives of Sexual Behavior, 35,* 647–658.

5. For some of the recent research on sex-dimorphic behavior and gender conformity or nonconformity in children, here are a few fascinating studies: Fridell, S. R. et al. (2006). The playmate and play style preferences structured interview: A comparison of children with gender identity disorder and controls. *Archives of Sexual Behavior, 35,* 729–737; Nuttbrock, L., et al. (2010). Psychiatric impact of gender-related abuse across the life course of male-to-female transgender persons. *Journal of Sex Research, 47*(1), 12–23; Ruble, D. N., Martin, C. C., & Berenbaum, S. A. (2006). Gender development. In N. Eisenberg (Ed.), *Handbook of child psychology: Vol. 3. Social, emotional, and personality development* (pp. 858–932). New York: Wiley; Wilansky-Traynor, P., & Lobel, T. E. (2008). Differential effects of an adult observer's presence on sex-typed play behavior: A comparison between gender-schematic and gender-aschematic preschool children. *Archives of Sexual Behavior, 37,* 548–557; Zucker, K. J., et al. (2008). Is gender identity disorder in adolescents coming out of the closet? *Journal of Sex and Marital Therapy, 34*(4), 287–290.

6. See this book for a fascinating and somewhat sad account of this boy's life: Colapinto, J. (2000). *As nature made him: The boy who was raised as a girl.* New York: HarperCollins.

7. See: Hyde, J. S. (2005). The gender similarities hypothesis. *American Psychologist, 60*(6), 581–592; Hyde, J. S., & Linn, M. C. (2006). Gender similarities in mathematics and science. *Science, 314,* 599–600; Hyde, J. S., et al. (2008). Gender similarities characterize math performance. *Science, 321,* 494–495.

8. Petersen, J. L., & Hyde, J. S. (2010). A meta-analytic review of research on gender differences in sexuality: 1993–2007. *Psychological Bulletin, 136,* 21–38.

9. Petersen, J. L., & Hyde, J. S. (2011). Gender differences in sexual attitudes and behaviors: A review of meta-analytic results and large datasets. *Journal of Sex Research, 48*(2–3), 149–165. (See last paragraph on page 163.)

10. Costa, P. T., Terracciano, A., & McCrae, R. R. (2001). Gender differences in personality traits across cultures: Robust and surprising findings. *Journal of Personality and Social Psychology, 81,* 322–331.

11. Guimond, S. (2008). Psychological similarities and differences between women and men across cultures. *Social and Personality Psychology Compass, 2,* 494–510; Guimond, S., et al. (2007). Culture, gender, and the self: Variations and impact of social comparison processes. *Journal of Personality and Social Psychology, 92,* 1118–1134.

12. Schmitt, D. P., Realo, A., Voracek, M, & Allik, J. (2008). Why can't a man be more like a woman? *Journal of Personality and Social Psychology, 94,* 168–182.

13. Jordan-Young, R. (2010). *Brain storm: The flaws in the science of sex differences.* Cambridge, MA: Harvard University Press.

14. Fine, C. (2010). *Delusions of gender: How our minds, society, and neurosexism create difference.* New York: Norton.

15. Snow, C. P. (1959). *The two cultures.* Cambridge: Cambridge University Press.

16. I found this article very helpful in teasing out the issues here: Boyd, B. (2006). Getting it all wrong: Bioculture critiques cultural critique. *The American Scholar, 75*(4), 18–30.

17. Lippa, R. A. (2010). Sex differences in personality traits and gender-related occupational preferences across 53 nations: Testing evolutionary and social-environmental theories. *Archives of Sexual Behavior, 39,* 619–636. doi: 10.1007/s10508-008-9380-7.

18. Details of Jay Giedd's research at the National Institutes of Mental Health may be found at: http://intramural.nimh.nih.gov/research/pi/pi_giedd_j.html.

19. Details of Larry Cahill's research at the University of California, Irvine, may be found at: http://cahill.bio.uci.edu.

20. Details of Bruce McEwen's research at Rockefeller University may be found at: http://rockefeller.edu/research/faculty/abstract.php?id=109. For the research on sex differences cited in this paragraph, I am indebted to this review by Diana Halpern of the Department of Psychology at Claremont McKenna College: Halpern, D. F. (2010). How neuromythologies support sex role stereotypes. *Science, 330,* 1320–1321.

21. This article helped me clarify my thinking and gave me the points I made in this paragraph. Laughlin is a professor of physics at Stanford and shared the Nobel Prize in Physics in 1998: Laughlin, R. B. (2010). What the earth knows. *The American Scholar, 79*(3), 18–27.

22. Balaban, E. (2008). The female equally with the male I sing. *Science, 319,* 1619–1620.

23. Everaerd, W., Both, S., & Laan, E. (2007). The experience of sexual emotions. *Annual Review of Sex Research, 17,* 183–199.

24. Zimmer, C. (2009). On the origins of sexual reproduction. *Science, 324,* 1254–1256.

25. Pennisi, E. (2010). Male rivalry extends to sperm in female reproductive tract. *Science, 327*, 1443; Manier, M. K., Belote, J. M., Berben, K. S., Novikov, D., Stuart, W. T., & Pitnick, S. (2010). Resolving mechanisms of competitive fertilization success in *Drosophila melanogaster. Science.* doi: 10.1126/science.1187096; denBoer, S. P. A., Baer, B., & Boomsma, J. J. (2010). Seminal fluid mediates ejaculate competition in social insects. *Science, 327*, 1506–1509.

26. Francis, R. C. (2011). *Epigenetics: The ultimate mystery of inheritance.* New York: Norton; Riddihough, G., & Zahn, L. M. (2010). What is epigenetics? *Science, 330,* 611; Bonasio, R., Tu, S., & Reinberg, D. (2010). Molecular signals of epigenetic states. *Science, 330*, 612–616; Miller, G. (2010). The seductive allure of behavioral epigenetics. *Science, 329*, 24–27; Books, LLC (2010). *Epigenetics: Sex-determination system, genomic imprinting, histone methylation, bisulfite sequencing, methylated DNA immunoprecipitation.* Memphis, TN: Author.

27. Wilkinson, L. S. (2010). Which parental gene gets the upper hand? *Science, 329,* 636–637; Gregg, C., Zhang, J., Butler, J. E., Haig, D., & Dulac, C. (2010). Sex-specific parent-of-origin allelic expression in the mouse brain. *Science, 329*, 682–685; Gregg, C., Zhang, J., Weissbourd, B., Luo, S., Schroth, G. P., Haig, D., & Dulac, C. (2010). High-resolution analysis of parent-of-origin allelic expression in the mouse brain. *Science, 329*, 643–648.

28. Bonnin, A., et al. (2011). A transient placental source of serotonin for the fetal forebrain. *Nature, 472*, 347–350; McKay, R. (2011). Developmental biology: Remarkable role for the placenta. *Nature, 472*, 298–299.

29. For some of the research data discussed in this paragraph, see: Hedges, L. V., & Nowell, A. (1995). Sex differences in mental test scores, variability, and numbers of high scoring individuals. *Science, 269*, 41–45; Kimura, D. (1999). *Sex and cognition.* Cambridge, MA: MIT Press; Levy, J., & Heller, W. (1992) Gender differences in human neuropsychological functions. In A. A. Gerall, H. Moltz, & I. L. Ward (Eds.), *Handbook of behavioral neurobiology: Vol. 11. Sexual Differentiation.,* New York: Plenum Press; Savic, I., & Lindstrom, P. (2008). PET and MRI show differences in cerebral asymmetry and functional connectivity between homo- and heterosexual subjects. *Proceedings of the National Academy of Sciences, 105*(27), 9403–9408.

30. Skidmore, W. C., Linsenmeier, J. A., & Bailey, J. M. (2006). Gender nonconformity and psychological distress in lesbians and gay men. *Archives of Sexual Behavior, 35,* 685–697.

31. McIntyre, M. H. (2003). Digit ratios, childhood gender role behavior, and erotic role preferences of gay men [Letter]. *Archives of Sexual Behavior, 32*(6), 495–497.

32. Rendall, D., Vasey, P. L., & McKenzie, J. (2008). The queen's English: An alternative, biosocial hypothesis for the distinctive features of "gay speech." *Archives of Sexual Behavior, 37*, 188–204.

33. Lippa, R. A. (2008). Sex differences and sexual orientation differences in personality: Findings from the BBC internet survey. *Archives of Sexual Behavior, 37*, 173–187.

34. Laumann, E. O., Gagnon, J. H., Michael, R. T., & Michaels, S. (1994). *The social organization of sexuality.* Chicago: University of Chicago Press.

35. Donaldson, Z. R., & Young, L. J. (2008). Oxytocin, vasopressin, and the neurogenetics of sociality. *Science, 322,* 900.

36. Everaerd, W., Both, S., & Laan, E. (2007). The experience of sexual emotions. *Annual Review of Sex Research, 17,* 183–198.

37. Robinson, G. E., Fernald, R. D., & Clayton, D. F. (2008). Genes and social behavior. *Science, 322,* 896–900.

38. Park, J. H., & Rissman, E. F. (2007). The male sexual revolution: Independence from testosterone. *Annual Review of Sex Research, 18,* 23–59.

39. van Anders, S. M., & Gray, P. B. (2007). Hormones and human partnering. *Annual Review of Sex Research, 18,* 60–93.

40. Young, L. J. (2009). Being human: Love: Neuroscience reveals all. *Nature, 457,* 148.

41. Cole-Turner, R. (2011). What defines us? *Science, 331,* 548.

INDEX

University of Hawaii, 45
University of Melbourne, 131
University of Michigan, 46
University of Pennsylvania, 46
University of Texas, Austin, 110
University of Wisconsin, 130

Vacuum pump, to treat erectile dysfunc-
    tion, 61
Vaginal canal, 126
Vaginal probe, 35
Values clarification, 65
Vasopressin, 144–45
Vatican, 69
Venereal disease, 68
Verbal fluency, and gender,
    130
Viagra, 61
Vibrators, 16
Victorian period, 44, 86
Vietnam, 8
Virginity pledges, 93

Visual spatial relations, and gender, 130
Voyeuristic behavior, 56
Vulva, 126

Wall, Judy, 65–66
Waxman, Henry, Rep., 92
Women's Christian Temperance Associa-
    tion, 86
Woodstock, 9
Worden, Frederick, 33
World AIDS Day, 70
World Health Organization Regional
    Office for Europe, 99
World War II, 7

YMCA, 86
Yolles. Stanley, 34
Youth: conservative religious, 108–15;
    myth of troubled, 5, 104–5; rebellious
    image, 122
Youth Risk Behavior Surveillance System,
    74

About the Author

GARY F. KELLY has been a sexuality educator and sex therapist for 40 years, publishing several popular books in the field. After a 35-year career as counselor, dean, and vice president for student affairs at Clarkson University and as headmaster of The Clarkson School, he retired from administrative work to devote more time to writing, teaching, and counseling. He continues to teach courses in human sexuality, psychoactive substances, and counseling psychology in the Department of Psychology at Clarkson University, where the Student Association honored him with its Outstanding Teaching Award in 2008. He also teaches courses on ethics and social problems in the Honors Program. Kelly was an innovator in developing graduate training in human sexuality for counselors. He is a licensed mental health counselor in New York State.

His work with students received national recognition with his election to the board of directors of the Sexuality Information and Education Council of the United States (SIECUS). Kelly served for eight years as editor of the *Journal of Sex Education and Therapy* and was one of the charter editorial board members of the *American Journal of Sexuality Education*. In addition to his books, he has authored 35 articles, book chapters, and booklets. He is a member of the American Association of Sexuality Educators, Counselors, and Therapists and of the Society for the Scientific Study of Sexuality.

Gary F. Kelly's website is www.garyfkelly.com

Other Books by Gary F. Kelly
Sexuality Today, 10th edition. 2011.
A Chinese translation of *Sexuality Today* was published in China in 2011.
Sources: Notable Selections in Human Sexuality. (Editor). 1998.
Sex and Sense: A Contemporary Guide for Teenagers. 1993. (Published in a Chinese edition, Taiwan, 1996.)
Good Sex: The Healthy Man's Guide to Sexual Fulfillment. 1979. Paperback: New American Library/Signet Books, 1980. (Also published in England, Holland, Italy, and Brazil in Dutch, Italian, and Portuguese.)
Sexuality: The Human Perspective. 1980.
Learning about Sex: The Contemporary Guide for Young Adults. 1976, 1977, 1986. Winner of American Library Association's "Best Book for Young Adults" award and listed by the New York City Library among "Best Books for Teens."

About the Series Editor

JUDY KURIANSKY, PhD, is an internationally known licensed clinical psychologist and adjunct faculty member in the Department of Clinical Psychology at Columbia University Teachers College and the Department of Psychiatry at Columbia University College of Physicians and Surgeons as well as a visiting professor at the Peking University Health Sciences Center and Honorary Professor in the Department of Psychiatry of the University of Hong Kong. A diplomate of the American Board of Sexology and fellow of the American Academy of Clinical Sexology (AACS), she was awarded the AACS Medal of Sexology for Lifetime Achievement. Dr. Judy is a pioneer of sex diagnosis, dating back to being on the committee for the *Diagnostic and Statistical Manual of Mental Disorders* (3rd ed.); sex therapy evaluation, including early Masters and Johnson therapy; and call-in advice talk about sexuality and relationships on the radio and television. A cofounder of the Society for Sex Therapy and Research and past board member of the American Association of Sex Educators, Counselors and Therapists, she has authored hundreds of article in professional journals, including the *Journal of Marital and Sex Therapy*; Sex Education Council of the United States (SIECUS) reports; and mass-market articles, including in *Cosmopolitan* and *Family Circle* magazines. She has written sexuality and relationship advice columns worldwide, including for the *South China Morning Post, Singapore Straits Times, Sankei Shimbun* newspaper, and the *New York Daily News*, and many books on interpersonal and international relations ranging from *The Complete Idiot's Guide to a Healthy Relationship, Generation Sex*, and *Sexuality Education: Past, Present and Future* to *Beyond Bullets and Bombs: Grassroots Peacebuilding between Israelis and Palestinians*. She has developed and led hundreds of workshops about sexuality and relationships around the world from China and Japan to India, Israel, Iran, Austria and Argentina, including an integration of Eastern and Western techniques for relationship enhancement and an HIV/AIDS education and girls' empowerment program for Africa. She is an award-winning journalist and news commentator, UN nongovernmental organization representative for the International Association of Applied Psychology and for the World Council for Psychotherapy, a fellow of the American Psychological Association (APA), and cofounder of the APA Media Psychology Division as well as a board member of the Peace Division and U.S. Doctors for Africa. Her website is www.DrJudy.com.